# THE MBI STORY

The Vision and Worldwide Impact of Moody Bible Institute

# THE MBI STORY

The Vision and Worldwide Impact of Moody Bible Institute

## JAMES VINCENT

MOODY PUBLISHERS

CHICAGO

© 2011 by
JAMES VINCENT

All Scripture quotations, unless otherwise indicated, are taken from the *New American Standard Bible*®, Copyright © 1960, 1962, 1963, 1968, 1971, 1972, 1973, 1975, 1977, 1995 by The Lockman Foundation. Used by permission. (www.Lockman.org)

Scripture quotations marked KJV are taken from the King James Version.

Edited by Elizabeth Cody Newenhuyse
Interior design: Ragont Design
Cover design: Moody Bible Institute
Cover image: Paul Brackley

PHOTO INSERT CREDITS—Page 9: International Student Fellowship by Emily Pine. Page 11: Moody Radio app. and Page 12: *Five Love Languages* and *Moody* magazine montage by Rhonda Elfstrand. All black and white photographs courtesy of Moodyana archives.

Library of Congress Cataloging-in-Publication Data

Vincent, James M.
  The MBI Story : The Vision and Worldwide Impact of Moody Bible Institute / by James Vincent.
     pages cm
  Includes bibliographical references and index.
  ISBN 978-0-8024-5101-9
  1. Moody Bible Institute--History. I. Title.
  BV4070.M76V56 2011
  267'.130977311--dc22
                                        2010043936

Moody Publishers is committed to caring wisely for God's creation and uses recycled paper whenever possible. The paper in this book consists of 30 percent post-consumer waste.

We hope you enjoy this book from Moody Publishers. Our goal is to provide high-quality, thought-provoking books and products that connect truth to your real needs and challenges. For more information on other books and products written and produced from a biblical perspective, go to www.moody publishers.com or write to:

Moody Publishers
820 N. LaSalle Boulevard
Chicago, IL 60610

1 3 5 7 9 10 8 6 4 2

*Printed in the United States of America*

# Contents

# Foreword

For more than two-thirds of my life I have been associated with the Moody Bible Institute. It has always been my proudest association.

MBI is not heaven. Anywhere hundreds of people work and study together is, by definition, imperfect. Yes, there are personality conflicts, turf wars, and all the other foibles associated with, well, people.

But there's something about Moody that makes nearly everyone who has ever been related to it wax nostalgic and trace many of the highlights of their lives to the place. That will make this updated history a treasure, especially to them.

In 1967 I became a seventeen-year-old freshman under President William Culbertson. I was less than successful as a student and yet maintain relationships to this day with two of my profs: Dr. Glenn Arnold and Dr. Wallace Alcorn. It was also during that school year that I met Dr. Gene Getz, who became a colleague and mentor decades later.

In 1974 I became an employee as editor of *Moody Monthly* under President George Sweeting, beginning a career as an MBI employee that would last thirty-two years and include roles as director of Moody Press and vice president for publishing.

In 2000 I became a member of the board of trustees, serving with MBI presidents Joseph Stowell, Michael Easley, and finally Paul Nyquist.

I rehearse those details only to point out that if anyone should have a handle on that elusive *something* about Moody, as a former student, long-term employee, and now trustee, I should.

So let me take a stab at it.

One thing I'm sure of is that it's not about Mr. Moody himself—as devout and dynamic as he was. It's not about the stellar presidents throughout the years. It's not even about the professors and fellow students and colleagues, many of whom have become lifelong friends.

Something about the place makes most associated with it remember the emotions stirred by the soaring music and dramatic messages that have highlighted chapel services and special events. But *it* is more than that.

What makes Moody my proudest association is that it has somehow maintained its priorities for 125 years. While many similar organizations, and especially other institutions of higher learning, have drifted so far from their Christian roots as to be nearly unrecognizable, Moody Bible Institute has stayed true to the essentials established from the beginning by D. L. Moody: the Bible and its gospel of Jesus Christ.

Mr. Moody was an evangelist, first and last. At MBI, the teaching, the training, the publishing, and eventually the radio ministry all serve the effort to share the love of God through the sacrificial death, burial, and resurrection of Jesus.

It falls to the gatekeepers at Moody to maintain above all the centrality of the Scriptures and the preeminence of Christ. The Moody trustees, of whom the president is one, annually sign a copy of the MBI doctrinal statement—as does every member of the faculty and senior staff—to individually affirm their continuing commitment to it. While this document has been annotated and clarified, it has remained virtually unchanged since 1927.

Is that the certain something that makes Moody what it is? Does this singleness of purpose—the centrality of the Bible and the preeminence of Christ—make all else about the milieu and the people that much richer and deeper?

May it ever be that when the name Moody Bible Institute is invoked anywhere in the world, people will know what we stand for: not for any individual who has ever been associated with the place, but rather for Jesus Christ, the Name above all names, and the Book that tells His story.

JERRY B. JENKINS
Chairman, Board of Trustees
The Moody Bible Institute
of Chicago

# Introduction

## There is no place like Moody.

I have believed that for many years. As a pastor, I was blessed by the exceptional conferences Moody hosted for Christian workers. As a mission agency president, I was pleased with the high-quality missionary candidates Moody produced for cross-cultural ministry. As a parent, I was delighted by the rich biblical training Moody provided my children. Now, as Moody's president, with a view from the inside, I am more convinced than ever: There is no place like Moody!

With 39,000 graduates ministering around the globe, Moody Bible Institute penetrates the world with the Word. Every continent has been marked by the ministry of pastors, evangelists, missionaries, educators, and aviators who are alumni of MBI. By God's grace, this legacy will only grow as MBI enjoys its highest enrollment in history. New campuses have been recently added into Moody's system in Spokane, Washington, and Plymouth, Michigan.

In addition to its global reputation as a leader in biblical education, Moody continues to use its substantial media ministries to proclaim the truth of God's Word to a needy world. The Moody Radio Network, along with its affiliates, blankets America with quality, biblically based programming. Moody Publishers uses traditional methods as well as digital formats to produce books that teach, encourage, and inspire believers in their faith.

As Moody Bible Institute celebrates its 125th anniversary, it remains firmly rooted to its biblical mission. Since its inception in 1886, MBI has always been committed to the proclamation of the Word of God. That will not change.

However, to remain relevant to a rapidly changing world, it is vital that MBI continue to adapt. Powerful forces are reshaping this planet.

Globalization has not only flattened the world but also linked it through a wireless, mobile web. Mammoth megacities are sprouting in dozens of locations as more people flock to urban centers. The global flow of communication is bringing an increasingly secularized worldview among all religious groups. City centers are no longer melting pots but resemble a patchwork quilt of different ethnic and linguistic identities operating side by side. The world has changed and the pace of change is accelerating. Moody graduates now minister in a multiethnic, multilingual, multicultural, urban-oriented world.

To continue its rich legacy into the future, MBI must be effective in this world that is and is becoming. Graduates must be intentionally trained to operate in a multicultural milieu without diluting the truth of the Bible. As the global church continues to grow and mature, MBI must have an increasing role in equipping international church leaders. New technology must constantly be evaluated so valuable tools can be selected and implemented. As an organization, MBI must become nimble and agile so it can adjust quickly and seize promising opportunities for the gospel. The organizations with most impact in upcoming years will be the ones with the greatest flexibility, wisdom, and courage.

This is not a time for MBI to relax or rest on its considerable laurels. False religions are making major global advances. Historic centers for evangelical Christianity are rapidly becoming post-Christian. Despite the encouraging growth of the church worldwide, it continues to be outstripped by population growth. Thus, the sad fact remains that there are more unbelievers alive than at any other time in human history. The Great Commission is still not accomplished.

Therefore, there remains an urgent need for preachers of the gospel. There remains a critical role for more missionaries, pastors, and teachers. There remains a vital place for those who can handle well the Word of God and proclaim its relevancy to man.

This is the gap MBI has sought to fill for 125 years. Until Jesus returns in the air, by His grace and with His enablement, this is the gap that Moody will continue to fill.

As you read this book chronicling Moody's history, may you rejoice in God's good hand on this institution. But may you also be reminded there is work that remains and there is no place like Moody.

J. Paul Nyquist
President
The Moody Bible Institute
of Chicago

# Preface:
## Invitation to a
## Quasquicentennial

Most Americans over the age of forty have firsthand knowledge of a *bicentennial* celebration—two hundred years of American independence in 1976 meant fireworks, parties, a parade of tall ships into Atlantic Coast harbors, and commentary about what makes America great. Those over the age of fifteen understand what a *millennial* celebration means, as they celebrated the second thousand years of the Christian era in the year 2000 with personal resolutions, reflection, and fireworks bursting throughout the world—hour by hour, thanks to the marvel of live satellite television coverage.

But only fans of Latin are familiar with a *quasquicentennial* celebration. A *quasquicentennial* is an anniversary celebrating an event that is 125 years old. This book celebrates 125 years of history following a major event in Bible school education: the founding of the Moody Bible Institute of Chicago. The celebrations in 2011 may not include fireworks, but for alumni and students alike, they probably will bring to mind lessons learned inside and outside the classroom—lessons about God's will, His grace, His plans—as well as personal friendships and compassionate professors. For those who never stepped into a Chicago classroom or attended an evening school class in Florida, Indiana, Illinois, Wisconsin, or Ohio, the celebrations may bring to mind Moody Radio broadcasts heard at one of the thirty-five owned-and-operated stations or one of over one thousand affiliates. Others may recall a book with an evangelistic message, like *An Anchor for the Soul*, or a book that restored a marriage, like *The Five Love Languages*.

Moody Bible Institute, which comprises an educational institution, a far-flung radio network, and a leading evangelical publisher—all dedicated to advancing Christ's kingdom—continues to have an impact on students, readers and listeners, and churches and Christian organizations across America and globally as it celebrates its quasquicentennial. *The MBI Story* seeks to remind readers of the vision of the Institute's innovative founder, D. L. Moody, and how that commitment to innovation pervades his Bible institute today.

After celebrating its first one hundred years in 1986, MBI senior leaders could have been content to simply hold the line. Instead, MBI stayed true to its mission but not complacent to its call. During the past twenty-five years the undergraduate school achieved accreditation and opened its first branch campus in Spokane; the graduate school offered a master of divinity degree; education joined the Internet revolution with online courses anytime, anywhere; and the Institute relocated and reinvented its signature flight school, Moody Aviation. Meanwhile the Moody Theological Seminary opened in Chicago and Michigan, Moody Publishers celebrated its first number one *New York Times* bestseller, *The Five Love Languages*, and Moody Radio jumped into the new world of communications technology.

The dynamic story of Moody Bible Institute and its founder has been chronicled by several qualified historians and biographers, but none better than Gene A. Getz and Lyle Dorsett. For the Institute's 1986 centennial, this writer was honored to update Getz's original *MBI: The Story of Moody Bible Institute*, written in 1969. Trained as an educator, Getz had penned a history that focused on the Institute's educational impact and drew on his doctoral dissertation (New York University). Portions of his original history and insights as well as our 1986 edition appear in several chapters of this book. Lyle Dorsett, a church historian and successful biographer, wrote the thorough and insightful biography of Dwight L. Moody, *A Passion for Souls*, in 1997. His research uncovered new information on the evangelist's vision, as well as Moody's skills, temperament, and character. Chapter 1 of this history, which explores Moody's ambition to create a Bible institute even as he remained involved in evangelism, is informed largely by Dorsett's deep yet winsome biography of the great evangelist.

With so many innovations at MBI in the past twenty-five years, I found helpful information from more than a dozen interviews with staff and managers at the Chicago and Spokane campuses. I am particularly grateful to Cecil Bedford and Jack Lewis at Spokane as they uncovered key elements of the recent history of MBI–Spokane (including the new Moody Aviation relocated to the Pacific Northwest). In Chicago, among the senior managers and directors, Ed Cannon, Larry Davidhizar, Charles Dyer, and Cynthia Uitermarkt granted extended interviews and reviewed portions of the manuscript. In media ministries, Doug Hastings (Moody Radio) and Greg Thornton (Moody Publishers) provided helpful perspective and information. I am also grateful to Phil Shappard, who offered great context and insight on developments in radio broadcasting and reviewed manuscript portions describing the Moody Radio expansion and implications of satellite broadcasting. Thanks, too, to John Jelinek for his insights on Moody Theological Seminary.

My thanks to the keepers of the Moody archives, better known as the Moodyana collection. Amy Koehler and Nikki Tochalauski opened the library's archive doors many times to let me explore portions of original writings and vintage historical photographs, many of which appear in the rich photo spread of this book. I am also grateful to Bailey Huckabee, my research assistant, who spent more time than I in the archives locating materials. Thanks too to Lysa Ellis, who provided valuable documents and background on the history of Moody Institute of Science. And special thanks to Betsey Newenhuyse, who offered wise counsel as well as the deft touch of her editor's hand.

Finally I appreciate the understanding and sacrifice of my three sons, who saw far less of their dad many summer weekends as he continued to research and write. Most of all, I appreciate my wife, Lori, who cleared time for me, explained my limited availability to Jonathan, Danny, and Tim, and showed compassion and forgiveness when my times with the project exceeded my times with the family.

Beyond giving a fuller context for understanding the history and legacy of Moody Bible Institute, may *The MBI Story* provide cause to celebrate God's gracious blessing upon the Institute and the servants who have ministered throughout its 125 years of teaching the Word and reaching the world.

JAMES VINCENT

# ( Part 1 )

## Quasquicentennial

# 125 Years of History
# at Moody Bible Institute

# The School That
# D. L. Moody Founded

Many institutions have been around longer than Moody Bible Institute, the school founded by evangelist D. L. Moody. Indeed, as MBI celebrates its 125th anniversary in 2011, ten colleges in America will have already celebrated their 250th anniversary—they began to offer bachelor's degrees before the thirteen colonies declared their independence from England. Moody Bible Institute, founded in 1886, is not even the oldest Bible school of higher learning. That honor goes to Nyack College of New York, founded four years earlier.[1]

Yet the impact of MBI in the annals of both higher and general adult education makes the school a leader in innovative training. Consider these firsts:

- The first program to train church musicians, in 1889. Northwestern University of Evanston, Illinois, launched the second church program in 1896.
- First correspondence courses offered by an evangelical school (1901). MBI became just the third correspondence school in America, preceded by Chautauqua and the University of Chicago.
- First Bible-oriented evening school, begun in 1903.

- First complete (three-year) program in Jewish studies (1923).
- Bible conferences, tracing back to 1897. Though such meetings began earlier, the extension department became one of the main promoters of such conferences, and influenced the Bible conference movement more than any other evangelical organization.
- First correspondence school course offered on radio (1926). *Radio School of the Bible* became the longest running educational radio program, offering on-air courses from the Moody Correspondence School for eighty-six years. First carried on Chicago station WMBI, it was later syndicated nationally. The final program aired in September 2002.
- First noncommercial educational and religious radio station, WMBI-AM (1926).

For Moody Bible Institute, which comprises educational, broadcasting, and publishing divisions, innovation is part of its DNA. All three branches serve to advance Christ's kingdom. The innovative approaches reflect the imprint of its founder and first president, Dwight L. Moody. Far better known as an evangelist than as a businessman or educator, Moody challenged the masses to come to the Savior.

Though sometimes plain-spoken and having a limited education, D. L. Moody displayed a humble attitude and a confidence in the Scriptures that would impress his supporters. They helped the onetime entrepreneur in his quest to serve Christ and His church. Moody's goals—to train Christian workers, spread the gospel, and distribute inexpensive books about the Christian life and the truths of Scripture—were accomplished partly during his lifetime. After his death, strong leaders he had appointed would further advance those goals and fulfill his vision; subsequent leaders would extend that vision with innovative programs throughout the twentieth century and beyond.

## SELLING SHOES AND SEEKING WEALTH

The compassion and directness of D. L. Moody may be due in part to his childhood in Northfield, Massachusetts. Dwight's father, Edwin Moody, died when Dwight was only four. His mother gave birth to twins one month later, giving Betsy Moody seven sons and two daughters. Though Betsy's brothers helped the family, the amassed debt made life difficult. Years later, Moody wrote, "My father died before I can remember.... He died a bankrupt, and the creditors came in and took everything as far as the law allowed. We had a hard struggle. Thank God for my mother! She never lost hope."[2] Young Dwight received perhaps four years of formal education at the local school before he joined his older brother Luther, who was boarding with a childless couple. Only ten years old, Dwight would spend most of his next seven winters staying with other families, as he and his older brothers helped neighbors with the farm chores to ease the burden on their mother, home with two young daughters.[3]

At age seventeen, Dwight Lyman Moody, restless and dissatisfied with farming and logging, left sheltered Northfield, Massachusetts (population 1,000 in 1850), for Boston, a metropolis of 150,000. He became a sales clerk in his uncle Samuel's shoe store. Within three months he had become the store's top seller of shoes and boots. Ever ambitious and out-going, he joined the Boston Young Men's Christian Association prima-rily to enjoy the YMCA's well-stocked library and its public lectures. Despite his limited education—or because of it—Moody wanted to learn. But he also wanted to make money. He learned about world markets and the selling prices of grain in New York, and even advised his broth-ers on what to plant and sell if they wanted to turn a large profit.[4]

## A TOUCH AND TEARS

Moody did honor his uncle Samuel's request to attend Sunday school and worship services at the local Congregational church. On Saturday afternoon April 21, 1855, his Sunday school teacher, Edward Kimball, was

| 1855 | 1860 | 1865 |
|---|---|---|
|  | Abraham Lincoln is elected president. | President Abraham Lincoln is assassinated. |
| Dwight L. Moody becomes a Christian. | Lincoln visits Sand Mission School and Superintendent Moody. |  |

preparing his Sunday lesson when he felt constrained to visit Moody and talk to him about receiving Christ. He obeyed the prompting, and arriving at the shoe store he found Moody in the back, wrapping and shelving shoes.

"I went up to him and put my hand on his shoulder," Kimball recalled years later, "and as I leaned over . . . I made my plea. . . . I simply told him of Christ's love for him and the love Christ wanted in return."[5]

Moody indicated Kimball's touch and tears made him tender to the gospel: "I recollect my teacher came around behind the counter . . . and put his hand upon my shoulder and talked to me [about] Christ and my soul. . . . I said to myself, 'This is a very strange thing. Here is a man who never saw me till lately, and he is weeping over my sins, and I never shed a tear about them.' But I understand it now, and know what it is to have a passion for men's souls and weep over their sins."[6]

## A STRUGGLE TO SURRENDER

In September 1856, Moody went west to Chicago, where his talent as a shoe salesman landed him a job at a thriving boot and shoe store in the downtown area. One of the owners noted, "His ambition made him anxious to lay up money. His personal habits were exact and economical. As a salesman he was . . . [a] zealous and tireless worker."[7] Soon "he was making more in one week ($30) than he was making in Boston in a month." Beyond selling boots and shoes for an astute entrepreneur, he was making much in real estate, buying land and selling it at a profit in a booming Chicago.[8] His personal ambition was to become wealthy—he hoped to make $100,000 in his lifetime, a princely sum in those days.

He was well on his way to achieving that goal when, in 1860, he decided to give up his business plans and devote his efforts entirely to Christian work. It was not sudden. He had given his Sundays fully to the

| 1871 | 1872 | 1874 |
|---|---|---|
| The Great Chicago Fire engulfs Chicago. | | Women's Christian Temperence Union founded. |
| | Moody challenged by Briton Henry Varley. | |

Lord's work soon after arriving, and his youthful energy and passionate commitment sustained him each weekend. He had joined the Plymouth Congregational Church and quickly rented one pew and made it his goal to fill it. He soon did, calling idle men on street corners and early risers in the rooming houses of downtown to join him. Eventually he "rented five pews and kept them filled with young men at every service. He also went out and hunted up boys and girls for the Sunday school."[9]

Next he started his own mission school for poor, underserved children living on the north side of the Chicago River in a vice-ridden section called the Sands and sometimes labeled "Little Hell." Some lived with one parent and skipped school to help at home. Moody, himself from a poor home and raised by one parent after his father's death, knew they needed the gospel. Unlike the typical church that did not know how to help these children who lacked discipline and interest, Moody's school accepted the occasional screams and scuffles and laughter, even as it focused on singing, Bible readings and stories, and prayer.

The Sands Mission School began in a vacant saloon but grew and soon moved to a large hall over the city's North Market, after Moody won the support of John Farwell, an entrepreneur who sold dry goods. The mission school soon had more than three hundred students. By late 1860, up to 1,200 students came each Sunday, and president-elect Abraham Lincoln, en route to Washington, stopped in Chicago to visit. At Moody's request, Lincoln gave an impromptu speech.[10]

Despite his zeal to spread the gospel, Moody still wrestled to surrender his ambitions to God fully. One of his mentors, Mrs. H. Phillips, known as Mother Phillips at her home church, had taught the relatively new believer in 1857 to be more faithful in prayer and also emphasized Scripture memorization, systematic Bible study, and the importance of disciple-making. That year Mother Phillips had urged him to quit business and wholeheartedly take up "the call." The same year J. B. Stillson,

| **1879** | **1881** | **1883** |
|---|---|---|
| Thomas Edison invents first functioning lightbulb. | | |
| *Moody begins Northfield Seminary for Young Women.* | *Moody opens Mount Hermon Boys' School.* | *Emma Dryer organizes the May Institute.* |

**MBI IMPACT**

( Radical Obedience )

For someone who had made it his goal in Chicago to earn $100,000, it seems surprising D. L. Moody resigned from his job, leaving behind a large annual salary and the big bank account he once hoped to nurture. But the call to radical obedience made total sense one day, as Moody watched the sacrifice of a teacher at his Sands Mission School.*

A loyal Sunday school teacher who managed to handle a noisy class of girls week after week missed a class one Sunday due to sickness, and Superintendent Moody took over. He appreciated how the teacher had calmed the unruly girls as they acted up on Moody himself. The next week the teacher came to Moody's store to announce he was leaving Chicago.

"I have had a hemorrhage of the lungs and the doctor tells me I can't live here. I am going home to my widowed mother to die."

Moody comforted the man and reminded him death was nothing to fear. The man agreed, but expressed his grief over the souls of the girls in his Sunday school class. Moody suggested that together they visit each of the girls "and tell them just how you feel."

Moody obtained a carriage and together they began to make the calls. At the first house the pale teacher said, "Mary, I must leave Chicago; I can't stay here any longer; but before I leave I want you to become a Christian." The teacher and student talked awhile, and then he prayed. Moody also prayed, and the girl became a Christian.

| 1892 | 1893 | 1894 | 1899 |
|---|---|---|---|
| Alexander Graham Bell establishes a telephone line between New York and Chicago. | | | |
| | Moody and his institute mobilize for the World Exposition in Chicago. | Moody opens Bible Institute Colportage Association. Joins Institute in 1899. | D. L. Moody dies. R. A. Torrey becomes the Institute's second president. |

During the next ten days, the teacher found some strength, and Moody assisted as the teacher made calls on other girls. One by one the girls surrendered their hearts to Christ. Finally the teacher visited Moody with the news he was leaving for home the next day. Moody wanted to arrange one last meeting of the class that night. The teacher, still weak, agreed to a farewell time of prayer, and Moody contacted all the girls.

"That night God kindled a fire in my soul that has never gone out," Moody said. The dying teacher explained how God had given him strength to visit each of them. The teacher then read some Scripture and began to pray. Moody explained what happened next:

"He prayed for me as superintendent of the school; after he prayed, I prayed; and when I was about to rise, to my surprise one of those scholars began to pray, and she, too, prayed for the superintendent. Before we rose from our knees every one had prayed. It seemed as if heaven and earth came together in that room.

"The next day I went back to the store, but, to my amazement, I had lost all ambition for business."

*Charles F. Goss recounted the episode in his 1900 book on Moody, *Echoes from the Pulpit and Platform* (Hartford, Conn.: Worthington, 1900); cited in Dorsett, *Passion*, 76–77.

| **1884** | **1886** | **1887** | **1889** |
|---|---|---|---|
| A ten story building in Chicago is the world's first true "skyscraper." | | | Jane Addams opens Hull House in Chicago. |
| | *Moody issues second call to train gap men; founding date of Bible institute.* | *Chicago Evangelization Society incorporates.* | *R. A. Torrey becomes general superintendent of Moody's Bible institute.* |

an evangelist twice Moody's age, taught D. L. the importance of tracts and New Testaments. The two men teamed to distribute the literature to the sick and to sailors lodging at night along the Chicago River; they also read the Scriptures to shut-ins.[11]

Now, in 1860, his struggle came to a head. Business travel, which he liked, increasingly was robbing him of time in ministry, which he loved. He could not forget the words of Mother Phillips to heed "the call." Biographer Lyle Dorsett attributes Moody's final step to full surrender to the example of a faithful Sunday school teacher (see "Radical Obedience"). Later Moody would say, "When I came to Jesus Christ, I had a terrible battle to surrender my will . . . [and then in 1860] I had another battle for three months." In one sermon he summarized the ultimate outcome: "Whenever God has been calling me to higher service, there has always been a conflict with my will. I have fought against it, but God's will has been done instead of mine."[12]

Moody entered full-time religious work with the same zeal he displayed in business. He soon became a leading figure in the national Sunday school movement, and in 1865 he was named president of the Chicago Young Men's Christian Association.

## MEETING MISS DRYER

In the midst of his busy schedule as a Christian leader and evangelist, Moody soon became keenly interested in educational endeavors. In 1870 he first met Emma Dryer, who had served on the faculty at Illinois State Normal University for six years as teacher of grammar and drawing, finally becoming principal of the women's faculty. Miss Dryer recently had resigned from the faculty after a debilitating bout of typhoid fever followed by complete healing. She believed the Lord restored her so she might "meditate on the needs of the dying world as never before. . . . And in my earnest prayerful meditation, God gave me new light from the Scriptures." She chose to commit her life to Christian service and left secular teaching.[13]

Her educational background, knowledge of the Bible, and dependence on God—like Moody, she had the courage to leave worldly success to serve Christ wherever He led—impressed the evangelist.

The Great Chicago Fire roared through the city on October 8, 1871, as Dryer visited friends there. Suddenly she found herself involved in various kinds of relief work. Sensing the great need, Miss Dryer began three busy years conducting mothers' meetings and children's industrial schools in Moody's Northside Tabernacle, which had been reconstructed at Ontario and Wells streets after the fire. As they worked alongside one another while helping the needy, Miss Dryer and Moody often talked about his special work in England, known as the Mildmay Institutions, which included the annual Mildmay Conference, thriving evangelistic and missionary enterprises in a large conference hall, and a nearby deaconess house, where women received training for home and foreign missions work.

Moody was particularly interested in the training home for female workers. He urged Miss Dryer to become active in this type of ministry. He told her he was planning to go to England for ten months but wanted to begin something similar to the Mildmay work. He asked Miss Dryer to begin such a training institute and promised that once he returned from England, he would build a home for the work.

## THE VISION FOR A COEDUCATIONAL BIBLE SCHOOL

Miss Dryer told Moody that she felt this proposed training school should be for young men as well as women. Moody, however, hesitated to start a coeducational program. He feared such a program would give the impression he was trying to compete with seminaries. Eventually this problem resolved itself in his mind, but it was Miss Dryer who raised the idea of coeducational training at the Chicago school.

Moody made a couple of visits to the British Isles in connection with his Sunday school and YMCA activities. When he returned for a third visit to Britain in 1872, he heard a challenge from evangelist Henry Varley: "The world has yet to see what God will do with a man fully consecrated to him." Varley's statement profoundly moved Moody, who reportedly said, "By God's grace I will be that man."[14] The next year he returned to Great Britain once more, this time for the first of his great evangelistic campaigns (1873–75), followed in 1875–1876 by his first American campaigns in New York, Philadelphia, and Chicago.

Meanwhile, Miss Dryer worked hard to develop what she called the "Bible Work" in Chicago. Though absent most of the time, Moody kept in contact, enlisting financial supporters for her and many students as he provided personal enthusiasm and prayers.

The ten months that Moody planned to be away from Chicago before he returned to promote this new work turned out to be more than ten years. His intentions were good, but his zeal for evangelistic work both at home and abroad dominated his schedule. Not until 1886 was he able to follow through on the plans he and Miss Dryer had talked about so enthusiastically in the winter of 1873.

Dryer conducted the first Bible classes in the temporary Northside Tabernacle, later in the Relief and Aid Society building, and eventually in a room provided in the new YMCA building. Moody urged friends in Chicago to support the expanding Bible work and its staff. Among his business friends were N. S. Bouton, Mrs. John V. Farwell, and the Cyrus McCormicks. Writing at that time, Miss Dryer reported: "Our workers had their appointed districts, in which they held meetings, and visited from house to house, cooperating with near churches."

She later described Moody's vision for the Bible work and his future Bible institute this way: "It was still Mr. Moody's hope to fill Chicago with Christian workers, who should competently instruct, and who working from missions, and selected stations, by house to house visitation, distribution of the Bible, teaching in homes and missions, should do a continued work for Christ here, and also in foreign fields."[15]

## THE VISION FOR NORTHFIELD

Moody's base of operations from 1871 to 1885 largely shifted from Chicago back to Northfield. The Moodys' home had been destroyed in the Chicago Fire, and he had relocated his wife, Emma Revell Moody, and their children to Northfield, his boyhood village. Between campaigns he now returned to Northfield. In a sense, Chicago was out of sight and almost out of mind. But his vision for educating the young and the poor for God's service was energized while home for two or three months a year. He sought to help impoverished New England girls with a college preparatory school—a rare type of institution for girls, especially girls in northern New England. He enlisted the help of Henry F. Durant, a wealthy Boston lawyer who founded Wellesley College in 1875, to give women a liberal arts education that included courses in English Bible and Christian doctrine.

Moody and Ira Sankey, his evangelistic song leader and soloist, donated the royalties from their popular hymnbook. Others offered funding, and several notable northern New Englanders joined the board of trustees. The Northfield Seminary for Young Women began on November 3, 1879. When officials dedicated the women's dormitory in September 1880, Moody concluded his address by saying, "The Lord laid it upon my heart some time ago to organize a school for young women in the humbler walks of life who never would get a Christian education but for a school like this."[16]

This was Moody's first school, but another would follow before the Chicago Bible institute would rise. People in the region pleaded for a school for boys and young men, and in May 1881 Mount Hermon Boys' School opened three miles from Northfield Seminary. Both schools included curriculum as well as extracurricular activities intended to help Christian students grow in their faith. Yet being a Christian was not a requirement for admission. Moody welcomed nonbelievers who could be loved into the kingdom. And in a society that offered limited educational opportunities to women and ethnic minorities, both schools enrolled Native Americans, students of Asian background, and African Americans.[17] Students paid only half the cost of tuition and room and board, but Moody found willing donors who paid all costs for the poorest boys and girls.[18]

In 1890, four years after Moody's supporters organized the Chicago Bible institute, Moody would launch a third school in the Northfield area. The Northfield Bible Training School (NBTS) focused on women with little or no formal training. Many times following his campaigns in New England and eastern Canada, Moody had learned about women who accepted Christ and within a couple of years sensed an ongoing call to home or international missions. Many were illiterate. "Moody wanted to connect those who were called with the locations needing workers," and these women assisted urban churches with evangelism and house-to-house personal work in the community.[19]

So as not to drain funds from Northfield Seminary, Mount Hermon, and the budding Chicago Bible institute, Moody found some wealthy Christians who owned the Northfield, a luxury hotel that hosted guests attending "deeper life" conferences. Moody had organized this conference program in Northfield, which hosted notable speakers during most of the spring and summer. During the six nonconference months (September through March), the hotel was empty. Moody put two women in each of the larger rooms and offered two three-month terms during the school year.

NBTS was a vocational school that taught skills such as sewing, cooking, music, and hygiene to prepare women to meet the physical needs of the urban poor they would serve. It had no endowment and no buildings of its own, yet it attracted an increasing number of women students. Historian Lyle Dorsett called it "one of Moody's most successful educational ventures."[20] Eventually Emma Moody would work closely with the women at NBTS. The school trained women for eighteen years before it was absorbed into the Northfield Seminary.

## MAY DAYS

Meanwhile the diligent Miss Dryer prepared for the coming Bible institute in Chicago. In 1882 she met the Reverend W. G. Moorehead, then a professor (and later president) at Xenia Theological Seminary in Ohio. Impressed with his teaching ability, she considered him as a possible teacher for a "test" institute in May of 1883. Later she approached Charles A. Blanchard, pastor of Moody's Chicago Avenue Church. Blanchard liked the idea of a preliminary institute and told her to forge ahead; he would be sure the necessary $500 to begin would be there when the doors opened.

The short-term "May Institute" opened with Moorehead in charge. Those institutes resumed each year in May until the year-round institute opened formally in 1889. However, other special events were occurring that soon would transform the Bible work in Chicago into a larger, more permanent organization.

## THE CHICAGO EVANGELIZATION SOCIETY

Moody's attention returned strongly to the proposed Bible institute in 1885 and again in 1886–87. Sometime in January 1885, Moody attended a special meeting in Farwell Hall to discuss city evangelization. T. W. Harvey, a prominent lumber merchant, presided. After two papers were read and discussed, Moody addressed the group. He laid the problem squarely on the line: If the leaders wished to carry on their plans to start the Chicago training school, the first step must be to raise the money to finance the work.

The need was there—of this he was convinced. But were the people of Chicago ready to support such an endeavor? He was not interested in starting the school without the full support and interest of the people in Chicago. According to Blanchard, Moody was candid in letting the people know that he himself would not spend time in Chicago raising money. His broader work was very demanding, and he felt it was up to someone else to raise the funds.[21]

Before departing, Moody told Emma Dryer, "Keep it before them, that I won't come until they raise that $250,000." Evidently Miss Dryer did this. Mrs. Nettie F. McCormick and her son pledged a total of $50,000. (Her husband, Cyrus H., inventor of the reaper that bears his name, had died just a year earlier.) John V. Farwell promised $100,000 in stock, and the long hoped-for and prayed-for training school was turning into a reality.

A year later Moody, again in Chicago, spoke at Farwell Hall on the subject of city evangelism. He kept the vision and the need before the audience: The next day, on January 23, 1886, a Chicago newspaper recounted Moody's address:

I tell you what I want, and what I have on my heart. I would like to see $250,000 raised at once; $250,000 for Chicago is not anything.

**MBI IMPACT** ( The San Francisco Preview )

While Moody was still in San Francisco, the local press interviewed him shortly before he left for Chicago to attend the final May Institute; his Bible institute would open four months later. The interview (abridged) contains many significant statements about the proposed Chicago Bible institute:

**Question:** What do you aim to accomplish through a Bible institute?

*Answer:* To raise up a class of men and women who will help pastors in their work: who will visit from house to house and reach the non-church goers. In other words, we must have a class of men and women between the laity and ministry to do the work that must be done.

**Question:** Will not such an organization antagonize theological seminaries?

*Answer:* I think it will help the seminaries. Many who go into the work will see the need of more training and study, and after a year or two will go into some theological seminary and take the regular course.

**Question:** What do you intend to teach at Chicago?

*Answer:* The great fundamental doctrines of the Bible, such as repentance, regeneration of the Holy Spirit, atonement, conversion,

---

Some will be startled, but see how the money is pouring in upon you. See how the real estate has gone up, and how wealth is accumulating, and how you are gaining in population, and a quarter of a million is not much. Take $50,000 and put up a building that will house seventy-five or one hundred people, where they can eat or sleep. Take the $200,000 and invest it at 5 percent, and that gives you $10,000 a year just to run this work. Then take men that have the gifts and train them for this work of reaching the people.

But you will say: "Where are you going to find them?" I will tell you. God never had a work but what He had men to do it. I believe we have got to have gap-men—men to stand between the laity and the ministers; men who are trained to do city mission work.[22]

justification, redemption, faith and assurance, law and grace, sanctification and consecration, resurrection. Of course a great deal of the instruction will be in methods of practical work, as "How to interest non-church goers," etc. Such matters will be discussed at many of the sessions.

**Question:** Do you intend to work independent of the churches?

*Answer:* No sir; but in full sympathy with all evangelical churches.

**Question:** What will be the cost?

*Answer:* Instruction will be free; the workers will board and lodge themselves.

**Question:** Do you know any scheme like this in the country?

*Answer:* I do not, nor in any other country, but I think it is the crying need of our churches today. Three-fourths of the workingmen in all our large cities are entirely neglected, and we must train men and women to reach them.

**Question:** Why not start such an enterprise right here in San Francisco?

*Answer:* I think Chicago is more central and less expensive to reach. San Francisco is too far to one side.

**Question:** Will you take persons of any nationality?

*Answer:* Yes; anyone who can understand the English language.

---

Just over a year later, on February 5, 1887, seven trustees signed the document creating the Chicago Evangelization Society. The first signature was that of Moody, who was also CES president. Others included Harvey, Farwell, Cyrus H. McCormick Jr., and Robert Scott, senior partner in what would become Carson Pirie Scott, a leading Chicago department store chain. Intentionally or not, the date honored Moody: February 5 marked his fiftieth birthday! CES began one week later, February 13, when the state of Illinois certified the organization.[23]

At its founding, CES established the Bible Work Institute, soon to be the Chicago Bible institute, the school D. L. Moody founded.[24] CES grew and thrived. Its workers held city tent meetings and visited homes with tracts and the gospel; some led Bible classes.

## AN UNEXPECTED DETOUR

The only setback occurred in July 1887, when Moody announced he would resign from the board of trustees. Moody and the board had disagreed about "some fundraising and construction strategies."[25] Later he received a letter from Mrs. C. H. (Nettie) McCormick in which she expressed some discontent regarding the constitution of the Chicago Evangelization Society along with some suggestions for improvement.[26] In his reply to Mrs. McCormick, Moody took issue with the board's plan to increase its size but also felt it would benefit the board if he resigned. The letter stunned Nettie, a loyal friend and major supporter, as well as Moody's fellow trustees. Mrs. McCormick immediately wrote and offered her own resignation in place of Moody's.

At this point the two Emmas, Dryer and Moody, close friends who knew D. L. well, interceded. Miss Dryer recognized that the plan for a year-round institute would not succeed without Moody's involvement. She sent a letter to Moody criticizing him for hurting the McCormicks and not respecting the decisions of others. She also wrote her good friend Emma Moody, "asking her to talk sense into her husband."[27]

Emma Moody played an important part in convincing her husband he should change his mind. Biographer James Findlay described her significant impact despite a quiet demeanor. "Emma Moody was shy and retiring in the extreme, and few people knew the influence she exerted on her husband. Little record is left of the esteem Moody held for his wife's opinions and the deep affection that existed between them. In her own special way Emma Moody acted constantly as a counterbalance to her ebullient spouse."[28]

Moody listened to both Emmas and apologized for his hasty response. He even telegraphed Dryer and McCormick to say he was "very sorry for the letter."[29] His heartfelt apology was readily accepted by Nettie McCormick and the board, and they continued to pour their energies into CES and the plan for a Bible institute.

## THE OFFICIAL FOUNDING DATE

On September 26, 1889, five months after Emma Dryer began her final May Institute (which actually commenced in April that year), formal classes began at the Chicago Bible institute. Although classes began in 1889, as early as 1905 a published annual report stated that the Institute was "founded by D. L. Moody in 1886, under the name of the 'Chicago Evangelization Society.'" This coincided with Moody's second Farwell Hall address and his public call for $250,000 for an institute to train "gap-men—men to stand between the laity and the ministers; men who are trained to do city mission work."

However, a school calendar published in 1894 had designated the founding date as September 26, 1889. In 1929, employee A. G. Olson wrote a letter to suggest that a special observance be held to celebrate the fortieth anniversary of the Institute, using the date of the "formal opening on September 26, 1889." A. F. Gaylord, the school's business manager, received the letter and then forwarded it to James M. Gray, president of the Institute. Gray wrote back the following informal note:

> I would not wish to reopen the old controversy as to the date of the founding of the Institute. We have always held it to be 1886, and although Mr. Olson is speaking of the date when it was "formally opened," yet it would be difficult to keep this distinction clear before the public.[30]

Thus the year 1886 has been accepted as the origin of Moody Bible Institute.

## FROM YALE TO LEIPZIG TO CHICAGO

Moody knew he would visit but not stay at the Bible Institute for Home and Foreign Missions—the Institute's formal name while he was alive—once it began. So he searched for the right person to lead the Institute. He soon settled on Reuben Archer Torrey, a powerful preacher who had directed a city mission in Minneapolis. Torrey combined evangelistic fervor with administrative experience and deep skill in biblical criticism. His training made some wonder why Torrey had accepted a city mission when he could be teaching in a college or university. After all, he had a BA from Yale University and a BD from Yale's Divinity School and was proficient in Greek and Hebrew. His mastery of German took him to two German universities, Leipzig and Erlangen, for postgraduate level studies in biblical criticism during the early 1880s. But Torrey sensed the call to this unique mission just as he had to Minneapolis.

This was a perfect match: the man who gave up business success initially to work with poor children had met a scholar who had given up an academic calling to serve God in urban ministry in Minnesota. Both men were preachers and evangelists. Torrey shared with Moody a passion for the urban masses and a belief that "the divinity schools, seminaries, and colleges that were providing academic training had simply failed to equip ministers and missionaries for the realities of wretched humanity at home and abroad . . . Except for rhetoric and homiletics, little was offered in practical theology."[31] From his days at Yale Divinity School, Torrey had a grasp of historical, biblical, and systematic theology.

R. A. Torrey joined as general superintendent and the primary Bible teacher; he also directed the men's department. Moody soon would recruit other teachers. With his preaching skills, Torrey also served as pastor of Moody's Chicago Avenue Church from 1894 until after Moody's death.

## THE STUDENTS COME

The Chicago Bible institute had room for fifty women and two hundred men by 1890, and these spaces soon were filled. At one point in 1898 Moody wrote Institute officials about a girl he had met in Pueblo, Colorado, who wanted to come to the Institute but was turned away because they were "full" now. "I want to see 1000 students at the Institute," he protested. He asked that they stop turning away students who were called to ministry and needed training.[32]

From its beginning, students paid for room and board only. Classes were tuition-free, thanks to donors who supported the students' education. This was Moody's vision. And 125 years later, undergraduate students at the Chicago campus still receive a tuition-paid education, paying only for room, board, books, and miscellaneous course and technology fees.

## THE WORLD COMES TO CHICAGO

Although D. L. Moody was away from the institute campus often in the 1890s, as president his fingerprints were all over campus—from the three-story 153 Building, the first structure built in 1889 (which quickly added two more stories in 1892), to the various evangelistic enterprises.

Moody and his institute mobilized for the 1893 World's Columbian Exposition in Chicago. Most remember the Exposition for its gleaming white buildings that inspired visitors to dub it the White City, and for its Palace of Fine Arts, which later became Chicago's famed Museum of Science and Industry. But Moody had a grand idea, "as novel as it was daring," his son Will later wrote: to make "such a carnival the scene of wide-spread evangelistic effort."[33]

The institute headquartered the crusade: Three hundred out-of-town workers and preachers stayed in the newly expanded 153 Building, displacing some students; and many students participated as counselors and helpers. Moody and his associates organized speakers and singers as well as recruited dozens of evangelists, including J. Wilbur Chapman, R. A. Torrey, and a young Billy Sunday. They were sent to theaters, halls, tents, and auditoriums. Moody associates and students alike invited tourists and locals to scores of venues. And the guests came. One Sunday morning in September more than 64,000 people attended seventy assemblies, and on another Sunday morning Moody preached to 20,000 in the Forepaugh's Circus tent. The World's Fair seemed to spark Moody's creativity and energy. He enlisted preachers from Germany, Poland, Russia, and France, who held services for international guests. He raised almost $70,000 to rent different venues at the Fair and throughout the city.[34]

Many Chicago believers argued for a boycott because the World's Fair was open on Sundays and the Parliament of Religions at the Fair would showcase the world's various religions. Moody, instead, saw an opportunity for evangelizing.[35]

The success there would motivate future MBI presidents and ministries to use world's fairs in the twentieth century as a means for creative advancement of the gospel. In 1939, Irwin Moon, then a member of the MBI extension department, presented Sermons from Science demonstrations to large crowds at the San Francisco World's Fair. Later Moon and his team, part of the popular Moody Institute of Science (MIS), would present films and science demonstrations at world's fairs in Seattle (1962), New York (1964), Montreal (1967), and Spokane (1974), all with an eye on how the God of creation formed this world that people might enjoy it and know Him, their Creator.

## BOOKS TO THE WORLD

Moody's other notable accomplishment at the Institute was to launch the Bible Institute Colportage Association (BICA) in 1894. "Colportage" refers to the making and distribution of religious literature. Five years later it incorporated within the Institute. The goal was to publish practical, inexpensive books on the Christian life for the masses.

The first paperback books were just ten cents, imitating the "dime novels" of the day. Yet the pricing was revolutionary for Christian books—one-third the price that was being asked for similar religious books. (The price was later raised to fifteen cents so that the colporteurs could make an adequate profit.) Early books included sermons by Moody and C. H. Spurgeon. In 1941 BICA became Moody Press and continued to expand. Today it is known as Moody Publishers, offering books, audio, and e-books. (For more on BICA, Moody Press, and Moody Publishers, see chapter 10.)

D. L. Moody died on December 22, 1899. Three months later the board of trustees voted to change the name of the school to the Moody Bible Institute of Chicago.

## NOTES

1. Nyack College was founded as the Missionary Training Institute by pastor and missionary advocate A. B. Simpson and is located in Nyack, New York.

2. As quoted in Charles F. Goss, *Echoes from the Pulpit and Platform* (Hartford, Conn.: A. D. Worthington, 1900), 495; cited in Lyle W. Dorsett, *A Passion for Souls* (Chicago: Moody, 1997), 34.

3. Dorsett, *Passion*, 34–36.

4. Ibid., 44–45.

5. Edward Kimball, "Reminiscences of Moody," MBI archives, as cited in Dorsett, *Passion*, 47.

6. D. L. Moody, as quoted in J. Wilbur Chapman, *The Life and Work of D. L. Moody* (Philadelphia: Winston, 1900), 76; cited in Dorsett, *Passion*, 47.

7. W. H. Daniels, *D. L. Moody and His Work* (Hartford, Conn.: American Publishing, 1875), 28–29; as cited in Dorsett, *Passion*, 55.

8. Dorsett, *Passion*, 56.

9. John Wilbur Chapman, *The Life and Work of D. L. Moody* (Philadelphia: Winston, 1900), 88, 91.

10. Lincoln had heard of the school's fame, but came with the understanding that he would not speak. At the end of his visit, as he readied to leave, Moody said to the school, "If Mr. Lincoln desires to say a word, as he goes out, of course all ears will be open." Lincoln moved to the center of the hall, seemingly disinterested. Then he stopped and began to address the teachers and children with humility. See John V. Farwell, *Early Recollections of D. L. Moody* (Chicago: Winona, 1907), 9; cited in Dorsett, *Passion*, 73–74.

11. Dorsett, *Passion*, 75.

12. Quoted in Joseph B. Bowles, *Moody the Evangelist* (Chicago: Moody Bible Institute, 1926), 17; cited in Dorsett, *Passion*, 75.

13. Dorsett, *Passion*, 166.

14. Bernard R. DeRemer, *Moody Bible Institute* (Chicago: Moody, 1960), 13; and Mark Fackler, "The World Has Yet to See . . ." Christian History.net; www.christianityto day.com/ch/1990/issue25/2510.html.

15. Unpublished manuscript by Emma Dryer, January 1916, 14, 19; cited in Gene A. Getz and James Vincent, *MBI: The Story of Moody Bible Institute* (Chicago: Moody, 1986), 20.

16. Dorsett, *Passion*, 285.

17. Ibid., 297, 287–88. Dorsett writes, "During some academic years the records reveal that promising students were brought to Northfield and Mount Hermon from Africa and Asia."

18. Ibid., 286. Sometimes, lacking a donor, Moody would cover the cost himself.

19. Ibid., 299.

20. Ibid., 300–301.

21. Unpublished manuscript of Charles A. Blanchard, February 1916, 12; cited in Getz and Vincent, *MBI*, 21.

22. *Record of Christian Work*, V, February 1886, 5–6. See also *Chicago Tribune*, January 23, 1886, 3.

23. Getz and Vincent, *MBI*, 54. A separate nine-member board of managers oversaw daily operation. Significantly, only two men were among the managers. The seven women managers included Emma Dryer, Mrs. C. H. McCormick, and Mrs. T. W. Harvey. See Dorsett, *Passion*, 274–75.

24. Most MBI students remember the hymnwriter Daniel B. Towner (known for such classic hymns as "Trust and Obey" and "Grace That Is Greater Than All Our Sins") for his hymn "One with the Lord" (popularly known as "God Bless the School"), with lyrics by MBI's third president, James M. Gray. The fourth verse begins, "God bless the school that D. L. Moody founded; firm may she stand, though by foes of

truth surrounded!" Written in 1909, it became the school song. A second "theme song" that traditionally has begun the academic convocation each school year is "Great Is Thy Faithfulness." More recently (2006) a third school song, "As One in Christ the Lord," by Timothy Dudley-Smith and David McCallister, is also sung at convocation and commencement.

25. Dorsett, *Passion*, 274.

26. Getz and Vincent, *MBI*, 24.

27. Dorsett, *Passion*, 274. In his letter to Mrs. McCormick dated July 18, 1887 (MBI archives), Moody explained he had two choices to resolve the board disagreement: "Either to go against my judgment and join with my board or stand aside and let the work go on without me. After due consideration I have decided to resign, and let me say in doing so, that I do it with the best wishes for the society."

28. James Findlay, "D. L. Moody," doctoral dissertation, Northwestern University, 1960, 331; see also James F. Findlay, *Dwight L. Moody* (Chicago: Univ. of Chicago, 1969).

29. Dorsett, *Passion*, 274. "Will withdraw [the letter]," he wrote. "Tell the trustees to do as they please . . . and I will come soon." Moody to McCormick and Dryer, July 27, 1887, MBI archives.

30. Original letters in MBI archive files; as cited in Getz and Vincent, *MBI*, 18.

31. Dorsett, *Passion*, 310–11.

32. Two letters from Moody to Miss Strong and Gaylord, November 24, 1898, MBI archives; cited in Dorsett, *Passion*, 299, 313.

33. William Moody, *The Life of Dwight L. Moody* (New York: Revell, 1900), 409; cited in Dorsett, *Passion*, 390. President Will Houghton would call the World's Fair outreach "the most audacious campaign of [Moody's] career"; in Will Houghton and Charles T. Cook, *Tell Me about Moody* (Chicago: Bible Institute Colportage Association, 1937), 68.

34. Houghton and Cook, *Tell Me about Moody*, 68–70; Dorsett, *Passion*, 391.

35. See Dorsett, *Passion*, 390–92.

# The Gospel Wagon
# and the E-book

D. L. Moody had visited his Chicago Bible institute several times after it opened in 1889, and he had captivated students while on campus (see pages 100–101), but he had put capable men in charge of daily operations. After the evangelist's death, they would lead the renamed Moody Bible Institute into the twentieth century.

R. A. Torrey was named superintendent when the school opened and became the second president after Moody's death, although his formal title remained superintendent. But his impact had been felt from his first day as superintendent, on September 26, 1889. Since Moody was often away in evangelistic work, the new superintendent was charged with developing the original curriculum and the program for practical Christian work. He supervised the men's department and served as the school's permanent Bible teacher, although many guest lecturers taught at the Institute in those early days. During the 1890s, Torrey moved toward establishing a resident faculty. This brought continuity and promoted unity in doctrinal positions, a wise substitute for Moody's plan to have guest teachers rotating at the school.

Equally important, Torrey led the Institute to a rock-solid position as the fundamental-liberal debate increased in volume. A number of ministers scattered throughout the land had introduced modern thinking to their congregations, and by the turn of the century some professors were openly teaching liberal theology in the seminary classrooms.[1]

With his training in historical criticism of the Bible at Yale, Leipzig, and Erlangen, Torrey had concluded the correct approach to interpreting the Scriptures was literal and conservative. After Moody's death, he became a strong spokesman for Moody Bible Institute and evangelical conservatives in defending the absolute authority of the Bible and other evangelical doctrines. Two of his popular books, *The Divine Origin of the Bible* (Revell, 1899) and *Difficulties and Alleged Errors and Contradictions in the Bible* (BICA, 1907) pointed to the inspiration and inerrancy of the Scriptures.

From the time of Torrey's arrival onward, the Scripture verse that appeared at conferences and before students through the years has been 2 Timothy 2:15: "Study to shew thyself approved unto God, a workman that needeth not be ashamed, rightly dividing the word of truth" (KJV). Torrey declared in 1911, "That text has been the motto of Moody Bible Institute from its beginning. . . . From the very first printed matter that went out from the Institute, that text stood at the top of it. The Institute has lived up to the text."[2]

## FITT TO FILL THE GAP

The newly named Institute faced two significant challenges following Moody's death. Without its founder and best promoter, the school lacked a recognized leader. Second, the school needed a solid, consistent base of donors to support MBI financially. Before his death, Moody had directed his son-in-law, A. P. Fitt, to lead the daily operations of the Bible Institute; the evangelist's older son, William Moody, would lead the Northfield schools. Fitt had served on the board in 1894–95, and agreed to return as trustee after Moody's death and to serve as full-time secretary. Although he did some teaching, he spent most of his time caring for executive and administrative details.

Fitt served well as a connecting link between the Institute and the Northfield schools, and as a liaison between the new school and D. L. Moody's interests and friends all over the world. He served the Institute in this position until he resigned in 1908 to go into business.[3]

## WISE COUNSEL FROM CROWELL

The most influential individual helping MBI mature into a strong and thriving institution was Henry Parsons Crowell. He joined the board of trustees on April 24, 1901, and was elected president of the board on April 24, 1904, a post he would hold for thirty-nine years.

The cofounder of Quaker Oats, Crowell lived only a few blocks from the Institute and with his wife, Susan, attended nearby Fourth Presbyterian Church on Michigan Avenue. Susan's friend Millicent Newell attended there with her husband, William, who was MBI registrar and later a professor. When Henry expressed a vague uneasiness about his spiritual life, Susan suggested they open their home to a Bible study where "we could invite your business friends, or people from church." He agreed, and beginning in fall 1899, Dr. Newell came to the Crowells' Rush Street home to lead a weekly study. The study had a great impact on the Crowells themselves. Susan, a regular churchgoer, became a follower of Christ. Henry rejoiced and found his own spiritual life renewed. Soon Crowell would move from "recognition as 'Christian businessman' to a 'Christian statesman.'"[4]

The wealthy and industrious Crowell—he also directed the successful Perfection Stove Company and Wyoming Hereford Ranch—prompted the Institute to look beyond prosperous donors to develop a corps of reliable, regular friends. Though he contributed great sums of

| 1900 | 1901 | 1903 |
|---|---|---|
| *Trustees name the institute Moody Bible Institute for its founder and first president.* | | *The Wright brothers make successful flight at Kitty Hawk.* |
| *The Institute Tie, forerunner of Moody magazine, begins publication.* | *Correspondence school established.* | *Evening school begins.* |

money to the work, he never allowed the Institute to become dependent upon him. The personal honesty and Christian ethics of H. P. Crowell are still reflected in the conservative and ethical financial policies of Moody Bible Institute. Designated contributions are spent where assigned, and no building projects are begun until at least 50 percent of funds are in hand, for example.

Crowell offered wise counsel in two other areas. His first was to James M. Gray, whom he urged to come to Chicago as the Institute's first dean. Gray had served as rector of the First Reformed Episcopal Church in Boston, as well as lecturer in English Bible at the Reformed Episcopal Theological Seminary in Philadelphia. He was not primarily interested in administrative work. He thought himself unable to handle the top position alone. But Crowell believed in Gray's abilities and encouraged the pastor and Bible teacher to reconsider. Because of that sincere support, Gray eventually accepted the position of dean of the Institute in 1904. He served as a strong and successful leader for the next thirty years.[5]

Educator Gene Getz credits Gray with playing a crucial role in planning the course of the school. "Although Moody's enthusiasm and R. A. Torrey's administrative and teaching abilities set the Moody Bible Institute in motion, James M. Gray probably did more than any other man to guide MBI through its most crucial years."[6]

Second, Crowell recommended the trustee board establish an executive committee to handle the affairs of the Institute between regular board meetings. They agreed. This arrangement proved to be both functional and successful; it continues to the present day. Originally the committee was composed of three members of the board who met each week at the Institute to consider matters brought before it by the executive secretary and to establish policies for that official to carry out.

After becoming president of the trustees and executive committee chairman, Crowell would meet every Tuesday at MBI with the commit-

| 1904 | 1906 | 1914–1918 |
|---|---|---|
| *James M. Gray appointed MBI dean, but has presidential role.* | Azusa Street Revival in L.A. births Pentecostal church. | World War I |

tee to monitor MBI's financial condition. For thirty years (1904–34), an alliance existed between the MBI president and the Quaker Oats president. "Dr. Gray would see to the educational and spiritual aspect of the Institute. Henry Crowell would look to the business side."[7]

## SCHOOL AFTER HOURS:
## BEGINNINGS OF THE CORRESPONDENCE SCHOOL

Within his first four years as president, R. A. Torrey supervised the creation of a correspondence school and evening school to prepare Christian workers who could not come to the Chicago campus. A correspondence program at Moody Bible Institute was considered as early as 1895, but it actually began in January 1901. Its stated objective revealed Moody's passion for training the common person: "The Correspondence Department has been organized for the benefit of those of both sexes who cannot, for financial or other reasons, attend the Institute personally. The purpose is to give them, as far as possible, all the advantages of the systematic methods of study here pursued." Moody Bible Institute launched its correspondence school just nine years after William Rainey Harper had brought such a school to the University of Chicago, making the MBI school-by-mail the "oldest of its kind in the Bible institute movement," according to S. A. Witmer of Accrediting Association of Bible Colleges.[8]

Torrey himself wrote the first two courses offered by Moody Correspondence School: Bible Doctrine and Practical Christian Work. The courses were divided into sections for easier study. The sections averaged forty-six pages each and were printed in separate pamphlets. Students often carried these pamphlets for study on the train or streetcar or would read them during their lunch hour.

When a student satisfactorily completed a course of study with a

| 1920 | 1922 | 1923 |
|---|---|---|
| Women vote; the first radio station, 8MK, begins broadcasting. | Pastors Course begins. | Jewish Missions Course begins. |

passing percentage, he received a certificate of progress, which was accepted for credit in the regular Bible Course of the Institute. A pupil studying two or three hours per week could complete the Practical Work Course in a year. Students devoting three hours per week to the Bible Doctrine Course finished that program in two years.

By 1915, the number of course offerings had doubled, from four to eight, including the first courses in apologetics, Christian evidence, and evangelism. By 1955, Moody Correspondence School offered approximately twenty courses. By 1965, more than forty were available. Today correspondence courses are still being offered—for personal enrichment only—through Moody Distance Learning.

## SCHOOL AFTER HOURS:
## BEGINNINGS OF THE EVENING SCHOOL

When MBI classes began in 1889, promotional literature advertised "special evening classes." Those classes continued for three or four years. However, the evening department began formally in 1903, with classes meeting four days a week. Attendance the first term averaged 125 each evening.

Beginning in 1904 three nights were set aside, with Tuesday and Thursday evenings being given over to Bible study and Wednesday evenings to the study of music. From 1952 to 1967 the evening school met two nights a week and then returned to three, Monday, Tuesday, and Thursday, the present schedule.

From the beginning of the regular evening program, students enrolling at night could choose either the Bible Course or the Music Course. Although the subjects offered were limited in number, Moody Bible Institute was attempting to offer "a similar course of training in

| 1926 | 1929 | 1933 | 1934 |
|---|---|---|---|
| Radio station WMBI-AM broadcasts first programs. | Stock market crashes. | Adolf Hitler seizes power in Germany. | James Gray retires. Will Houghton becomes the third MBI president. |

evening classes" as those offered in the day school. However, only from the fall term of 1918 to 1924 did the evening school parallel the day school curriculum.

When first established, the evening department had a general objective similar to that of the day school. The main purpose was "to furnish a practical course of training in Bible study and approved methods of aggressive Christian work for men and women employed during the day." Still, the day school was geared to preparing students for full-time church vocations. The evening school, on the other hand, trained lay workers who would, though active in secular work, become more effective workers in their churches and in other types of Christian service.

## THE DEAN WHO WAS PRESIDENT

In 1923 MBI Dean James M. Gray was designated president—up to that time the term *president* was reserved for the president of the board of trustees. But just as Torrey remained the "superintendent" but acted with the powers of a president in 1899 after D. L. Moody's death, so Gray remained "dean" but acted as president beginning in 1904. Torrey remained at MBI until 1908, but Gray's arrival freed the superintendent to conduct more frequent evangelistic campaigns.

During his years as president and superintendent, R. A. Torrey preached in Australia, Canada, Great Britain, and New Zealand. His evangelistic campaigns brought great fruit for the kingdom. In Massey Hall in Toronto, for example, sixteen-year-old Oswald J. Smith heard Torrey on Isaiah 53:5 and believed Jesus was the Christ, beginning a long ministry as evangelist, missions advocate, and founder and pastor of the Peoples Church of Toronto.[9] Torrey's frequent campaigns made Gray effectively the president upon his arrival in 1904.

Torrey remained with MBI until 1908, when he left to devote himself to full-time evangelism. But the heart of an educator remained. In 1912 he became the first dean of the Bible Institute of Los Angeles (today Biola University). As President Will Houghton would write later, that made Dr. Torrey "the only man to have been head of the two largest Bible institutes in the world."[10]

## NAME THAT COURSE

In 1900 the Missionary Course became part of the curriculum. For one hour each week, students learned about home and foreign missions. The Biblical, Musical, and Practical Work courses remained essentially the same, except that new subjects were added and the staff of teachers was increased, particularly for the Biblical Course. Two years of study and satisfactory completion of either the Biblical or Musical Course were still required in order to obtain a diploma.

Beginning in 1906, the term *course* was reserved for a full program of study covering a two-year cycle. As a result, the Missionary Course became missionary study, and the Practical Work Course became practical work. The Biblical Course and the Musical Course remained essentially the same but were called simply the Bible Course and the Music Course.

Students soon were classified as Bible students, Bible-music students, or music students. The minimum period for study and recitation was twenty-seven hours per week. Those preparing primarily for Bible work were advised to take the full Bible Course. Those interested in a combination of Bible and music were advised to take eighteen hours each week in the Bible Course and a maximum of nine hours in the Music Course. Students interested in preparing for a ministry in music enrolled in the Music Course and were required to take eighteen hours each week in the Music Course and a maximum of nine hours in the Bible Course.

In 1912 missionary study again became the Missionary Course, with a dual focus: First-year classes helped all students build an interest in missions, and final-year classes were designed for those who were planning to become foreign missionaries.

The foreign missions emphasis concentrated on answering the new demands in missionary training. MBI continued to add subjects to its Missionary Course over the years. Under Director William H. Hockman (1927–45), the Missionary Course offered increased medical training, reflecting the needs of and demands on the mission fields during this time. Students could elect either a short or a long course in special missionary preparation. The short course was in essence the program offered previously, while the long course included a number of additional medical subjects, such as anatomy and physiology, diseases of digestive organs, diseases of eye, ear, nose, and throat, minor surgery, obstetrics, and tropical diseases.

This curriculum resulted in a seven-term Missionary Course and a nine-term Missionary Medical Service Course, both offered until 1930. The two programs then merged into one course of eight terms, designated the Missionary Course.

## MISSIONARY UNION FOR ALL

In addition, all students were involved in missions through the Missionary Study and Prayer Union (begun in 1900). Originally the MSPU program had corresponded closely with the regular curriculum, since the outline for the MSPU meetings formed the basis for the first informal Missionary Course.

By 1913 all students were required to attend the union meetings at 9 a.m. on Wednesdays and received one half-hour credit per term. MSPU became Missionary Union in 1914, with the former MSPU subject requirements shifting to the General Course in Missions.

Until 1921 Missionary Union continued to be both a student organization and a part of the curriculum. At that time the General Course in Missions was rendered Missions and became an introductory subject required of all students. Missionary Union then became a student organization under faculty guidance. Its membership was voluntary.[11]

## LOOKING FOR PASTORS

President Gray and his team instigated a couple of major curricular—and philosophical—changes. In 1922 the Institute established the Pastors Course, a full pastoral training program. This represented a shift from previous policy: Just one month after the school opened in 1889, Moody and his collaborators took pains to avoid giving the impression that the new training was to compete with seminaries. MBI officials clarified the purpose of the school with an article in the Christian newspaper *Record of Christian Work*.

It is not to train preachers that the school is established nor to furnish a short-cut to the ministry. We say, therefore, to young men
who intend to be ministers, do not come here to prepare for the ministry. If you are ready for the ministry and want to take a short course
of practical training, come to the Institute. If you intend to study for
the ministry and desire the practical training before taking your seminary course, then come, but do not come thinking this is a substitute for a theological or a college education.[12]

The new program began in order to meet a real need, particularly to
prepare men as pastors in rural areas and to serve smaller churches
among "lower" socioeconomic groups. These were places to which many
seminary-trained men hesitated to go.

The changing impact of denominationalism also contributed to the
formation of a Pastors Course at Moody. Denominational walls rose high
during the late nineteenth century, but congregations were gradually
developing a new attitude toward selecting their pastors. Dargan calls
this "the voluntary principle in the choice and maintenance of pastors."[13]
In many instances individual congregations began to ignore denominational authority and to control their own affairs on a more decentralized
basis. This religious trend began to create pressure on MBI leaders to
inaugurate a Pastors Course—even against their desire to do so.

The voluntary principle and the lay movement both helped to break
through denominational walls. These trends also contributed to the success of the Moody school, which from its beginning had as its objective
the training of a certain type of layperson.

The goal of this new course was "to provide adequate pastoral training for the benefit of certain qualified students" who wished to enter the
Christian ministry. Initially the Pastors Course represented an additional
year of specialized studies for graduates of the regular Bible, Bible-Music,
or Missionary courses. In addition, qualified students who had taken
comparable training elsewhere also could enroll for these specialized
subjects. Later, a full program was offered especially for those interested
in the pastoral ministry.

## JEWISH MISSIONS

The second course added under President Gray was the Jewish Missions Course. It began in 1923 with Solomon Birnbaum, a first-generation Jewish follower of Jesus, as director.

In the early years, the Hebrew Christian Alliance of America (today the Messianic Jewish Alliance of America) partially funded the program,[14] but later it became a course offered by MBI. The three-year course proposed "to prepare workers to carry the Gospel of Christ to the Jews" at home or abroad. Two events helped spur the creation of the course: the Balfour Declaration at the end of World War I and the British Mandate calling for a Jewish homeland. Bible dispensationalists (including MBI leaders) saw this as part of God's fulfillment of His plan for His chosen people prior to Christ's return.[15]

In addition to the biblical studies and other courses already required in the general course, Jewish Missions offered the following specialized subjects: Hebrew, Yiddish, Rabbinics (a study of the rabbinical writings), Jewish history, Messianic prophecy, and Jewish feasts and customs.

Five Messianic Jews have led the Jewish missions program: Solomon Birnbaum, course director from 1923–40; Max I. Reich, course director from 1940–46; Nathan J. Stone, course director from 1946–66; Louis Goldberg, professor of Jewish studies, who continued the program as a major within the department of world missions from 1967–93; and Michael Rydelnik, who has been professor of Jewish studies since 1994.

The Jewish Missions Course—now Jewish studies—represented the first complete training program for ministry in Jewish missions. Stone noted, "Though other schools offer a subject or two on Jewish missions, the Institute provides an entire three-year course for those interested in this type of ministry." By 1936 about 50 percent of those in Jewish ministry in the U.S. were former MBI students, Stone had estimated. Chaplain and rabbi David Max Eichhorn wrote of MBI, "A high proportion of the most active American missionaries to the Jews . . . have been trained in this school" through 1975.[16]

Today half of the students enrolled in Jewish studies are Messianic Jews who want to learn the Bible in a way that integrates their faith and their heritage. "The other [Gentile] students have a love for Jewish people and Israel. They see the Jewish studies major as a way to study the Bible with Jewish eyes and also to understand the Jewish roots of their faith," writes Professor Rydelnik. He says all students desire to serve the Jewish community, some in Israel, some in America, and still others in various Jewish population centers. Although some are outreach workers, others "serve in the messianic Jewish world as worship leaders, congregation planters, spiritual leaders in congregations, [and doing] educational work with children and adults."[17]

In addition to these two courses, three others were developed during Gray's tenure, later to be discontinued or incorporated into academic departments. Those three courses—the English Course (1913), the Sunday School Course (1914), and the Swedish-English Course (1916)—are described in chapter 6.

## DIVINE WORK AND "DUM WORK"

During the early decades of the twentieth century, students were required to do their practical Christian work (PCW)—the forerunner of today's department of field work and practical Christian ministry—five days a week, Tuesday through Saturday. Assignments ranged from helping in city and rescue missions, teaching Sunday school classes, visiting hospitals and jails, and conducting evangelistic services.

One of the more noteworthy PCW assignments was the open-air campaigns, when students would move into the city to distribute Colportage Association literature and present the gospel. Their vehicle of choice was the gospel wagon, featuring a desk for a pulpit, a small organ, and chairs for a student choir. Once under way, the gospel wagon would stop at strategic locations on Chicago's North, West, or South Side for fifteen to twenty minutes. As Flood and Jenkins wrote, "If the people would not step inside a church, the Moody Bible Institute would take at least a semblance of the church to the people."[18] It was a novel and successful idea, which soon spread to Europe. One British publication credited MBI with creating this "church" on wheels: "The idea of the Gospel wagon probably originated at the Institute, but has become so popular that it is now seen in nearly all of the large cities of the U.S. and some in Europe."[19]

For students, the Institute owned both the carriages and the horses, which boarded in a stable on the southwest corner of Wells and Chestnut—today the location of the five-story Moody parking garage.

The gospel wagon soon became the gospel car, as gas-propelled vehicles replaced the horse-pulled wagon. The cars generally offered smoother rides, quicker transit, and more comfortable seats than the wagons that preceded them, but they held the same occupants: a small choir of men and women, a musician (typically a trombonist rather than an organist), and a speaker. The singers drew the attention of the crowd; the speaker gave a short message, and then the students would offer tracts to the audience. Soon MBI had four gospel cars.

Years earlier, colporteurs had used gospel wagons to sell books, witness to those who showed interest, and distribute tracts. The fleet of horse-drawn wagons had the following sign on each side: "Gospel and Colportage Carriage/ D. L. Moody President/ From the Bible Institute/Chicago."[20]

By 1926 larger gospel buses replaced the gospel cars. The buses transported more students to work assignments. The trombonist often had other brass and sometimes string players giving musical support to the choir.

Over time, the vehicles, used for hospital and jail visits as well as evangelism outings to Chicago street corners and factories, became worn gospel buses. In 1935 each of the four gospel buses was refurbished with a new Ford V8 chassis, and fresh paint, with a prominent seal displaying 2 Timothy 2:15, the school verse.[21]

It's unclear when the gospel buses disappeared from PCW open-air assignments and the Colportage Association ministry. Yet as a delivery system of literature and good news, the gospel bus and its predecessor, the gospel car, were both effective and innovative, true crowd-catchers in the early twentieth century. In the second decade of this century, e-books seem to have become modern echoes of the gospel wagons and cars of the early decades of last century. Electronic books offer easy transport, the ability to be read on many different devices, and the power

## MBI IMPACT — A Day in the Life of a Student

What was life like for an MBI student in the early days? For a student in 1915, daily life included several times for private and group devotions and worship. A typical day in the Women's Building began at 6:15 a.m. Tuesdays through Saturdays, the days classes met; for men the rising bell sounded at 6:30 a.m. Fifteen minutes later the bell rang again for "'Quiet Time,' which is observed for 15 minutes, during which students are expected to be quiet and in their rooms except for where assigned duties conflict," the 1915 Information Booklet explained. On Sunday and Monday, the wake-up bell rang fifteen minutes later.

Students held separate worship exercises in their respective dining rooms after breakfast, "when students are required to be present unless excused by the superintendent. On Saturday morning this service is held at 8:30 a.m. in the gymnasium, when the entire Institute household, faculty, students, business staff, and other employees unite so far as is possible."

After a 5:30 p.m. "supper," male students had evening devotions, known as fellowship meetings, in the lecture room, and women held their devotions in the chapel. In addition, "various prayer bands of the Missionary Union" met weekly, and special prayer meetings were held "from time to time in offices, dormitories, or class rooms, for particular objects."

Most classes ended at noon (several music classes were at 1:30), and "dinner" was served at 12:30. Afterward, those not on practical Christian work assignments (which could be in the afternoons or evenings) or working might study; study hours were from 2:30 to 4:30 and 7:30 to 9:00. "During these times there shall be no visiting and the house shall be as quiet as possible."

---

to reach people all over the world with the push of a button. Like the gospel car of the past, the e-book can grab people's attention and deliver vital messages that can change lives.

Beyond the divine work of PCW for God's kingdom, there was the daily work in the dorms and dining room that all students had to do;

But despite the schedule, play and visiting were included. In fact, "daily exercise to the extent of at least 45 minutes is *expected* to be taken by all students" [italics added]. The Information Booklet recommended that students "join the 'Recreation Club,' which arranges games, excursions, skating parties, etc. in their season, and which usually occur on Monday."

Although male and female students sat in separate portions of the classroom and had separate group devotions, they had opportunities to mingle and romances did develop. The Women's Building was "no man's land," but it also became known as the "match factory." As historian DeRemer noted, "'Matches' were indeed made there; where better could one obtain a life's partner than at MBI, among the cream of the crop of Christian young people?"

The Information Booklet laid out a few guidelines: "Women students attended by gentlemen, either singly or in small groups, are not permitted outings and picnics, or to take meals in hotels, cafes, or other public places, without permission of the superintendent. When not at the homes of friends or in attendance at entertainments, they are expected to be in the building before 9:00 p.m."

A later Student Information Booklet (1924–26) detailed practical matters of lodging that echo several standards of Houghton and Culbertson Halls today: "Rooms are cared for by the occupants, and must be kept clean and orderly; walls must not be defaced by nails, pins, paste or any markings; rugs may not be shaken out the windows and no articles placed in the outside sills." And in one concession to men students, shoes almost always stayed shiny: "A room is provided on the first floor (rear) of the Men's building, where men will find shoe blacking and brushes for polishing shoes, and electric irons for pressing clothing, without charge."

---

they referred to these daily tasks as *dum work*. In the dining room students emptied tables, washed glasses, and cleaned silver; in Institute offices, students would dust and clean. Many other tasks existed, and the daily, one-hour jobs helped the Institute maintain a small staff. Student assistance through dum work continued until about the time of World War II.[22]

## "PRACTICAL AND PERPLEXING QUESTIONS": MOODY IN PRINT

From its beginning, the Moody Bible Institute understood and used the power of media to educate and challenge the Christian public, as well as promote its ministries. BICA, founded in 1894 to publish practical, inexpensive books on the Christian life, joined the Institute in 1899. The next year the Institute began publishing *The Institute Tie*, a monthly magazine that focused on interests and programs of MBI. It included "all the news about the Institute, including letters from students on home and foreign fields, lectures, and activities by the instructors, outlines, and suggestions for sermon and prayer meeting talks."

The focus of the periodical changed significantly beginning in July 1907, when James M. Gray and R. A. Torrey became coeditors. The contents of the magazine began to reflect more of an educational mission, rather than being only a "tie" between the Institute and its former students and friends. Though still a mirror of Moody Bible Institute, the magazine began to meet MBI objectives by including feature articles and regular departments focused primarily on Bible study and Christian living. Torrey answered "Practical and Perplexing Questions" in most issues and later "Studies in the Life and Teaching of Our Lord." In each issue Gray wrote a biblical exposition titled "The Layman's Bible Commentary" that progressed book by book through the entire Bible.

Gray became editor-in-chief after Torrey left the Institute in 1910, and *The Institute Tie* was renamed *The Christian Workers Magazine*. Articles instructed and encouraged Christian workers, and practical helps for Sunday school teachers became common. The magazine was retitled *Moody Bible Institute Monthly* in 1920 (to be shortened simply to *Moody Monthly* in 1938). Gray would continue as editor for twenty-eight years until his death (1935).

## "WE THINK IT IS OF GOD": MOODY ON THE AIR

President James Gray clearly was a progressive. He had been a guest superintendent for four months in 1898 even as he taught Bible classes.

In 1905, one year after being appointed dean yet filling a presidential role, Gray merged the men's and women's departments, and required English as part of the curriculum. He raised entrance requirements to include having a high school diploma, despite a storm of protest that the action would exclude many for whom the school had been intended.[23]

But on some issues Gray remained the traditionalist. He could not support radio broadcasting, for example. Like many other Christian leaders, he regarded the airwaves as mysterious, even sinister. After all, the New Testament had defined Satan as "the prince of the power of the air" (Ephesians 2:2).

But shortly before MBI broadcast its first program from its own studio, Gray explained his change of heart. When a North Dakota resident wrote the school in 1926 and asked, "Is radio of God or the devil?" President Gray answered, "We think it is of God."[24]

Some credit S. A. Woodruff with the original idea of broadcasting via radio, but the man who played the most important role was young Henry Coleman Crowell, son of Henry Parsons Crowell and an assistant to the president in 1925. Young Henry Coleman had an engineering degree from Yale and was given charge of developing the radio work. Although the Institute was hesitant at first to venture into the field of broadcasting, during the early part of 1925 donations started to come in designated for this purpose. The possibilities were reevaluated, and eventually the board of trustees approved the construction of a radio station. The Institute began constructing a five-hundred-watt Western Electric transmitter near campus and a broadcasting studio was completed.

Convinced of the right position and having the full support of the trustees, the president began to accept the medium. Gray, along with Reverend J. C. Page of the faculty, delivered the first message on March 3, 1926, from 8 to 10 p.m. The two-hour broadcast (actually carried on station WENR as the Institute awaited its own wavelength from the Federal Radio Commission) evidently made President Gray a believer in the benefits of radio. After Gray had somewhat skeptically delivered his message, he walked from the studio across Institute Place to his office in the 153 Building. No sooner had he entered the office than the phone rang.

The voice on the other end of the line, to Gray's astonishment, came from Florida reporting that his message had just been received. Other calls and correspondence followed, dispelling any doubt in Gray's mind as to the value of radio. WMBI itself had its maiden broadcast three months later, on July 28, one day after a telegram from Washington informed MBI leaders that a frequency in Chicago was available.

That first year the AM station began broadcasting the program *Radio School of the Bible* (RSB). This was one of the earliest correspondence study programs ever offered by radio in America. Two class sessions aired each week, and the correspondence school selected teachers, mailed materials, and scored exams for all listeners. The program grew quickly in listeners and enrolled students.

Eventually MBI faculty taught the RSB courses, which later would air nationally on the Moody Broadcasting Network in more than 250 cities. Students received a textbook and notes upon enrollment and completed periodic exams during the academic quarter. They earned correspondence school credits for successful completion of each course. The RSB program continued for eighty-six years (concluding the third quarter of 2002) and became the longest running education program in radio. More on the history of Moody Radio, now part of the media division of Moody Bible Institute, appears in chapter 9.

When James Gray retired in 1934, the Institute was almost fifty years old. Earlier that year he had spotted his successor after a Moody-sponsored Bible conference at Calvary Baptist Church in New York City. He stayed Sunday morning to listen to the well-known pastor. Will Houghton, the preacher who was also an author and evangelist, soon would become college president as well as head of a publishing company, radio station, correspondence school, and magazine. Three years later President Houghton would lead the Institute and all its ministries during its golden anniversary celebration.

## NOTES

1. Henry Kalloch Rowe, *The History of Religion in the United States* (New York: Macmillan, 1928), 191.

2. Reported in *Chicago Christian Worker's Magazine* (later *Moody* magazine), February 1916; cited in Bernard R. DeRemer, *Moody Bible Institute* (Chicago: Moody, 1960), 61.

3. William M. Runyan, *Dr. Gray at Moody Bible Institute* (New York: Oxford Univ. Press, 1935), 136.

4. Joe Musser, *The Cereal Tycoon* (Chicago: Moody, 1997), 119–20.

5. Richard Ellsworth Day, *Breakfast Table Autocrat* (Chicago: Moody, 1946), 167.

6. Gene A. Getz, *MBI: The Story of Moody Bible Institute* (Chicago: Moody, 1969), 77.

7. Musser, *The Cereal Tycoon*, 130–31.

8. S. A. Witmer, *The Bible College Story* (New York: Chanel, 1962), 129.

9. "Oswald Smith," http://www.christians.com/oswaldsmith/main.

10. Will H. Houghton and Charles T. Cook, *Tell Me about Moody* (Chicago: BICA, 1937), 68.

11. Early in the history of the Institute, students had organized a missions group called the Bible Institute Foreign Missionary Band, a branch of the national organization known as the Student Volunteer Movement for Foreign Missions. By 1911 SVMFM had bands of students in nearly a thousand institutions of higher learning in North America. Moody Bible Institute was one of these schools, which is not surprising since D. L. Moody was a key figure in helping to found the national movement.

    Membership in the band at Moody was limited to those who were planning on becoming foreign missionaries. The organization thrived until 1927, when the Student Volunteer Band ceased to function at MBI, probably because of the liberal theological views that had permeated the national Student Volunteer Movement.

12. *Record of Christian Work*, November 1889, n.p.

13. Edwin Charles Dargan, *A History of Preaching*, vol. 1 (New York: Hodder & Stoughton, 1905), 563.

14. Yaakov Ariel, *Evangelizing the Chosen People* (Chapel Hill, N.C.: Univ. of North Carolina, 2000), 94.

15. Ibid., 100. Michael Rydelnik, MBI Jewish studies professor, believes Moody's premillennial, dispensational understanding of the Scriptures was crucial both to the creation of the Jewish studies program (then Jewish Missions Course) and his own hiring to direct the program in 1994; telephone interview, August 12, 2010.

16. David Max Eichhorn, *Evangelizing the American Jew* (Middle Village, N.Y.: Jonathan David, 1978), 140.

17. Michael Rydelnik, e-mail response, August 11, 2010.

18. Robert G. Flood and Jerry B. Jenkins, *Teaching the Word, Reaching the World* (Chicago: Moody, 1985), 48.

19. DeRemer, *Moody Bible Institute*, 43.

20. Lyle Dorsett, *A Passion for Souls* (Chicago: Moody, 1997), 342.

21. File 47, Moody archives, "PCM—Transportation: Gospel Wagons."

22. As cited in DeRemer, *Moody Bible Institute*, 42.

23. Dorothy Martin, *Moody Bible Institute: God's Power in Action* (Chicago: Moody, 1977), 67, 70–71.

24. James M. Gray, "Radio," *Moody Bible Institute Monthly*, March 1926, 309.

# Growing Tall

U.S. Treasury Secretary Timothy Geithner called it "the worst economic crisis since the Great Depression." Democrats and Republicans added words like "catastrophe" and "calamity." During the 2008–2009 recession, Americans watched as banking and other financial institutions foundered and the values of their homes plummeted by as much as 30 percent, putting many homeowners "underwater," owing more on their mortgages than their homes were worth. Meanwhile, one of every ten workers was jobless throughout 2009.

Still, the recent economic downturn, as hard as it has been, pales in comparison to the scope of the 1929–39 Great Depression. At its peak, one of every four workers was jobless. The annual unemployment rate during the final eight years of the Depression never went below 14.3 percent, cresting at 24.9 percent (in 1933).[1] And although fortunes and retirement savings were wiped out in the twenty-first-century Great Recession when the stock market lost almost half its value (48 percent), during the Great Depression the Dow Jones Industrial Average would plunge 89 percent.[2]

In D. L. Moody's home state of Massachusetts, unemployment surpassed 25 percent in 1934, and more than half of those without jobs had been so for at least a year.[3] Yet Moody Bible Institute seemed providentially protected, and it actually thrived in this environment. Will Houghton, now MBI's fourth president, declared, "A remarkable fact is that 'depression years' have enrolled new students in near-record numbers." He cited three notable achievements during the thirties:[4]

1. The day school enrollment hit its highest number to date in the fall of 1935.
2. Similarly, the evening school had a record enrollment in 1935. Reviewing graphs of evening school enrollments since 1919, Houghton marveled, "While there are 'downs' for certain school terms . . . the 'ups' predominate, especially since 1929."
3. Campus expansion had continued. The Institute owned thirty-two buildings in 1931, up from eight in 1904, and it leased three others.

The correspondence school did suffer slight declines in enrollment[5] during the Depression's early years, yet the decreases were minimal. In 1930, the National Home Study Council reported that while enrollment in other correspondence schools (religious and secular) dropped between 50 and 70 percent, at MBI the declines were far less: 3.5 percent in 1930, 7 percent in 1931, and 9.5 percent in 1932. But in 1933, enrollment again increased 8.7 percent.[6] So while the Great Depression affected the correspondence study in general, the impact on MBI was relatively mild.

## A BUILDING BOOM

MBI's physical expansion over the years echoed the growth in Chicago, the city of big shoulders, big plans, and bigger buildings. City officials had approached the Institute in early 1930 to explain LaSalle Street needed bigger shoulders of its own. Commuters had been driving LaSalle to the downtown financial district in increasing numbers after Henry Ford's Model T made automobiles affordable for the masses. Its successor, the Model A, featuring brakes on all four wheels, would sell more than four million between 1927 and 1931. Now cars by Ford, Chevrolet, and Chrysler were bigger and traffic was heavier. Auto sales would soon flatten under the Depression's pressing weight, but Chicago was still feeling the traffic pinch in 1930.

Later that year the growth became apparent to MBI leaders as they eyed large land movers widening LaSalle Street. The city had agreed to pay an undisclosed amount of cash for properties the school would have to level once the wider road was in place. After Dr. Houghton arrived in 1934, the board of trustees, Institute leaders, and Houghton agreed this was an opportunity to grow the campus. The city had mandated that present buildings come down, so leaders planned for a new centralized administration building to replace most of them. The new building would house business and educational offices previously spread along an entire city block, as well as additional classrooms, new studios for radio station WMBI, and a larger library. And so, following the blueprints of architect F. J. Thielbar, workers began constructing a twelve-story administration building. Its signature entry would be a seventeen-foot-high arch that took students, staff, and visitors into the school that D. L. Moody founded. Visitors walking within the archway could enter the administrative building or continue through a nearly identical arch onto Institute Place, entry point to other campus buildings.

When it was dedicated on February 4, 1939, Trustee Board Chairman Crowell laid the cornerstone. The structure was simply called "the Administration Building," despite Crowell's fund-raising efforts and his own contribution of 50 percent of the money needed. He politely refused President Houghton's request that the words "Crowell Hall" be carved in the stone arch entry on LaSalle. After hearing the president's request, he had paused perhaps two minutes, then lifted his head and said, "No . . . no . . . ; years ago I told the Lord that if He would allow me to make money for His service, I would keep my name out of it, so He could have

| 1935 | 1936 | 1937 |
|---|---|---|
| Social Security Act becomes law. | Celebration of MBI's fiftieth anniversary. | Centenary celebration of D. L. Moody's birthday. |

the glory."[7] The building was renamed Crowell Hall in 1945, when Crowell went to join his Lord.

The same year that the Administration Building/Crowell Hall made its debut, the most famous campus structure came down. The former Moody Church, on the corner of LaSalle and Chicago, had remained a valuable auditorium for campus and community events until the end of 1938. In fact, the first set of graduating students to walk through the arch did so in spring 1938 (before the formal dedication of Crowell Hall), en route to the auditorium for the commencement ceremonies. The historic church-now-auditorium fell, and next year's graduating class would change direction for commencement, heading north through the arch to the newly constructed basement of Torrey-Gray Auditorium. Though only a basement, Torrey-Gray was an auditorium able to seat 1,800 for meetings. When the present auditorium was completed in 1955, seating increased to over 1,900 (excluding choir loft), but the low basement ceiling gave way to a huge interior featuring a choir loft, balcony, and a roof fifty-five feet above ground. After removing a couple dozen seats for AV use, the auditorium today has exactly 1,886 seats.

The most unusual deconstruction and rebirth occurred between the new Torrey-Gray Auditorium and the Administration Building. The women's dormitory, known as the Women's Building (and later the 830 Building), also faced LaSalle, and the wider roadway made walking to the entrance a tight squeeze. In 1939 workers shaved fourteen feet from the front of the building, top to bottom, for all seven floors and created a new exterior. Here future women students would lodge until 1951 when a new women's dorm named after President Houghton opened, occupying the spot of the original Moody Church. The original Women's Building eventually became Smith Hall, where today staff and faculty offices occupy the lower floors and married students live on the upper floors.

| 1938 | 1939 | 1941 |
|---|---|---|
|  | Television invented; World War II begins. | Japan bombs Pearl Harbor. |
| Sermons from Science joins the MBI extension department. | Twelve-story Administration Building dedicated; named Crowell Hall in 1945. | The Bible Institute Colportage Association becomes Moody Press. |

## THREE THEOLOGICAL CONTROVERSIES

The same year construction began on the Administrative Building, President Houghton released *Tell Me about Moody* to coincide with what would have been the evangelist's 100th birthday. His book addressed the controversial social gospel, one of three contentious theological issues the president would face. Twenty-five years after the school's silver anniversary, it remained an issue: Is the gospel's mission to promote social change and relief for the world? Gray had said the way to resolve global injustice was to preach the gospel. Houghton echoed him and affirmed the unchanged course of the school as he looked back to Moody's evangelistic mission: "As every form of human relief followed after the great Moody-Sankey missions in Great Britain and the United States, so the Institute held steadfastly to the doctrine that works of love and mercy spring from the hearts in which the love of God has been shed abroad by the Holy Spirit."[8] Good deeds spring from changed hearts, Houghton argued, and the best way to help those in other lands is to let them hear and respond to the life-changing gospel of Jesus Christ.

Two other theological controversies bubbled up during Houghton's tenure as president. Neoorthodoxy upheld the practicality of the Scriptures while dismissing the reliability of the Scriptures. Like the liberals, neoorthodox theologians accepted modern science. They believed the theory of evolution and accepted the destructive aspects of higher biblical criticism. The Bible was not totally inerrant; some of the miracles recorded could be explained by natural phenomena. Karl Barth's famous statement "The Bible is God's Word so far as God lets it be His word"[9] attacked the idea that one can know the truth by the Scriptures alone.

At the same time, Frank Buchman started the Oxford Group Movement. "Buchmanism," as some called it, was cultlike in pulling

| 1942 | 1945 | 1946 |
|---|---|---|
| National Association of Evangelicals founded. | US drops atomic bombs on Japan. World War II ends. | |
| | Irwin Moon founds the Moody Institute of Science. | Paul Robinson founds the Missionary Aviation Course (Moody Aviation). |

people from churches to start Buchman's own following. He denied his was a church or a religion, wanting only to uphold the four standards of absolute honesty, absolute purity, absolute unselfishness, and absolute love, but he was pulling collegians and other intellectuals away from churches. Buchman believed good works assured heaven and that his group could lead the way. He spoke of "moral re-armament" and caught the attention of *Time* magazine, making their April 1936 cover and receiving lengthy coverage in the article "Cultist Frank Buchman: God Is a Millionaire." Buchman and his Buchmanites lost much credibility in 1936, when Reinhold Niebuhr quoted Buchman praising Adolf Hitler for opposing the Soviet Union and "the anti-Christ of communism."[10]

Houghton and other MBI representatives resisted liberalism, neoorthodoxy, and cultism by standing on their position that the Scriptures are inerrant and made known through the Holy Spirit alone. In its Chicago day and evening classes as well as through correspondence courses available throughout the United States, MBI advocated a literal interpretation of the Bible and the primary role of the church to spread the gospel. Moody speakers at the annual Founder's Week conference as well as other Bible conferences preached from the Scriptures.

## A TWIN CELEBRATION

Two significant opportunities arose in the thirties to proclaim the true gospel and the vision of D. L. Moody and his school. The golden anniversary of MBI was in 1936; the centennial anniversary of Moody's birth was 1937. President Houghton decided to highlight both in a two-year celebration. The twin anniversaries offered a chance to inspire supporters and the general public with the evangelist's hope for the spiritually and socially poor, declare anew the mission of Moody Bible Institute, and answer the liberal and neoorthodox critics.

The celebration took place on two continents, reminding listeners of Moody's witness in the United States, United Kingdom, Canada, and Mexico. Speakers addressed crowds in Chicago during Founder's Week conferences in 1936 and 1937. On Moody's centennial, February 5, 1937, 12,000 came to the Chicago Coliseum to celebrate. Two days later churches in every state and thirty countries observed "Moody Day." During the two years, MBI-sponsored rallies and conferences ranged from Carnegie Hall to London's Royal Albert Hall. There were Christian conversions at several of the venues.[11]

Still another way MBI sought to proclaim the biblical gospel clearly and strongly was through publishing. In 1941, Houghton and his leadership team aligned the successful Bible Institute Colportage Association more closely with the Institute, renaming it Moody Press. The Press would become a vital inner component of MBI to help Christians in their everyday lives, seek to strengthen Christian families, and aid churches. Through its books, Moody Press would promote biblical truth and reject heresy. (For more on Moody Publishers, see chapter 10.)

## AN EYE FOR INNOVATORS

As the Moody chief executive, Houghton had a keen eye for talented innovators. Two whom Houghton championed before the board of trustees were Irwin Moon and Paul Robinson.

### An Eye on Science

Houghton met Moon while visiting the Church of the Open Door in Los Angeles, the church former president R. A. Torrey had pastored three decades earlier. Moon was touring churches with his "Sermons from Science." These science demonstrations focused on the gospel by showing how the wonders of creation were the work of God, not the result of evolution. Moon was himself a pastor who at times illustrated his sermons with simple yet riveting scientific demonstrations. Eventually he recognized God could use him as a science "evangelist" while reinforcing the faith of Christians who wondered if science and Christianity were incompatible.

Houghton observed Moon in action at the Church of the Open Door and afterward urged him to join the MBI extension staff of speakers. Moon hesitated. He thought coming to Moody would limit his access to the secular public. Houghton eventually convinced him the opposite was

**MBI IMPACT** ( Promoting Christ )

He had received Christ at age fourteen during an evangelistic crusade, yet a few years later, he joined a touring company in spite of his mother's pleas. Soon he became a seasoned performer with his own comedy act.

The vaudeville circuit had its charms, but young Will Houghton could not escape the conviction of the Holy Spirit. When he revisited his mother's church at age twenty-three, the sermon gripped him. Houghton left the stage for good.

Eventually he became a song leader, singer, and preacher. When he candidated for a pastoral position at what would become his first church, nine people were converted. Houghton was not afraid of his past. In fact, his most popular sermon was "From Stage to Pulpit," his "I Surrender All" story. Listeners appreciated the honesty and drama of his spiritual turnaround.

When President James Gray heard Will Houghton, then pastor of Calvary Baptist Church in downtown Manhattan, preach one Sunday morning, he declared, "There is the man to follow me at the Institute."

Houghton, an accomplished preacher who learned the value of promotion during his vaudeville years, "early saw the tremendous possibilities for stimulating evangelism and revival by holding a great two-year celebration in 1936–37 for the golden anniversary of MBI and the centennial of D. L. Moody's birth," wrote MBI historian Bernard DeRemer in *Moody Bible Institute: A Pictorial History*. Rallies were held in more than seventy-five American cities as well as London's Royal Albert Hall.

That may be why Houghton's successor, William Culbertson, described the fourth president of Moody as the "promoter pastor." He was a master promoter whose goal was to honor the Master while preparing students at MBI to do likewise.

true. Moon joined the extension department in 1938.

Within a year his popular demonstrations would be featured at the San Francisco World's Fair, when MBI loaned him to Christian Businessmen's Committee International. At the 1939 Fair, the demonstrations often began hours ahead of the scheduled time because early arrivals had filled up the auditorium, and more people were waiting outside. Crowds listened quietly to his thought-provoking questions repeated after each experiment: "Can you believe these miracles are the result of chance or accident? Or are they a part of a divine pattern? What do you think?"[12]

After the World's Fair, Moon traveled across the country holding meetings in major auditoriums. When war broke out in 1941, he turned toward the servicemen on military bases. For five years he ministered to young GIs, giving them an opportunity to receive Christ as Savior before going into combat overseas.

This ambassador for Moody soon realized he could reach only so many people by touring. He noticed that the military was using training films to reach its troops in various locales. Why not put his own material onto film? President Houghton liked the idea, and convinced the trustees that Moon needed a platform bigger than the extension department. They approved a new department in 1945, the Moody Institute of Science. A year later MIS released the first of what would become thirty "Sermons from Science" films. *God of Creation* was a hit, and would eventually be translated into nine languages for international viewing.

Moon located quality coworkers to aid with his budding film production. He began with good friend F. Alton Everest, a conservative Baptist and professor of electrical engineering at Oregon State University; together they cofounded MIS. Moody Institute of Science would include both its own production studio and science laboratory. The lab staff would perform scientific studies and develop photographic equipment and techniques for its live and filmed demonstrations of God's creative power in nature. Everest became the first director of research and later executive director of MIS.

MIS films would win many awards for innovative techniques, including trailblazing time-lapse photography and unique equipment to photograph the inside of the human heart. By 1961, *American Cine-matographer* magazine would describe the production unit of MIS as "the biggest little studio in the world."[13] Its phenomenal look at the life of honeybees, *City of the Bees*, alone would win fourteen awards in 1963, including honors at the Edinburgh Film Festival and the International Film Festival of Vancouver.

While still a traveling representative of Moody's extension department, Moon asked President Houghton whether the Institute would encourage the formation of an evangelical organization for science educators. Moon explained to Houghton what he had told Everest during a meeting after a Sermons from Science demonstration in Salem, Oregon. "The young people flocked to [me] with their questions, eager for reassurance that modern scientific knowledge does not rule out faith."[14]

Houghton, aware of the evolution-creation controversy and impressed by the vision of Moon and Everest, invited five scientists, including Everest, to a three-day meeting in September 1941 at MBI. Houghton explained the objective of the group in a letter to Everest.

> Some of us believe the time has come for a meeting of science teachers who are Christians and who feel that some scientific facts are not bearing proper recognition, while some hypotheses are being presented as laboratory truth. It might be that eventually an organization will come into being, but this is not the immediate plan of the two or three in back of this letter. Our thought is of an annual meeting which could be a kind of clearing house for ideas. There should be the presentation of papers, and a discussion of those papers.[15]

With the encouragement of Houghton and MBI vice president H. Coleman Crowell, the meeting was key to the founding of the American Scientific Affiliation later that year. Everest served as its first president. The organization remains active today, its members forming "a fellowship of men and women of science and disciplines that can relate to science who share a common fidelity to the Word of God and a commitment to integrity in the practice of science." Its purpose is to "investigate any area relating Christian faith and science" and "to make known the results of such investigations for comment and criticism by the Christian community and by the scientific community."[16]

## An Eye on Flight

President Houghton and Coleman Crowell (now executive vice president) had their eye on missionary flight in 1946 after a Moody-trained pastor approached Crowell during Founder's Week. Paul Robinson had felt God's call to missions service, specifically Brazil. As his wife and he prepared, he recognized a small airplane could help them reach into the jungle interior, so he began flight training. But three days after he completed his solo flight, Japanese bombers attacked Pearl Harbor. The next day President Franklin Roosevelt declared war on Japan, grounding all civilian aviation. Robinson continued as a pastor but also joined the Civil Air Patrol to get further training. When Brazil reopened to missions after the war, Robinson was too old to go. But he had a plan for helping missionaries reach places where roads did not exist or were in disrepair. Small aircraft could make primitive trails a nonissue, and planes could transport missionaries to their station in a few hours instead of days or even weeks via rivers or jungle brush. Small aircraft could also help villagers and missionaries in need of prompt medical treatment and vital supplies.

Robinson explained all this as he met Crowell during the Founder's Week meeting. MBI had been his first choice for a missionary aviation program, both because of the school's stellar missions program and his own experiences as a Moody student and graduate (class of 1936). He started at "the top," thinking he would work down a list of schools. "But I never got off the top. Moody bought the idea."[17]

Crowell caught the vision and shared the concept with Houghton. The president saw the potential and asked Robinson to explain his plan to the Institute's executive committee and finally to the board of trustees. Robinson recalled his nervousness as "a country preacher from the boonies" standing before the august board members. "Yet, they must have sensed how I felt, for I have never been put more at ease than when I was in the presence of those great men of God."[18]

The board members liked what they heard. One stood, voiced his approval, and then offered to pay for the first two airplanes to get the program started. The missionary aviation program took flight that summer with three students learning with a J-3 Piper Cub. The program would be based at Elmhurst Airport, in a suburb twenty miles northwest of campus.

MBI allowed Robinson to make a fundamental change during the first years of what would become the missionary technical course. Many candidates for training either lacked mechanical aptitude or assumed that, like learning to drive a car, they would need only occasional flight time in the cockpit to master a plane. He realized missionaries who wanted to be pilots were not the same as prospective pilots who wanted to be missionaries.

"I knew we had two choices: quit or go all the way with a professional maintenance and pilot training school."[19] It was an easy decision, and one that would pay dividends for the rest of the twentieth century. Moody aviation would continue to supply almost half of all trained missionary pilots and mechanics to Mission Aviation Fellowship, JAARS (originally Jungle Aviation and Radio Service), and other missionary pilot–sending agencies.

## MORE THAN A SCHOOL

The third talented leader Houghton recruited was his successor. William Culbertson caught the president's eye as a speaker in 1939. Three years later Houghton asked Culbertson to become the dean of education. In June 1946, the president suffered a heart attack. Though Dean Culbertson kept Houghton informed of events, the president would not return to his office in Crowell Hall as other illnesses sapped his strength. On June 14, 1947, Will Houghton died, and five days later William Culbertson became acting president. The following February the board of trustees elected Culbertson the Institute's fifth president.

The trustees and Houghton had smoothed the way for Culbertson with a major reorganization of the corporate structure. Under Houghton MBI had become more than a school with day, evening, and correspondence courses. It had developed into a media enterprise as well, offering its first radio broadcasting course (1939), moving to full daytime broadcasting on its Chicago AM station (1941), and operating the first noncommercial religious FM station (1943). MBI now supervised a thriving book publisher as well, Moody Press.

The current structure had become unwieldy. For example, the business manager had served as a liaison between the functional departments and the top administrative position and the board of trustees. By 1944, he supervised nine large departments—too much supervisory responsibility and power for effective administrative action.

The board of trustees, after consulting with top administrators, adopted a new organizational structure in 1946. These sweeping organizational changes took place toward the end of the Houghton presidency and in response to significant advances under Houghton. The new corporate structure implemented a branch system. Those heading each branch were designated vice presidents. Within their respective areas of operation, these men had great creative liberty and responsibility. They reported to an executive vice president. It was the responsibility of this person, "in the absence of the president of the Institute, or his inability to act," to "perform all duties which would be performed by the president . . . were he present or able to act."

Coleman Crowell, son of Henry Crowell, became the first executive vice president in 1945 and enacted the plan in President Houghton's absence. Under the new plan, the president became "subject to the control of the Board of Trustees," but had "the general charge and supervision of the affairs of the corporation." William Culbertson no doubt welcomed these efficiencies as he embarked on growing the Institute in an expanding postwar America.

## NOTES

1. *Historical Statistics of the United States*, ed. Susan Carter et al. (Cambridge: Cambridge Univ. Press, 2006), cited at www.shmoop.com/great-depression/statistics.html.
2. Ibid. The Dow Jones Industrial Average fell from its high of 381.17 in September 1929 to 41.22 in July 1932. The DJIA would not recover to its 1929 peak until November 1954, a full quarter century after the market crash. In 2008–09 the DJIA

fell from 13053 on April 30, 2008, to 6783 on March 2, 2009; see www.dowjones
.close.com, and Alexander Twin, "Dow Below 7,000," www.money.cnn.com/2009
/03/02/markets/markets_newyork/index.htm.

3. Tom Juravich, William F. Hartford, and James R. Green, *Commonwealth of Toil*
(Amherst, Mass.: Univ. of Mass, 1996); cited in www.massmoments.org.

4. Will H. Houghton and Charles T. Cook, *Tell Me about Moody* (Chicago: Bible Institute Colportage, 1937), 77, 81.

5. "Enrollments" designate the number of courses in which individuals are enrolled and
may not represent the total number of people involved, since a person may have
enrolled in more than one course.

6. Gene A. Getz, *MBI* (Chicago: Moody, 1969), 87.

7. Bernard R. DeRemer, *Moody Bible Institute* (Chicago: Moody, 1960), 80–82.

8. Houghton and Cook, *Tell Me*, 73.

9. Karl Barth, *The Doctrine of the Word of God, Church Dogmatics*, vol. 1 (London:
T & T Clark, 1956), part 2, 123; cited in "Neoorthodoxy—History," http://mb-
soft.com/believe/txc/neoortho.htm.

10. Reinhold Niebuhr, "Hitler and Buchman," in *Christianity and Power Politics* (New
York: Charles Scribner Sons, 1946); adopted from a Niebuhr article in *Christian
Century*, October 7, 1936, 1315; as cited in www.orange-papers.org/orange
-rroot870.html.

11. Robert G. Flood and Jerry B. Jenkins, *Teaching the Word, Reaching the World*
(Chicago: Moody, 1985), 60.

12. Ibid., 199.

13. Darrin Scot, "World's Biggest Little Studio," *American Cinematographer*, August
1961, 4.

14. F. Alton Everest, "The American Scientific Affiliation—The First Decade," *Journal of
the American Scientific Affiliation* 3 (September 1951): 33–38; cited in www.asa3.org
/ASA/PSCF/1951/JASA9-51everest.html.

15. Wilbur M. Smith, *An Annotated Bibliography of D. L. Moody* (Chicago: Moody,
1948), 142.

16. www.asa3org/ASA/about ASA.html.

17. Kay Oliver, "Paul Robinson: Winging It," *Moody Monthly*, September 1975, 122.

18. Ibid., 122–23.

19. Ibid., 123.

# ( 4 )

1947–1986

# The Next Forty Years

The two men who would guide Moody Bible Institute the next forty years had one thing in common. Each was commended by his predecessor for the office he would soon assume.

But in every other way they seemed different.

William Culbertson had presided over the Reformed Episcopal Church's New York and Philadelphia synods. George Sweeting led city churches in New Jersey and Chicago. So one had administrative gifts; the other pastoral gifts. Culbertson was a scholar, who first came to MBI as dean of education; as president he served on the editorial team that would update the Scofield Reference Bible. Sweeting was the personable pastor who greeted members before the service; his shoulder clasp and warm greeting made people in Chicago's large Moody Church (one mile north of the Institute) feel much closer to the front than they were. Ever the teacher, Dean Culbertson would still teach a Bible geography course when he became president. Ever the pastor-evangelist, Sweeting would travel to evangelism conclaves and host annual pastors conferences at MBI over the years.

During Culbertson's final years, the school would remain a beacon during the psychedelic and war-ravaged 1960s. During Sweeting's opening

years, Moody would ride out the shock waves of a presidential resignation, heightening Arab-Israeli tensions, and economic recession.

Yet both leaders would bring innovation to the Chicago campus that
allowed MBI to float steady in the turbulent waters of their eras.

Culbertson's earliest innovations revised the curriculum and boosted
the school's academic reputation. During his first full year as president,
Culbertson traveled 120 miles to Winona Lake, Indiana, to dialogue with
representatives of forty Bible schools. On the campus of Grace College,
they formed the Accrediting Association of Bible Institutes and Bible
Colleges. Their goal was to standardize Bible school credits and courses
and to raise educational standards. Moody Bible Institute received
accreditation in 1950, just three years after the association began. In
1962, John Mostert, then director of admissions at MBI, was named
president of the accrediting association, and served there twenty years.
In 2004 the Accrediting Association became the Association for Biblical
Higher Education (ABHE) as the association expanded to include graduate education accreditation.

Today both the undergraduate school and the Moody Theological
Seminary and Graduate School (MTS) are accredited by the ABHE. The
undergraduate school also has received full accreditation by the Higher
Learning Commission of the North Central Association of Colleges and
Schools. Accredited course work benefits undergraduate students
greatly, whether they transfer to another college or later enroll in a graduate school or seminary. The other schools recognize the MBI training
as meeting national standards for faculty, facilities, and undergraduate
training and typically will grant credit for courses completed at Moody.
Similarly, graduate-level students in MTS know the quality of their education is nationally recognized and that other institutions will accept
their course credits.

## THE THREE-YEAR DIPLOMA

The subsequent interactions among the Winona-based accrediting
association as well as the needs of postwar students drove MBI to a
major change in its course calendar. The school moved to a semester

schedule in 1951. In place of the year-round "term plan," students now could enroll two semesters per year plus an optional summer school. The new course calendar allowed students a summer away from books, when they could engage in local church ministry and other work while resting from intense classes.

Eight courses existed at this point: general Bible (previously the "General Course"), missionary, pastors, music, Christian education, Christian education–music, Jewish missions, and missionary technical (for prospective missions pilots and mechanics). Except for the missionary technical course, each required six semesters of work, or three years to complete. Some new studies were added, but many of the one-hour subjects offered under the term plan were reorganized and formed into two- and three-hour subjects.

The objective of the general Bible course remained the same—to give students a growing knowledge of the Bible and skills to be effective Christian workers—though students now chose an "emphasis" in music, home missions, Christian education, or the Bible. This new curriculum approach meant the general Bible course was nonspecialized, while the other courses would train people for specific church vocations—pastors, missionaries, church musicians, directors of Christian education, directors of youth, children's workers, and specialized home and foreign missionaries.[1]

## MISSIONARY TECH CHANGES

At the same time, the missionary technical course expanded to a four-year program. Students devoted two years in direct study of the Bible, as well as in missionary subjects, followed by two more years of technical training in one of four areas: radio and communications, photography, aircraft maintenance and repair, and flight and groundwork, which would lead to a commercial pilot license. The course was designed

| 1947 | 1948 | 1950 |
|---|---|---|
| Billy Graham begins evangelistic crusades. | *William Culbertson becomes fifth president of Moody Bible Institute.* | *MBI accredited by the Accrediting Association of Bible Institutes and Bible Colleges.* |

"to meet the recognized need for missionaries who have technical knowledge as well as Bible institute training."

By 1954 the tech course included two distinct majors: aviation flight and mechanics, and radio and communications. Students in the aviation flight and mechanics major could concentrate either in aircraft and engine mechanics or in flying during their third year.

The technical curriculum continued to develop, as Paul Robinson and President Culbertson sought to provide the most practical program for the missionary enterprise. Robinson's staff regularly consulted missionary aviation agencies concerning the changing field needs.

As interest increased in the technical course and more applicants competed for limited openings, Robinson and his faculty realized they needed a filter to find the best-qualified candidates. Now the first-year program would include aptitude tests and a one-week flight camp the following summer. Leaders then reviewed the aptitude results, flight camp tests, and spiritual qualifications for missions service, and finally interviewed candidates. Based on the outcomes, a select, qualified group of students entered formal training during their second year at Moody.

To screen students even more carefully, by 1960 all students admitted to the aviation program were required to successfully complete a two-year pre-aviation curriculum in the regular missionary course. Those who did not qualify would continue in the regular MBI curriculum; those who did continued in the program, and the Institute was assured that higher-quality students remained in the technical major.

In 1961, the Federal Aviation Agency awarded the Moody Aviation faculty examining authority for private pilots. This appointment placed Moody Aviation among the limited number of aviation schools in the United States that met the stringent training standards that authorize them to issue certain airman certificates without further government (FAA) examination. A few years later an FAA administrator told the

| 1951 | 1954 | 1960 |
|---|---|---|
| *Houghton Hall dedicated as new women's dormitory.* | *Brown v. Board of Education sets legal basis for integration of public schools.* | *Station WDLM joins WCRF and WMBI to create the Moody Radio Network.* |

*Chicago Tribune* the Moody aviation program ranked among "the most comprehensive and exacting training programs anywhere."[2]

The Moody aviation program quickly outgrew its Elmhurst airfield and relocated its flight school at nearby Wood Dale Airport in 1954. But in less than a decade a neighboring airport would create congestion. The new airport, named after World War II flying ace Butch O'Hare, opened in 1955; a major expansion would add to O'Hare International Airport all flights from crosstown Midway Airport by 1962. Tiny Wood Dale Airport, just five miles away, was close to O'Hare's flight paths. O'Hare threatened to crowd the small flight school, limiting air routes and flight times.

After an extensive search, MBI trustees approved the purchase of land in Elizabethton, Tennessee, in 1967. The hilly terrain of eastern Tennessee clearly simulated the flight conditions of typical missions work—primitive settings and changing elevations—while providing room for the flight school to expand. There Moody pilots would train for the rest of the century, until the missionary aviation program relocated to Spokane in 2005. (For more on the new program, see chapter 12.)

## FROM DIPLOMA TO BACHELOR'S DEGREE

In the 1960s, the school wrestled with a critical education decision: Should it go beyond granting diplomas to granting bachelor's degrees? A self-study report by the educational branch in 1961 had examined the academic programs, while an alumni survey by Professor Gene Getz in 1964 had evaluated the educational experiences of graduates. Both reports revealed that students needed an undergraduate degree for many types of ministry.[3]

| 1963 | 1966 | 1967 | 1969 |
|------|------|------|------|
| Martin Luther King Jr. leads March on Washington. | | | Neil Armstrong takes first steps on the moon. |
| *MIS film* City of the Bees *wins first of fourteen awards for pioneering photography.* | *MBI begins offering bachelor of arts degree.* | *Moody Aviation relocates flight center to Elizabethton, Tennessee.* | |

Controversy soon surrounded the proposed shift in curriculum. Some wondered whether adding a degree program might cause MBI to lose its distinctive, specialized education. Many argued that a degree program would transform MBI into a liberal arts school that included Bible but did not focus fully on it. Among the fears were that a "Moody Bible College" could "subtly change the campus atmosphere, spread resources too thin, and sacrifice the distinctives of its rich heritage."[4] Yet academic degrees seemed essential to training men and women for a fully informed ministry.

Administration and faculty dialogued. As the former dean of education at Moody, President Culbertson helped oversee the discussion. Along with the board of trustees, he ultimately agreed that D. L. Moody's vision for workers required the institute model to continue. Yet the benefits of a baccalaureate program needed to be incorporated, so MBI adopted an innovative solution: a three-year's study at MBI and two years of liberal arts courses at a college or university.

The new bachelor of arts option allowed students to complete an additional sixty semester hours of course work in the liberal arts at an accredited college or university. They could earn those academic credits before coming to Moody Bible Institute or after finishing the three-year diploma program. All course work for a BA degree would be completed within five years. Thus Moody would remain a Bible institute yet offer a degree to those who finished the liberal arts courses elsewhere.

The new program began in 1966, the same year MBI replaced the historic "course" plan with a system of majors offered by academic departments. The new plan gave students greater flexibility in their choice of subjects. A diploma or a BA degree could now be earned in eight majors, including Bible-theology, Christian education, pastoral

| 1971 | 1973 | 1975 | 1978 |
|------|------|------|------|
| George Sweeting becomes sixth president. | Moody Evening School expands into Ohio.<br><br>Moody Pastors' Conference begins. | Saigon falls to communists; war in Vietnam ends. | Moody Press releases the Ryrie Study Bible. |

training, church music, foreign missions, and communications. Major changes in the late 1980s (see chapter 6) would make it possible for MBI students to receive their undergraduate degree entirely on campus in four years.

## FACING THE POSTWAR SURGE

Even before MBI leaders began to revise their curriculum, the school's reputation was drawing a growing student population. Students traveled to the Chicago campus in record numbers following World War II. During 1945, the final year of the war, student enrollment had fallen to under eight hundred students, as many men and women served their country abroad and on the home front. The next year, though, total enrollment jumped 90 percent and stayed at then-record levels for two years.[5] Many men had delayed their education and ministry plans during World War II. Now they had the time and the resources, as the GI Bill of Rights offered financial assistance to veterans. Though MBI remained tuition-paid, the GI Bill covered most miscellaneous expenses.

The surge of applicants taxed dormitory space. Men lived in two of the campus's oldest buildings, the 153 Building, constructed in 1890, and the 152 Building, constructed in 1909. Those in the 153 Building shared space with classrooms, offices, the library, and the campus dining room. Though the 152 Building was primarily a men's dorm, it included offices and a gymnasium. Meanwhile, the Women's Building was full and some women lived in various smaller buildings around campus. Sensing the need, Moody leadership launched a drive to build a new residence for women students. On October 20, 1951, officials dedicated Houghton Hall with room for 448 women. Now all women could be in

| 1981 | 1984 | 1985 | 1986 |
|------|------|------|------|
| Sandra Day O'Connor becomes the first woman appointed to the Supreme Court. | Chicago Mayor Harold Washington visits campus, speaks to students. | Moody Graduate School begins. | Challenger space shuttle explodes.<br><br>MBI celebrates its centennial anniversary. |

one ten-story building with room for more women students in the future. And in a clever but odd exchange, the men moved out of the 153 Building to the former Women's Building, now renamed the 830 Building. What had previously been No Man's Land was now men only.

Meanwhile, the men and women continued to sit separately for breakfast, mingling in the dining room only during lunch and dinner. But in a curious change born out of convenience, women started sitting near the south end of the dining room, closest to their Houghton Hall homestead, and men migrated to the north end, nearer to their 830 Building home. Their new dining locations were exactly the opposite of their seating just weeks earlier!

The number of students remained strong through the 1960s.[6] The seven-story 830 Building was straining to hold all the male students, and plans began for a new men's dormitory. Finally in 1969, a new men's dorm opened with room to grow—the modern brick building soared twenty stories, becoming the largest structure on campus. In 1971 it was named Culbertson Hall in honor of the president. And in a touch of irony, that same year the men's dorm was renamed, a new subterranean dining room opened just north of the first men's dormitory, the 153 Building, which itself had been demolished in 1969 to open up the campus plaza.

## BROADCASTING: THE NETWORK EXPANDS

It took awhile for President James Gray to embrace radio as a God-given technology to teach and preach to Christian and seeker alike, as well as uplift with gospel songs. In contrast, President George Sweeting welcomed radio broadcasting in the 1970s and 1980s. When he arrived as president in 1971, two owned-and-operated stations existed outside Chicago and two within. Station WCRF, Cleveland, had begun broadcasting November 23, 1958, after a group of Christian businessmen asked the Institute to operate a Christian station they were funding. Institute officials accepted the Cleveland proposition, if the station would be supported locally. It became the second station owned by MBI.

In 1960 MBI officials decided to expand within Illinois, where

WMBI was joined by its sister station WMBI-FM. That same year, in East Moline, Illinois, near the Mississippi River and Iowa, WDLM initially received programs by direct wire from Chicago and carried much of the WMBI broadcast schedule. Today the station is locally operated for superior audio signal and to localize programming. It receives selected Moody Radio programs as well.

The addition of WDLM created what became the Moody Radio Network. In 1973 and 1974 President Sweeting and the department of broadcasting welcomed stations from Tennessee (WMBW-FM, Chattanooga) and Washington (KMBI and KMBI-FM, Spokane).

By the end of the Sweeting presidency there were eleven stations across the United States owned and operated by MBI. Later the radio network would expand into most of the U.S. through the advent of satellite broadcasting (see chapter 9).

## BOOM TIMES FOR THE EVENING SCHOOL

The evening school that had been anchored in Chicago through the 1960s expanded during the Sweeting years, first within Illinois and later into other states. In September 1972 a satellite campus opened in Joliet, a distant southwest Chicago suburb. During the initial evening registration, more than 140 students came through the doors of the Joliet YMCA, keeping the registrar and his staff busy until nine at night enrolling first-time students.

The year following the Joliet opening, the program expanded into Ohio. A group from the Center for Christian Studies asked MBI leaders to start a school in Akron, Ohio, following the closing of the Akron Bible Institute. The group provided initial funding, and MBI agreed to the plan. The active search by the CCS and Joliet's immediate success confirmed the wisdom of expanding the evening school. "The success in Joliet showed that going into a suburban location was a viable approach. In Ohio we were going four hundred miles away from the central campus and the historic strength of Moody Bible Institute," recalled Jay Fernlund, then director of the evening schools. The success in Joliet assured officials that the school could succeed at remote locations.[7]

Enrollment figures soared in the 1970s. From 678 students in 1970, more than 1,800 had enrolled in evening classes by 1977. Throughout the 1970s the expansion of extension campuses continued, aided by an unusual ruling of the Federal Communications Commission. The FCC announced that educational FM radio stations must have an educational branch of their organization in the area to be eligible for a station license. Evening school officials started classes in the Iowa-Illinois Quad Cities area in 1977, which allowed licensing of WDLM-FM. In 1980, an extension campus opened in Boynton Beach, Florida, in connection with the Moody FM outlet, WMBW.

During the 2000s there have been seventeen extension campuses in Illinois, Wisconsin, Ohio, Washington, and Florida, now known as regional classrooms.[8] Six of the regional classrooms are in middle and southern Florida.

## "KEEP THE MAIN THING THE MAIN THING"

The Institute continued to hold firmly to biblical inerrancy during the four decades under Presidents Culbertson and Sweeting. At the 1966 Founder's Week conference, Culbertson cautioned denominations that were considering other views of the Scriptures. "As president of Moody Bible Institute, I want to sound again the word of warning. If we as orthodox, as evangelicals, as fundamentalists move from this doctrine—the inspiration of the Word of God—we are doomed to disaster." Culbertson served on the editorial committee that updated the *Scofield Reference Bible*, and he subscribed to the 1967 preface, which declared, "Every member of the board believes in and teaches the plenary inspiration and inerrancy of the Scriptures. . . . Aware of the problems of biblical criticism, the committee is unshaken in its adherence to the authority of the infallible Word of God in respect to both faith and practice."[9]

George Sweeting continued to uphold the doctrinal position of the Institute concerning the Bible, God, man, salvation, and the church. Sweeting's refrain at key points in his administration was, "Remember to keep the main thing the main thing." He was talking about the Bible and its gospel of Jesus Christ. The "main thing" also implied evangelism, a cornerstone of Moody's ministry when he founded the Institute. Evangelism had been Sweeting's personal focus since his teens and became his passion for students and the school. Keeping "the main thing the main thing" meant holding to the founder's vision for the lost.

Sweeting, the only president who was an alumnus of MBI (class of 1945), had served as a traveling evangelist for almost a decade after graduation, and sometimes used colorful chalk drawings with dramatic, shifting lighting to illustrate the gospel and, with the help of the Holy Spirit, transport some listeners emotionally to Calvary.[10] Several times during his sixteen-year presidency he would turn the weekly President's Chapel into an artistic presentation. With his white shirtsleeves rolled up, a piece of thick chalk in hand, and several more on the easel ledge, Sweeting drew a scene of a city or a hill with a cross in the background. Then the auditorium lights darkened, and the hushed crowd in Torrey-Gray Auditorium watched the colored lights play on the drawing as Dr. Sweeting sang a hymn about Calvary. The glowing, changing lights alternately silhouetted and highlighted the cross, creating a three-dimensional scene that would turn serene, then powerful, and finally subdued. Some students called it the highlight of their President's Chapels.

His evangelistic fervor was like that of MBI's founder. Both Moody and Sweeting used world expositions as evangelistic forums. During the twentieth Summer Olympiad in Munich, Sweeting sent fifty student counselors to the Moody Institute of Science pavilion to interact with viewers after watching MIS films shown in all five official languages. "Tragedy struck when terrorists stormed the quarters of Israeli athletes, but even this opened unexpected doors for the gospel."[11] The effort resulted in decisions for Christ from thirty-five countries at the 1972 Olympics.

Ten years later Sweeting led a powerful evangelistic campaign in South Korea. Korean Christians had invited Dr. Sweeting to celebrate the 100th anniversary of Protestant missionary influence in the land. He spoke to large churches in Seoul during his eight days in the country, which culminated with a four-evening evangelistic crusade in Inchon (now Incheon). One thousand people made decisions to receive Christ during the crusade.[12]

## STAY—OR GO?

During the mid-twentieth century, the board of trustees started exploring the question of MBI's remaining in its location close to downtown Chicago. The debate began during President Culbertson's tenure. The board recognized several benefits of relocating the campus: lower costs of operation, valuable revenues from selling a downtown campus, a quieter locale outside the city. Yet they also knew the mission and heritage of their founder, who chose Chicago to reach the poor and the masses, while helping local churches. The Institute was literally within one mile of the poorest and richest housing in the city. Many of the wealthy lived to the east in elegant apartments on the Gold Coast, near the Magnificent Mile of shops along Michigan Avenue. Just two blocks to the west stood public housing. In 1962 the last of ten Cabrini-Green public housing projects rose, soon to be followed by poverty and crime. Eventually, the board voted to stay in inner Chicago, a mission field outside its own front door.

Under President Sweeting, the trustee board again would discuss and once more affirm MBI's call to the city. Other seminaries and Bible colleges were exiting the urban environment for suburban or rural settings. Such moves offered economic savings, as well as profits for selling valuable city property. And much easier commutes awaited faculty and staff who could not afford housing in the city or preferred a suburban community. Moreover, Cabrini-Green was infested with gangs and drugs. So Moody's leadership again considered the option of moving.

But the discussion also recalled D. L. Moody's vision for the city, and the ongoing impact of students in the community and of leaders on local government. Downtown Chicago remained an outstanding training ground for Bible teachers and evangelists—a world-class city with more than thirty-five ethnic groups, with public housing and lakefront condos in walking distance. It was a compact snapshot of modern America.

The trustees decided the school would remain in the heart of the city, where students served in churches, shelters, retirement homes, youth organizations, and other settings with the gospel and hands-on assistance (through practical Christian ministries, chapter 8). Leaders once more recognized that the Institute's influence and power rested partly in its location. Future students would have many opportunities to tutor and provide encouraging models for the children at Cabrini, and many have helped children and teens throughout the city through the Big Brother/Big Sister programs and other local agencies.

President Sweeting clearly articulated the Institute's commitment to the city in a convocation address to faculty and students in 1981:

> As spokes in a wheel lead to the hub, so all roads lead to the urban centers. The city is where the action is. . . .
>
> In his work *The Meaning of the City*, the French social critic and commentator Jacques Ellul points out that the first biblically recorded cities were founded by men who rejected God. They were products of self-will and self-ambition. But Ellul goes on to acknowledge, "Our task is therefore to represent Him [God] in the heart of the city." . . .
>
> We believe that it is no accident that we are in the city these momentous days. With God's help and upholding, we intend to stay.[13]

Sweeting noted that God established the school in the city, where MBI began as "a school keyed to meet the spiritual needs of the city." Of course, the school today also embraces international and rural evangelism, he said, "but not at the expense of the unreached masses of the cities."

## MOODY GRADUATE SCHOOL: APPLIED ACADEMICS

In June 1985 MBI welcomed eighty-one pastors, missionaries, and evangelists to the newly formed Moody Graduate School. With graduate courses offered in one-week modules four times a year, the school represented a combining of the practical and the theoretical, a hallmark of the Moody educational tradition. Students earning thirty-six semester hours earned a master of arts in ministry (MA Min), a professional degree.

"The program reflects the Moody tradition of providing people to stand in the gap," said B. Wayne Hopkins, first dean of the school. That gap had developed as seminaries offered an increasingly academic curriculum, Hopkins explained when the school opened. The master of theology

(ThM) degree had emphasized research; the master of divinity (MDiv) historically was designed to be a practical degree. "But it is becoming more academic. Therefore, students are coming away from seminary campuses with not a lot of preaching, little counseling, and probably no courses in management."[14]

Two kinds of students enrolled in the inaugural classes. Many students were seminary graduates who enrolled "to receive training they did not receive on the seminary level," according to Hopkins. Other students had only a Bible college degree and were active in a Christian ministry. This type of student did not want seminary training since he already had completed several of the Bible and theology courses. Yet the student needed more training.

Instructors did not overlook the theoretical and historical framework, but they emphasized the practical application. Each course had two instructors, one an academician, the other a practitioner. "So the student has someone who is an expert in theory and someone who is an expert in the application of that theory," Hopkins explained. The instructors included successful pastors, missionary leaders, authors, and management consultants.

## A CENTENNIAL CELEBRATION

Chicago leaders recognized the Institute's continual contributions to the city as the MBI centennial anniversary approached. In 1984 Mayor Harold Washington visited the campus and thanked the school for its continued presence and impact in the city. Speaking in Torrey-Gray Auditorium, the mayor described MBI as "a pillar and model for the entire community. . . . Chicago desperately needs the enduring compassion, humility, and wisdom of your institution." He pledged the city's support in any expansion program on campus, adding, "We are thankful that you are here, that you are growing, and that you represent a vibrant voice of Christianity."[15]

The Sweeting years closed with three great events in 1986, as MBI celebrated its first one hundred years. City leaders again lauded the Institute as the centennial approached. The Chicago City Council sent

**MBI IMPACT**

## ( The Evangelist on the Evangelist )

Most historians call Dwight L. Moody and Billy Graham the greatest evangelists of the nineteenth and twentieth centuries, respectively. As the final speaker at the centennial celebration during Founder's Week 1986, Dr. Graham spoke about Moody and his impact. Here are some of his comments:

"Moody is the man in evangelism I have admired the most and patterned a great deal of our evangelistic work after."

"His example and single-minded zeal to preach the gospel has influenced my own life tremendously."

"Relatively few men in the history of the church have had such a profound impact as Dwight L. Moody. Directly he touched thousands in his day. Indirectly, through all the things he has started, he has touched millions."

Graham noted that even his home community of Montreat, North Carolina, was founded by Moody. The evangelist, who held many Bible conferences in Northfield, Massachusetts, "sent two people down from Northfield to find a location in the south that would be suitable for a conference center," according to Graham. They helped birth the Mountain Retreat Association, from which Montreat received its name. In 1898, the second year of summer conferences, R. A. Torrey led the sessions and spoke frequently.

Graham felt much of Moody's power derived from his prayer life and unshakeable belief in the reliability of the Bible. "D. L. Moody had a childlike faith in the Bible as the inspired, infallible Word of God. It was largely because of his immense knowledge of the Bible and his practical application of the Bible that he drew such large crowds.

"Moody was a man of prayer—not pompous, not to impress others, but it flowed from a daily walk with Christ. His assistant, Ira Sankey, said, 'Moody is a far greater pray-er than an evangelist.'"

a resolution of thanks and congratulations; Mayor Washington issued a proclamation commending the school. The mayor proclaimed Founder's Week 1986, February 3–9, as "Moody Bible Institute Week in Chicago." In the proclamation, Mayor Washington noted the centennial anniversary and urged "all citizens of Chicago to remember and honor the work that Dwight Lyman Moody and all those associated with Moody Bible Institute have done on behalf of their neighborhood and the City of Chicago."

Second, Founder's Week featured prominent speakers, including apologist Josh McDowell and pastors James Boice, Charles Swindoll, and Warren Wiersbe. It concluded at the Rosemont Horizon with a Sunday crowd of more than 16,000 to hear evangelist Billy Graham. The evangelist talked about how the Institute has continued "Building on the Rock," his sermon title. He described six rocks that build on each other: The Lord Jesus Christ, faith in the Bible, devotion to prayer, the Spirit-filled life, a missionary vision, and looking for the second coming of Christ.

Third, throughout the year representatives of MBI, including President Sweeting and Board Trustee John MacArthur, toured the country to celebrate one hundred years of ministry at the Institute.

That summer Sweeting spoke at the second International Conference for Itinerant Evangelists, known as Amsterdam '86. Eight thousand itinerant evangelists—75 percent from the non-Western world—listened to the MBI president describe "The Evangelist's Passion for Lost Souls."[16]

> When I go to the cross . . . and enter into His passion, then my passion is revived and my vision is renewed. . . . Our calling as evangelists is not to silver or satin or silk or stones precious, but to blood, toil, tears, and sweat. May our commitment be so complete that we will make hell gasp for breath. Yes, our commitment needs to be that complete. . . .[17]

His keynote address finished, Sweeting turned from the podium to loud, sustained applause. On the platform, Billy Graham passed George Sweeting a note as the moderator concluded the meeting. The short note read: "Dear George, thank you for one of the greatest sermons I've ever heard. Thank you. Thank you. Love in Christ, Billy."[18]

In a President's Chapel during his final semester leading MBI, Sweeting watched as staff and students honored the president and included a video clip of his closing words at Amsterdam '86 and the international audience's warm response. When the lights came up in Torrey-Gray Auditorium, Sweeting came to the podium and thanked the students and staff for the kind words. He ended by quoting a verse from Psalm 115:1 that summarized his response—and MBI's as well—to such recognition: "Not to us, O Lord, not to us, but to Your name give glory".

## NOTES

1. Gene Getz and James Vincent, *MBI: The Story of Moody Bible Institute* (Chicago: Moody, 1986), 70–71.

2. Kay Oliver, "Paul Robinson: Winging It," *Moody Monthly*, September 1975, 123.

3. Getz and Vincent, *MBI*, 71.

4. Robert G. Flood and Jerry B. Jenkins, *Teaching the Word, Reaching the World* (Chicago: Moody, 1985).

5. Note: Enrollment figures typically include part-time students and probably are inflated. However, they provide valuable year-to-year comparisons. Enrollment in the fall of 1945 was reported as 786 students. In fall 1946 and fall 1947, 1,428 and 1,426 students, respectively, attended MBI. Enrollment fell just slightly the next two years, to 1,374 and 1,331 students in 1948 and 1949, respectively. Data obtained from annual education report to board of trustees; compiled by Patrick Friedline for the MBI Alumni Association in 1996.

6. Enrollment averaged 1,350 students for the ten years ending in 1967.

7. Getz and Vincent, *MBI*, 77.

8. In 2006 the Spokane regional classroom (since 1993) became a branch campus of MBI. It had always offered courses during day hours only, and thus was distinct from the other "regional classrooms" that provided courses during evening hours. More on the development of regional classrooms appears in chapter 6.

9. *The New Scofield Reference Bible* (New York: Oxford Univ. Press, 1967), v.

10. While a student at MBI, Sweeting took one class at Chicago's Art Academy and later another at the Art Institute of Chicago to sharpen his artistic skills. It made for long school days; he often went to bed after midnight. Yet despite getting only five hours' sleep, he was "still making time for personal devotions" in the morning. See Jerry B. Jenkins, *A Generous Impulse* (Chicago: Moody, 1987), 59.

11. Flood and Jenkins, *Teaching the Word*, 91, 263.

12. Lisa Livingston, "Celebrating a Centennial in Korea," *Moody Monthly*, September 1983.

13. George Sweeting, "The Challenge of the City," pamphlet, 11–13.

14. Getz and Vincent, *MBI*, 195.

15. Dan DeSmyther, "Mayor Visits Campus," *Moody Student*, May 18, 1985, 1.

16. "Records of the International Conference for Itinerant Evangelists" (Amsterdam '86), Billy Graham Center Archives, Wheaton College; http://www.wheaton.edu/bgc/archives/GUIDES/560.htm.

17. George Sweeting, "The Evangelist's Passion for Lost Souls," the International Conference for Itinerant Evangelists, Amsterdam, the Netherlands, July 19, 1986.

18. Jenkins, *A Generous Impulse*, 142.

# The Halls of Presidents

Joseph Stowell finished his first year as the president of Moody Bible Institute with a series of chapel messages on Jonah. Stowell told the students the prophet had "repented of his relationship toward God, but he never repented for his attitude toward his fellow man" when he resented God's withholding punishment from Nineveh. "Jonah accepted the call of God [but] refused the character of God."

Something was lacking deep inside Jonah, the president said, and he compared the prophet to people who tamper with Oreo cookies. He described the time Nabisco began to make "Double Stuff" Oreo cookies with double the cream filling. "A lot of people like to eat Oreos by pulling them apart and licking out the frosting. The Oreo people ran the advertisement and warned us, 'Don't fiddle with the middle!' Jonah's problem was he never let God fiddle with the middle.

"Jonah said, 'God, I will obey You.' But he never let God turn his heart toward the compassion God showed His enemies. . . . There is no value to a Christian life that is committed to the call of God but not the character of God."[1]

The message of change from the inside out and maintaining an intimate walk with Jesus formed a major theme of the Stowell presidency, and the seniors listening in chapel apparently got the message. One month later, on May 27, 1988, Stowell was the keynote speaker at the MBI commencement (his first as president). Later he shook hands with each graduate as he or she received the diploma. Some of the students appeared to be handing something to the president, but parents and friends couldn't tell what.

Finally the president stepped to the microphone to announce: "Whoa, I don't have any place to put these cookies anymore, so the rest of you can keep your cookies."[2]

"Early on you're the president and you're trying to build relationships, and you're there for the students," says Stowell, who called the march of Oreo cookies during commencement "a very affirming, relational thing. They felt comfortable relating to me on that level. They didn't see me as someone far removed who would have taken this the wrong way."[3]

Although cabinet meetings and travels at times kept Stowell away from the students, his warm, genuine greetings connected personally with students and MBI staff. He once said his desire as president was to bring students a fresh "reality of Jesus Christ . . . so that we would not only proclaim Him and not only know His theology, but we would live Him out so the city of Chicago and this campus would radiate with the personality and the ethic, and the characteristics of the person of Jesus Christ."[4] He wrote fourteen books while president, including *The Trouble with Jesus*, which won the Christian Booksellers Association Gold Medallion Award for its post-9/11 call that Christians name Jesus in public prayers and proclaim Him in a pluralistic society without fear of offense.

## BUILDING FOR THE FUTURE

During the Stowell presidency, three new buildings expanded the educational mission of Moody Bible Institute. The Solheim Center, a new life sciences/urban outreach center, opened in 1990. It replaced aging, cramped North Hall, a former Masonic temple that had been retrofitted for recreational and intercollegiate sports as well as offices for student organizations and rehearsal space for music groups. The MBI Archers had played on a basketball court so tight that players had to brace themselves for the wall just a few feet beyond the end lines.

For the players, the new center was like trading in a Ford Pinto to drive a Lincoln Continental: three basketball courts, a fitness/weight training room, women's and men's locker rooms, women's and men's varsity team rooms, an elevated running track, four racquetball courts, and a twenty-five-yard swimming pool, as well as classrooms. As an urban-outreach center, it began to host summer basketball training camps. During the past twenty years the center has welcomed local youth organizations and ministries year-round to its facility.

Word quickly got out about the three basketball courts, ideal for simultaneous practice games. The National Basketball Association (NBA) soon arranged to have their predraft camp at MBI's Solheim Center. NBA coaches, general managers, and pro scouts came each year for fourteen years, 1991–2005, to evaluate college talent they would sign into the pros. And the 1994 and 1996 USA men's basketball teams both practiced at the Solheim and both won gold medals, the '94 team the world championship (Toronto) and the '96 team the summer Olympic Games (Atlanta).[5] The Solheim also hosted the 1996 women's USA basketball team. Today many NBA teams practice at the Solheim before they play their night game against the Chicago Bulls.

Karsten Solheim, who designed and manufactured industry-leading golf clubs, gave a major gift to MBI to jump-start the life sciences/urban outreach center that would become the Solheim Center. Solheim's generous seed money for athletic centers at other Christian colleges included a design/build blueprint that could be adapted to any school's building site for quick construction.

In 1986, the Century 2 campaign had commemorated the school's centennial anniversary with plans for a new educational building. Dubbed the academic/learning resource center, it would be 112,800

| 1987 | 1989 | 1991 |
|---|---|---|
| Joseph Stowell named seventh president.<br><br>Moody Undergraduate School earns accreditation with NCA. | Berlin Wall comes down. | Sweeting Center for World Evangelization opens doors. |

square feet for thirty classrooms, a large library, and faculty offices. The Century 2 contributions began almost immediately, yet the center opened one year after the Solheim Center due to its size—twice the area of the Solheim—and the Solheim's fast-track construction schedule using the design/build model. When the academic center opened in 1991, it had a new name, the George Sweeting Center for World Evangelization, in honor of the former president and chancellor.

The Sweeting Center includes computer labs, a media center, television studios, video editing suites for communications classes, and 32,000 square feet of library space, holding 155,000 books, numerous journals, volumes, and newspapers. Builders included the infrastructure for "smart classrooms" that would give professors quick access to multimedia tools for teaching, including PowerPoint, video, and lighting. "The equipment came later. That was good because it came after technology had developed," said Bruce Cain, vice president of facilities when the Sweeting Center opened. "We could do it more efficiently and [buy] more of a smart classroom.[6]

He called the library furnishings, including the much larger shelving area for books and additional study carrels for students, "the big thing."[7] Card catalogs dating back more than seventy-five years were dumped as librarians and assistants transferred all holdings onto digital catalogs. Today students, faculty, and guests can go online to learn what holdings are available, obtain call numbers, and read publishing information before even stepping into the library.

The Alumni Student Center (ASC) opened in 1999. Funded largely with gifts from alumni as well as other interested supporters, the two-story building is like a traditional student union. The second floor includes a coffee shop, lounge area for students to mingle, game room, and activity and meeting rooms. A large employee/student cafeteria anchors the first floor. The Commons seats 625 diners and serves breakfast and lunch.

| 1994 | 1996 | 1998 |
|---|---|---|
| Rwanda genocide devastates that nation. | Moody Monthly *renamed* Moody Magazine, *continues publishing until 2003 and wins multiple awards.* | India and Pakistan test nuclear weapons. |

Despite its size, architects succeeded in tucking the ASC between Smith Hall and Torrey-Gray Auditorium. Howard Whaley, director of the project, and his team worked with designers to keep the Alumni Plaza open, allaying fears this new building would cramp the area and clash with existing buildings. The signature clock tower marks the southwest corner of the center.

## GIVING CREDIT WHERE IT'S DUE

President Stowell joined Moody as the undergraduate school completed its initial accreditation process with North Central Association of Colleges and Schools (NCA) and the graduate school started its steady growth. The undergraduate school had continued its affiliation with the Association for Biblical Higher Education (ABHE) that it began in 1950 (see previous chapter), benefiting from seminars for college deans and presidents. But in 1986, under the leadership of Dean of Education Howard Whaley and Dean of Faculty Robert Woodburn, MBI sought broader accreditation with NCA, one of six regional accrediting agencies. Previously the NCA had made it difficult for private and religious schools with smaller resources to achieve accreditation. But in the mid-1980s the Higher Learning Commission of the NCA set new criteria that would measure a school's qualification in terms of meeting its mission. St. Paul Bible College (now Crown College) made application under the new criteria and won approval. Moody would become the second Bible college to achieve accreditation. "Now a majority of Bible colleges have regional accreditation under the new criterion that the school meets its mission," notes Larry Davidhizar, vice president and dean of the undergraduate school.[8]

The process was demanding, requiring that the undergraduate school conduct an extensive self-study of its programs to determine how

| 1999 | 2000 | 2001 |
|---|---|---|
| *Alumni Student Center opens. Moody Graduate School offers MDiv program.* | *Moody online courses offer students classes anywhere, anytime.* | Pentagon and World Trade Center attacked by terrorists. |

effective it was in achieving its mission. Evaluators who came onsite to visit would ask, "Do you have the resources? Do you have a strategic plan?" Then they would evaluate and measure the effectiveness of the programs. They earned accreditation in 1987—renewed in 1992 and 2004. Its next review will be in 2014.

The accreditation process remains demanding, and the educational services branch now has a director of accreditation and assessment and a director of institutional research who assist both the undergraduate school as well as the graduate school and seminary as they prepare for upcoming accreditation reviews. But it benefits students who transfer from MBI, knowing their course credits are acceptable at most colleges, as well as alumni who apply to graduate schools and seminaries that recognize the quality of the MBI courses.

## A GROWING GRADUATE SCHOOL

During the Stowell years (1987–2005), the graduate school grew, adding almost a half dozen master's degree programs: MA biblical studies, MA intercultural studies, MA spiritual formation and discipleship, MA urban studies (all requiring sixty course hours, as well as a master's of ministry), and the master's of divinity (MDiv). The MDiv is a professional degree, requires ninety-six academic hours, and offers "in-depth biblical and practical preparation for those desiring to minister in churches or parachurch organizations." Students could choose from one of four emphases: biblical studies, intercultural studies, spiritual formation and discipleship, or urban studies.

In 2010 Moody Graduate School acquired the Michigan Theological Seminary and became the Moody Theological Seminary and Graduate School (MTS). For more on MTS, including its graduate studies certificate program, see chapter 11.

| 2003 | 2005 | 2006 |
|------|------|------|
| *Moody Aviation begins its relocation to Spokane.* | *Michael Easley named eighth president.* | *Moody Bible Institute-Spokane opens as first branch campus.* |

## PRESIDENT EASLEY ON
## THE GOSPEL AND THE SCRIPTURES

Michael Easley came to Moody from a successful pastorate in suburban Washington, D.C., where the echoes from the 2001 terrorist attacks left some in his congregation unsure how to respond to true, devout Muslims who prayed boldly in the name of Allah through the prophet Muhammad. As the eighth president, he encouraged students to have the same boldness in declaring Jesus. "We need in the same kind, gentle, and firm way to say, 'I am the way, the truth and the life, and no one comes to the Father except through Me.' And one of the great challenges and privileges at the Institute is to empower these young men and women in our undergrad and grad schools—to say to them, 'You can do this. You can stand gently and firmly in the gospel on Christ, and on His Spirit, through these very challenging times.'"[9]

Two-thirds through his tenure as president (2005–2008), Michael Easley described to a radio audience his focus and hope for students as being the Bible itself. "It's from this Word that we understand the revealed Jesus Christ. And to me, I hope in God's kindness and in His history, we'll look back on this as a time when we refocused and re-centered the Scripture as our authority." In Moody Radio programs and Moody Publishers books, as well as President's Chapels and speaking dates, Easley charged all MBI ministries to continue to emphasize the reliability and practicality of the Scriptures for daily living.

President Easley suffered back pain beginning twenty months into his term. A medical leave, surgery, therapy, and rest gave him only temporary

| 2007-2008 | 2008 | 2009 | 2010 |
|---|---|---|---|
| *Moody Radio launches three worldwide audio channels.* | Barack Obama elected first African-American president of the United States. | *J. Paul Nyquist inaugurated as ninth president.*<br><br>The Five Love Languages *(Moody Publishers) reaches number one on* New York Times *bestseller list.* | *Moody Graduate School acquires Michigan Theological Seminary and becomes Moody Theological Seminary.* |

relief. He resigned after three years, explaining in a letter, "Surgery has already once interrupted my tenure for several weeks, and unfortunately it has become clear that more treatment is required. I have come to the difficult conclusion that under the circumstances I cannot be as effective a president as the Institute deserves."

A yearlong search brought the MBI community to J. Paul Nyquist, a former pastor of two large churches and president of Avant Ministries, a global missions organization. When Jerry Jenkins, chairman of the board of trustees, announced the selection to Moody faculty, staff, and students, he said, "Dr. Nyquist's skill set and character uniquely match our search committee's profile." A brief profile of the ninth president appears at the end of this chapter under "Meet the President."

## A WALK WITH THE FIRST THREE PRESIDENTS

The nine presidents who have led Moody Bible Institute during its first 125 years brought different gifts and skill sets to the Institute. Yet all have demonstrated a passion and vision for teaching biblical truth and spreading the gospel. All made contact regularly with students in the hallways and in some cases the classrooms as well.

The evangelist and first president of the Institute visited the school several times once year-round classes began in 1889. Often when he visited, D. L. Moody would take charge of classes, according to one student, who added, "He would not lecture us but talked in a fatherly way about practical things." Once "he told the men students not to try to preach like someone else but to maintain their own individuality. He also told them not to lie on the pulpit when preaching but to stand erect and keep their hands out of their pockets."[10]

Tradition says Founder's Week, the weeklong Bible conference that began in 1911 to commemorate Moody's birthday, harkens back to one visit when the evangelist dashed into a classroom and shouted, "It's my birthday; let's go for a sleigh ride!"[11] The story may be legend (one version says an excited Moody burst into the student dining room to give the invitation), but it's clear D. L. Moody loved his students and was available when he was present on the Chicago campus.

*The Institute Tie,* forerunner of *Moody* magazine, announced in 1901 the first Founder's Day celebration: "A new day for annual observance has been decided upon by the faculty—Feb. 5th, Mr. Moody's birthday—Founder's Day. While Mr. Moody was with us, it was his custom to out-vote the entire faculty of the Northfield schools and give a general holiday in both institutions on his birthday. Some of the most playful and kindly reminiscences about him cluster around those anniversaries.

"While the Institute usually has not observed the occasion in similar fashion, the faculty have now inaugurated this memorial movement and beginning with . . . this year, the day will be observed with special exercises."[12]

Moody's care for the students traces back to the first graduate of his institute. William Evans was given the coveted number one diploma in 1892, ironic since Evans hesitated to enroll due to the sacrifice required—he would be forced to surrender his position as a typesetter for the *New York World* and begin with no income. Moody had given an impassioned call at Fifth Avenue Presbyterian Church in New York for young men and women to give their lives to God's service. Looking into the audience, the evangelist sensed Evans's doubts and singled him out. "Young man, I mean you."

After the message, Moody found William. "Young man, somehow or other God told me He meant you. Have you never been called to give your life to service of Jesus Christ?"

Evans had been helping in missions work for weeks, but he was unsure about the financial sacrifice of moving to Chicago and becoming a student without a job. Then a friend volunteered that William's funds were small.

"Did I say anything about money? Young man, you pack up your trunk and go to my school in Chicago. Never mind about money."

Evans agreed, and when he arrived the financial office reported an allowance of $25.00 a month was being provided (a gift from the compassionate Moody). Evans eventually completed his training (and no longer needed the allowance after his cornet playing at the Pacific Garden Mission eventually earned him $5.00 a week). Later Evans would become a noted Bible teacher at Moody Bible Institute.[13]

With his frequent travels as an evangelist, D. L. Moody walked the halls less frequently than the second and third presidents. R. A. Torrey became president upon Moody's death in 1899, but he had been in charge of developing the school curriculum since being named the first superintendent in 1889. Though president in function, Torrey retained the title of superintendent, just as his successor James Gray would carry the title of dean but act as president beginning in 1904.

Both men walked the halls regularly, Torrey as the school's permanent Bible teacher and director of the men's department, Gray as the dean who would give direction to daily operations. Torrey remained as superintendent until 1908, but was increasingly away from campus for evangelistic campaigns overseas. After Torrey left Moody Bible Institute, he continued his evangelistic campaigns for four years. In 1912 he became dean of the Bible Institute of Los Angeles (now Biola University) and served in that role for twelve years. Getz notes that Torrey soon was "recognized as one of the outstanding early leaders of Moody Bible Institute."[14]

As dean, Gray decided to combine the men's and women's departments in 1905, effectively making classes coeducational—though men and women continued to sit on opposite sides in classrooms.

## EARLY IN THE MORNING

Students who rose early enough on weekday mornings could often find President Houghton walking through the arch of Crowell Hall. The president began his workday early. Often he would arrive on campus before 7 a.m., the first of three hundred staffers to report.

One such morning Wilbur Smith, faculty member and close associate, spotted Houghton in the archway of Crowell Hall.

"And how are you this morning?" he asked Houghton.

"I guess I am all right," the president said, leaning heavily against the brick wall. "I did not sleep all night—but there is work to do."[15]

Clearly Houghton's motto could have been 1 Corinthians 15:58: "Be ye steadfast, unmoveable, always abounding in the work of the Lord" (KJV). He endured migraine headaches throughout the presidency. Indeed he suffered from recurring headaches during his final thirty years, but they became more frequent and intense during his final five years.[16] Yet he remained steadfast in the work at MBI.

## THE PRESIDENT IN THE CLASSROOM

Maybe it was not surprising to MBI staff that as president William Culbertson would spend two or three hours a week teaching students. He had begun to walk the halls of the Institute as dean of education on September 1, 1942. When he became president more than five years later, he chose to stay close to the students by continuing to teach one course on campus: geography of Bible lands. During those early presidential years in the classroom, he developed a strong rapport with his students, many of whom would soon scatter around the globe as missionaries and Christian leaders.[17] He visited several during a world missions tour in 1960.

Of the nine presidents, perhaps Culbertson best summarized the distinctives of the Bible institute:

Bible institutes from the time of their origin . . . have stressed those things needed for vital Christian witness: the study of the English Bible, the winning of souls, spiritual living, missionary outreach, and gospel hymnody.

While certain elements have been added to the course of study, these basics remain intact. As I see it, the Bible institute is a specialized school, distinct from the liberal arts college, from the theological seminary, and from a scientific institute. Some speak of it as a religious, undergraduate, professional school.[18]

## PASSING THE BATON

When it was time for Culbertson to pass the baton, he met with George Sweeting, then senior pastor of Moody Memorial Church. As Culbertson explained how the reluctant pastor might fit in as the next president of Moody Bible Institute, he summarized the gifts and passions of the first four MBI presidents:

George, if you'll notice the rhythm of the Moody Bible Institute, you'll know we were founded by an evangelist. D. L. Moody was succeeded by R. A. Torrey, another evangelist. Then we had James M. Gray, an administrator/educator, then Houghton, a promoter pastor. We need now the gifts you have.[19]

Culbertson did not speak of his own training, but Sweeting knew the successes of this humble pastor, church leader, and academic. What did Sweeting have in common with Culbertson and his predecessors? Most of them were either evangelists or pastors. All had a passion for building God's kingdom through the local church and reaching those who were spiritually lost. It took George Sweeting more than one hundred days to be assured this step was God's leading and not his own. Then he finally said yes, confident not in his own abilities but in God's provision.

"I didn't feel qualified, and I suppose I would have been more scared if I had," President Sweeting later told his biographer. "No one should come into a responsibility like that one feeling as if he is perfectly capable in himself. I knew better. I knew the only way it would work would be with my total dependence on God."[20]

## A HEART FOR PASTORS AND EVANGELISTS

Sweeting came to MBI with the shoes of an evangelist and the heart of a pastor. Within two years of becoming president, he initiated the Moody Pastors' Conference. His conference team anticipated three hundred at the inaugural conference. But more than six hundred came on campus from thirty-seven states, Puerto Rico, and Scotland.[21] Sweeting's legacy continues; the conference approaches its thirtieth anniversary with attendance well above 1,100 pastors.

In 1973 Sweeting began a three-year community evangelistic campaign called the Chicago Evangelism Outreach (CEO). The campaign featured a personal letter from Dr. Sweeting that summarized the plan of salvation and offered a free correspondence lesson, "The Good Life." The first year the letter went to 400,000 homes on Chicago's North Side. As part of the follow-up, students and staff visited scores of homes, and

CEO 1974 culminated with a large rally. CEO continued its efforts on the city's West and South Sides in 1975 and 1976.[22]

## THE PROVOST AND THE THREE PRESIDENTS

Perhaps no one has worked closer with the three most recent presidents than Charles Dyer, provost and dean of education from 2000–2010. As he prepared to welcome in June 2010 incoming provost Junias Venugopal, Dyer talked about Drs. Stowell, Easley, and Nyquist, the three presidents he served during his decade of ministry.[23] Like many senior managers at MBI, Dyer knew the presidents as colleagues and friends; so he spoke of each by their first names.

"Joe brought two things. He brought the care for people. He was the consummate people person. When he was with you, for ten seconds you were the focus of his world. He looked at you, he knew your name, he would ask how things were going. He modeled what it meant to care for people.

"He also moved Moody into a national arena. I think Dr. Sweeting started that process, but Joe catapulted us into some arenas we would not have been otherwise because of his incredible giftedness as a communicator." He noted Stowell's involvement as a member of the trustee board at the Billy Graham Evangelistic Association, service as a contributing editor to *Christianity Today*, and presence as a featured speaker at several Promise Keepers men's conferences in the 1990s.

While Dyer credits President Stowell with bringing Moody into greater national prominence, he credits President Easley with focusing MBI strongly on the Bible and truth. "Michael's greatest strength at Moody was the reminder that you can get so soft around the edges that you can make the foundation crumble. Michael focused back on the Word of God and truth. In broadcasting, Dr. Easley called upon a focus on biblical truth; in publishing, upon books that would change lives." Because of health issues, "his was a very short tenure as president," Dyer acknowledges, "but that reenergizing our focus on the Word of God and the life-changing power of it was a very necessary thing."

**MBI IMPACT** ⟨ In Their Own Words ⟩

Three presidents representing nearly four decades of leadership (1971–2008) met for a historic interview on Moody Broadcasting Network's *Open Line* program on April 10, 2007. George Sweeting, Joe Stowell, and Michael Easley talked about their times and themes. In their own words, here are some of their thoughts.

**On their times. GS:** "During the 1960s and early 1970s, three political assassinations and war in Vietnam created turmoil in the cities and just outside the Moody campus. I remember staying at Moody Church over one night and looking down North Avenue, just seeing the sparks flying in the night, and the National Guard was here, hippies came for the Democratic Convention, fifteen thousand camped in the park across from the church.

"So they were very difficult, precarious days, and yet, the work of God went on, and we saw some come to faith. Dr. Culbertson was president, I was pastor of Moody Church in those days, and it overlapped into my time as president. We endured those times and I would say Moody kept its commitment to being in the city. It would have been easy to flee to the suburbs or some other city, but in the spirit of D. L. Moody, MBI stayed in the city, and continued its presence in the urban area."

**JS:** "I think [the terrorist attacks of] 9/11 was certainly the pinnacle national disaster in my time in serving Christ here. [Yet] there was the joy of being able to walk our students through a biblical perspective on this. The joy of knowing God is God, and that His Word is true, in a time like that, is huge. And to be able to have something of authority, to say to people, 'This is God in the midst of this. And we don't have all the reasons why, but these are the ways of God in moments like this.'"

**ME:** "The tragedy in the wake of 9/11 is in the [continuing] culture of postmodernity and what I call pan-modernity. Everything is being pounded flat. My fear is that the culture we're in is loath to Christianity. We're the one last bastion you can still whale upon and not suffer any backlash. It's okay to be anything today except a believer in Christ. We are in a very interesting fulcrum, theologically and culturally. How are we going to recapture this generation, this culture to [bring it back] to a biblical theology? That's our greatest challenge in a culture that's washed in relativism."

**On their themes. GS:** "It was *evangelism*. I was trying to go back and get hold of the passion of Moody and share it with our students, because he talked about shoe-leather evangelism. Sharing your faith intelligently, lovingly, but definitely doing that.

"Another word that characterized my time was . . . excellence. I mentioned that we want to do things in an excellent way—not extravagant, but excellent. The challenge was to do our best . . . to excel for the glory of God."

**JS:** "In my eighteen years here, my passion was to lead our students to the real Jesus. We're called Moody Bible Institute, and I think one of the things we kind of get caught up in and sidetracked with is we're Moody *Bible* Institute, as though the *Bible* is the end game. And I'm not depreciating the Bible, but the Bible is *not* the end game. It's God's revelation to us to lead us to Himself. Jesus is the central theme of the Old Testament and New Testament of the Bible. My desire was to bring the reality of Jesus Christ.

"I had a second passion, and I get this right from D. L. Moody: I wanted us to be as broad as the gospel. D. L. Moody was as broad as the gospel. He was beyond the denominational barriers. He was beyond cultural barriers. He was beyond gender barriers, and he embraced as wide as the gospel embraces."

**ME:** "While I agree with everything Joe said about Christology being our center, I am a biblicist. I think the only way we get to this Jesus Christ is a clear understanding of the Word of God. . . . It's not just a book, it's not just theology, it's the very Word of God. And it's from this Word that we understand the revealed Jesus Christ."

Charlie Dyer lauds Dr. Paul Nyquist's global perspective: "What Paul brought is the international focus. Joe was focusing on the urban environment; Paul is now saying the international environment is where we need to be looking. He is [saying] 'God didn't just call [us] to be salt and light to the U.S. but to the entire world.' It has always been part of Moody, but it is being reemphasized by Paul. I suspect over the next decade . . . that's what you are going to see."

Dyer believes their different leadership gifts and perspectives have been matched by distinctive personalities. "Joe had a warmth about him that characterizes few people. I don't know anyone who wasn't Joe's friend. . . . Michael had an absolute commitment to truth. Truth trumps all. So what is the Word of God saying? That is what we need to focus on—and that is not necessarily going to make friends, because Jesus said, 'If the world hates you [remember that it has] hated me' (John 15:18). So if I'm a follower of Christ, there is a divisiveness at times that comes through that, but I've got to make the commitment to be the follower of Christ.

"Paul is pastoral. He's quieter. He's not the outgoing, gregarious Joe. But there is a genuine warmth and pastoral dimension with Paul that you just sense he's a caring individual. He came out of the pastorate too. So he's had church and nonchurch experience."

Even with his pastoral heart, President Nyquist will find some keen differences at Moody, Dyer says. "It's still a different animal. It's huge and has three major legs, all different. He has experience in corporate management, so it's a matter of learning."

## THE NINTH PRESIDENT

J. Paul Nyquist began his service as president on June 1, 2009, and soon led the charge to develop a strategic plan for all the ministries of Moody Bible Institute, assisted by Ed Cannon, executive vice president and chief operating officer. Both the board of trustees and Dyer say the new president's skills highly qualify him for the challenge. Board Chairman Jerry Jenkins described Nyquist as "a proven leader, team builder, and visionary who also happens to be a theologian. We look forward to many years of inspired leadership."

Before becoming the ninth MBI president, Nyquist directed Avant Ministries, an evangelical missions agency that began as Gospel Missionary Union in 1892. "Avant was an organization with a century of history that had to reinvent itself," says Dr. Dyer. Under the leadership of Nyquist, Avant began to ask, How do we stay the same as a mission that's committed to planting churches to reach the world and do it in a new paradigm, with short-cycle mission opportunities? As a result of that question, Nyquist "has had the opportunity of helping an organization think strategically, keep the foundational elements, and yet embrace a new way of strategically moving," Dyer says.

## MEET THE PRESIDENT

Paul Nyquist was formally inaugurated on October 23, 2009, in a stirring ceremony including former presidents Stowell and Easley and distinguished guests from other academic institutions. His vision for MBI during the next decade is suggested by the title of his inaugural address, "Biblical Mission, Global Vision" (see excerpts on pages 240–41). His passion for the worldwide church has been fueled by his eight years as president and chief executive officer of Avant Ministries. From 2001 to 2009 he visited more than thirty countries and witnessed vibrant churches in many lands, including India and in Africa. He believes MBI and other ministries can have a renewed global impact on churches, but he emphasizes the Institute must come alongside as a servant:

> In the last twenty years, the church around the world has grown rapidly [and is maturing]. And they don't need us dictating to them, "Here's what you need to do." We need to be serving them, asking, "How can we help you reach your people for Jesus Christ? We've got . . . educational resources, people resources—but how can we serve you?"[24]

Looking ahead, Nyquist believes a key step in beginning to implement the "Biblical Mission, Global Vision" theme is to work with the strategic initiative teams tasked with coming up with recommendations for their respective divisions—broadcasting, publishing, and education (both seminary and undergraduate). The teams met for six months in 2010 to evaluate existing programs and consider new approaches, under the vision outlined in the new president's inaugural address. Nyquist, Cannon, and other senior MBI leaders continue to discuss and refine these initiatives, and look forward to working closely with the entire Moody family on the new challenges and opportunities God may bring the Institute in the next few years.

## FINDING FELLOWSHIP WITH GOD

But a truly biblical vision begins with leaders who find guidance in the Scriptures and through personal fellowship with God. Nyquist finds his own personal devotions in the Bible refreshing, even though as a Bible expositor and speaker he has studied some passages over and over. Recently he recalled his daily study of the book of John:

I'm going through the gospel of John. And just the last two or three days, chapter 8 two days ago, chapter 9 yesterday, chapter 10 this morning, and I'm just [thinking], *Wow! It's almost like some of these things I've never seen before.* Every time you go through a portion of Scripture—I don't know how many times I've read that book—you just go, "This is fascinating! The dialogue that Jesus has with the Pharisees here and how He was just able to turn their arguments around."

So I try to make sure that in my time alone with the Lord I'm reading for me. I'm not reading for preaching, I'm not reading to study it for some other application. I try to keep those very different. It's for me, "What is it that God has for me today in His Word?" And sometimes there's just so much of it, I go, "Wow! I wish I had another couple of hours here to just dig into this deeper."

His favorite passages are on the greatness of God, especially Isaiah 40—he had faculty member Rosalie DeRosset read all thirty-one verses during his inauguration. He declares his favorite New Testament book is

Romans. With a passion befitting someone who holds a ThD in system-atic theology, he recounts the joys and inspiration of a study of this major letter by the apostle Paul:

> For example, Romans 5:8, "For God demonstrates his own love to us, in that while we were yet sinners, Christ died for us." What a verse! Or Romans 8:1, "There is now no condemnation for those in Christ Jesus." I mean it's just *packed* with those incredible truths. Like Romans 12:1, "Now offer your bodies as living sacrifices." Bang, bang, bang, bang, all the way through that book. And not only that, but it tells you about the wisdom of God's plan of redemption that has worked out. Not only as it relates to all of us being sinners . . . but then in chapters 9 through 11, how He's going to bring Israel in; and then the ramifications of that in chapters 12 through 16. There's no book, in my mind, like the book of Romans.

For the former pastor and missionary leader who is now the ninth president of Moody Bible Institute, such passion and familiarity with the Bible seem altogether fitting.

## NOTES

1. Joseph Stowell, President's Chapel, video recording, April 27, 1988, archives, MBI library.
2. Joseph Stowell, telephone interview on July 1, 2010. Dr. Stowell says he is unsure of the exact wording of his announcement, but he does remember that he was stacking cookies on the side of the pulpit as well as on the table where the diplomas rested.
3. Ibid.
4. As quoted on "Leading a Legacy," *Open Line*, Moody Broadcasting Network, April 10, 2007.
5. Known as Dream Team II, the 1996 Olympic team featured six future Hall of Fame players: Charles Barkley, Karl Malone, Hakeem Olajuwon, Scottie Pippen, David Robinson, and John Stockton. All practiced at the Solheim Center.
6. Bruce Cain, personal interview, July 8, 2010.
7. Ibid.
8. Larry Davidhizar, personal interview, May 7, 2010.
9. All statements by Michael Easley are from "Leading a Legacy," *Open Line*, Moody Broadcasting Network, April 10, 2007; hosted by Wayne Pederson.

10. Bernard R. DeRemer, *Moody Bible Institute* (Chicago: Moody, 1960), 31.

11. Ibid., 46.

12. Ibid., 45–46.

13. Jim Vincent, "The Man Who Learned to Stick," *Moody Monthly*, June 1985, 43; Bernard R. DeRemer, *Moody Bible Institute*, 32, 34. Evans joined the faculty in 1903 and became director of the Bible Course a few years later; see DeRemer, *Moody Bible Institute*, 38.

14. See Gene Getz, *MBI: The Story of Moody Bible Institute* (Chicago: Moody, 1969), 76.

15. Wilbur M. Smith, *Will H. Houghton: A Watchman on the Wall* (Grand Rapids: Eerdmans, 1951), chapter 22; as cited in DeRemer, *Moody Bible Institute*, 95.

16. Ibid.

17. Robert G. Flood and Jerry B. Jenkins, *Teaching the Word, Reaching the World* (Chicago: Moody, 1985), 80.

18. Warren Wiersbe, *William Culbertson* (Chicago: Moody, 1974), 67.

19. Jerry B. Jenkins, *A Generous Impulse* (Chicago: Moody, 1987), 132.

20. Ibid., 133.

21. Flood and Jenkins, *Teaching the Word*, 92.

22. Ibid.

23. All statements by Charles Dyer are from a personal interview on May 6, 2010. Dr. Dyer continues in 2011 to serve as professor-at-large of Bible. His new responsibilities include teaching modular and online classes and continuing to lead MBI-sponsored tours of the Holy Land.

24. All quotations by Paul Nyquist are from a personal interview, June 11, 2010.

( Part 2 )

Inside Moody Bible Institute

# 6

# The Around-the-Clock
# Undergraduate School

Most people agree the heart of Moody Bible Institute is its undergraduate school. If so, the heart has had plenty of vigorous exercise through the years, as leaders have expanded and reshaped the curriculum, always keeping in mind the needs of the Christian community they serve. Programs have been added; others have been dropped when they no longer served a purpose.

In the first decade of the twenty-first century, though, technological and cultural changes reshaped the undergraduate learning experience. In 2000, online classes, courtesy of the Internet, appeared for "rooted learners" outside Chicago. Soon undergraduate-level courses also appeared, allowing MBI resident students to take selected classes online.

In 2004 the undergraduate school started requiring all students to complete an internship to graduate; and in 2009, each academic department began to offer interdisciplinary studies. These final two changes acknowledge the increasing specialization within American society and its impact on church and ministry. Internships enable students to go into the field and, in a real-world setting, become more proficient in a specialized area (and along the way perhaps earn a recommendation from their mentor). An interdisciplinary major affords valuable cross-training. A missions major, for example, can go outside her twenty-seven credit hours (plus an internship), replacing up to twelve hours with youth ministry courses or women's ministry courses. Either specialty could be useful on the mission field.

Specialization at Moody has also meant the addition of focused majors within different departments. For example, students in the Bible department can take a biblical languages major (added in 2001); students in world missions and evangelism can learn to teach English overseas through the TESOL major (teaching English to speakers of other languages; added in 1999); and students in educational ministries can choose to major in youth ministry to learn to serve youth in a church or parachurch organization (added in 1993).

## AT THE FOUNDATION

Yet the Bible remains a foundational text and the foundation of training. All students complete a minimum of thirty-six hours of Bible and theology (which is drawn from the Scriptures). Bible and doctrine courses are the core of every major. Rounding out the course work for a BA or BS degree are general studies classes necessary to prepare a student to relate to the needs of people and to be effective in his or her ministry of the Word of God. The mission of the school is "to provide a Bible-centered education that enables students to know Christ and serve Him through His church in vocational ministry."[1]

There have been major changes to curriculum through the years, as the undergraduate school moved from a year-round school that invited students to "enter at any time" during the calendar year to a two-year semester-plan campus (in 1951); to a school that offered diplomas in three years and undergraduate degrees in five (in 1966 in coordination with other colleges); to a full baccalaureate degree in four years (in 1985), first through an articulation arrangement with nearby colleges and eventually by offering all general studies (liberal arts) courses on campus.

But the focus on Bible remained unchanged from its earliest days.

After its opening as a year-round Bible institute in 1889, the school published its curriculum, described in part this way:

> The English Bible is the principal textbook. The study of the Bible is divided into five departments:
>
> 1. Introductory. The Inspiration of the Bible. The Structure of the Bible. Methods of Bible Study.
> 2. Study of Bible Doctrine. God, Attributes, Trinity, etc. Divinity of Christ, Person and Work of the Holy Spirit.
> 3. Study of the Bible—in sections and in books. The first year study [included] Luke [through] Romans, Colossians and some other Pauline Epistles. All of the general Epistles and Revelation.
> 4. The Analysis by the students of texts and passages of Scripture, together with exercises in the construction and delivery of Bible Readings, addresses, etc.
> 5. The Study of the Bible in its application to various classes of men, the special object of this study being to give the students facility in using their Bibles in the Inquiry room, home workshops, etc.[2]

Beyond the Bible emphasis, students also studied music and "methods of city, home and foreign mission work." Classes were open to all men and women who wished "to acquire proficiency in Christian work."

Today the Bible is still at the center of a Moody education. Yet some wonder if one day, with all its bachelor of arts and bachelor of science degrees, Moody Bible Institute might become Moody Bible College. That, education leaders agree, will not happen. Former Dean of Education Charles Dyer acknowledges that some regard the term *institute* as a lesser, or limited, place of learning. "Institute [seems to imply] a level that is a step below a college, but there are some exceptions, and Moody and MIT happen to be two of them." Like MIT (Massachusetts Institute of Technology), known for its science and technology courses, MBI is known for its Bible courses. The Institute name emphasizes MBI's distinctive strength, a Bible school that trains students to understand and apply the Bible for future lives of ministry.[3]

"We are a college; we are considered a level 2 college, because we have graduate and undergraduate programs." Yet *institute* remains part of the name, Dyer says, as MBI keeps Bible courses at its center, even as such undergraduate departments as communications, music, and educational ministries train students for vocational ministry.

In a sense, students have a double major—thirty-six semester hours in Bible (including Bible-heavy theology courses) and thirty to forty-plus hours in their major.

## THE EARLY "DEPARTMENTS"

Today there are eight departments that offer bachelor of arts degrees: Bible, communications, educational ministries, music, pastoral studies, sports ministry, theology, and world missions and evangelism. A final department, missionary aviation technology, offers a bachelor of science degree.

Recall that in the early years the undergraduate school curriculum was offered in "courses" rather than departments. Four courses/departments existed by 1900: the Biblical, Musical, Practical Work, and Missionary Courses. Three other early courses emerged in the 1910s.[4]

First, an *English Course* appeared in 1913. This was not a full-fledged program, but several subject areas that were offered to meet student needs. Classes emphasized grammar, rhetoric, and composition, as well as conversational speech for foreign-speaking students. The following year, proficiency in rhetoric and composition became a requirement for graduation. During those formative years of the MBI curriculum, school officials were concerned with training students who could communicate competently in both speaking and writing and thus serve effectively in Christian service.

Second, a *Sunday School Course* began in 1914, following the counsel of the International Sunday School Association. (Various subjects directly related to Sunday school work had been offered at the Institute since 1900.) The purpose of this course was to prepare young men and women "to make Sunday school work their life calling." Students who wished to enroll in this program did so at the beginning of their fourth term of study. Graduates of the course received both the diploma of the Institute and a teacher training diploma from the Illinois State Sunday School Association.

In 1916, the third new course of study appeared, the *Swedish-English Course*. The largest grouping of Swedish immigrants to America had settled in Chicago. During the 1880s the Swedish population had exploded to more than 43,000 people, trailing only the German, Irish, and British settlers. Networks of friends and relatives eased their transition to urban life, helping newcomers find housing, jobs, and social connections. Significantly, the largest enclave was north of the Chicago River on the Near North Side, just blocks from the Moody Bible Institute.[5] Designed to train Swedish young men for Christian work, the Swedish Course included the regular subjects offered at the Institute, plus special courses in English, Swedish language and literature, New Testament Greek, homiletics (in the Swedish language), and history.

By 1918 this program became more formalized with a working arrangement between MBI and the Swedish Evangelical Free Church of America (EFCA); in effect, MBI served as the training school for the denomination's young men who wished to prepare for the ministry or for missionary work.

By 1930 almost 66,000 Chicagoans were Swedish-born and there were more than 140,000 children of Swedish immigrants. The Swedish-English Course continued until 1928, when it became part of a separate school in Chicago, as the EFCA began a four-year liberal arts program. Many years later the EFCA school Trinity College emerged. Today it is part of Trinity International University, located in Deerfield, Illinois, with its sister seminary, the Trinity Evangelical Divinity School. (MBI still offered a limited Swedish-English Course until 1934.)

## HOW THE "MISSIONARY COURSE" GREW INTO THE WORLD MISSIONS AND EVANGELISM DEPARTMENT

Two departments that trace back to the first twenty years of MBI— the department of world missions and evangelism and the department of educational ministries—provide case studies in how the Institute modified its offerings to meet the needs of the era. The Missionary Course of 1900 remained largely unchanged for sixty-five years, although in 1929 it absorbed the missionary medical service course (see chapter 2). The related missionary technical course that appeared in 1949 prepared specialists for mission-field operations in aeronautics, radio communications, and photography. With changing mission and curriculum needs, aeronautics eventually would be replaced by the existing missionary aviation technology course begun by Paul Robinson; photography would move into the department of communications. When the new baccalaureate program began in 1966, the missionary technical course became the department of missionary technical training.

Two separate departments appeared in 1971: missionary aviation technology and missionary radio. The objective of the missionary radio department was "to prepare missionary technologists in point-to-point communications and missionary radio broadcasting." Initially enrollment was strong, but as student attendance began to decline, officials became aware of a decreasing need. Electronics training had become available at numerous community colleges and technical institutes.

Furthermore, students with technical skills now came to MBI for specialized training in Bible and theology as one-year special studies or advanced studies students. Clearly the department no longer needed to train radio technologists, and in 1978 the department of missionary radio was discontinued.

Similarly, the missionary nursing program ended in 1981 when it was clear that many students were arriving at MBI as nurses already, seeking biblical training prior to missions service. To help these nurses, the department of world missions eliminated a nursing major but offered practical supplemental electives on subjects such as tropical diseases and nutrition in developing countries.

After the Missions Course became the department of missions in 1966 and began to offer a BA degree, the department began to evaluate all its majors. The missions faculty soon concluded that the program at MBI was emphasizing foreign missions, with home missions regarded as preliminary training. In 1976 the department renamed the home missions major the American intercultural ministries major, or AIM. The name recognized the growing multicultural diversity of the United States. AIM would provide cultural and ministry skills by offering students emphases in one of six areas: black American, Asian American, native American, Hispanic, rural American, and urban American ministries.

With this new emphasis in place, the department leadership began to reexamine the entire program and concluded the label "foreign missions" major was also misleading. Raymond Tallman, later the chairman of the department, explained, "'Foreign' had become the term for missionary work that was thought to be cross-cultural. However, with the American intercultural ministries we had taken the first step in identifying . . . home missions as cross-cultural."[6]

To recognize the equality between foreign and home missions, in 1981 the foreign missions major became international ministries, while the AIM major eventually narrowed its focus to become the urban ministries major. Both became part of the new department of world missions. Years later the department of personal evangelism merged with world missions. Today the department of world missions and evangelism offers those two majors and four others: applied linguistics, evangelism/discipleship, Jewish studies, and TESOL. For the impact of missions on all MBI students, see "MBI Impact" on pages 124–25.

## HOW THE "SUNDAY SCHOOL COURSE" GREW INTO THE EDUCATIONAL MINISTRIES DEPARTMENT

*The Sunday School Course. The Religious Education Course. The Christian Education Course. The Christian Education-Music Course. The department of Christian education.* The changing names for today's department of educational ministries (so named by faculty vote in 1991) all reflect the changing needs of the times, a hallmark of MBI's innovative educational model.

The Sunday School Course was developed in 1914 "with the advice and assistance of . . . representatives of the International Sunday School

Association [ISSA]." It was the forerunner of what would be called departments of Christian education in evangelical schools of higher education—a term that would endure into the 1980s. The Sunday School Course itself ended in 1922, as the ISSA had merged with another Sunday school council to become the International Council of Religious Education. No other outside organization would affect professional church education at MBI. Instead, the Institute itself became the influential agency in promoting evangelical professional church education.[7] That year Clarence H. Benson joined the MBI faculty, and two years later he helped to organize the Religious Education Course (1924). In 1928 the course name was changed to Christian Education Course due to reaction in the evangelical world against the liberalizing term "religious."

As the Christian education program evolved, changes took place in the basic curriculum structure. In 1931 a new three-year course came alongside the Christian Ed Course. Called the Christian Education-Music Course, it helped to prepare students for the dual position of director of Christian education and director of church music.

When MBI began its program of departmental majors in 1966, a new department of Christian education replaced the Christian Education and Christian Education-Music Courses. Students now could receive a degree in Christian education by completing the MBI three-year curriculum and sixty hours of liberal arts courses at an accredited college or university.

The department was renamed educational ministries in 1991 for two reasons, according to Chairman Dennis Fledderjohann. First, the phrase *Christian education* tended to be equated with just Sunday school, and the department mission had been "broadened to include education in various venues—Christian schools associated with churches and parachurch organizations, such as Lydia Home [for children]." Second, the phrase "seemed to be a dated term with some negative baggage."[8]

Today the department of educational ministries offers majors in children's ministry, educational ministry, elementary education, pre-counseling, and youth ministry. Students completing course work in the elementary education major fulfill certification requirements of the Association of Christian Schools International. In 1984 an Alumni Association survey found that 53 percent of graduates from the then-Christian Education Department had held at least one position in full-time Christian service.[9] A 2009 survey of the elementary education graduates conducted by the educational ministries department found that during the five years ending in 2008, 73 percent of the graduates taught full-time their first year. Of those, 20 percent taught overseas. The remaining 27 percent who did not teach full-time the first year after graduation worked part-time in day care, were teacher assistants, or served as substitute teachers.[10]

## GENERAL EDUCATION COMES TO MOODY

The next big move for all academic departments came in 1987. The education team, led by Dean of Education Howard Whaley and Dean of Undergraduate School Robert Woodburn and encouraged by President Stowell, had achieved regional accreditation of its undergraduate programs in 1987. And through mutual arrangements with local Chicago schools like Harold Washington College and Roosevelt University, students now could earn baccalaureate degrees in four years. Students took their science, language, and history courses at local colleges while still enrolled at MBI.

Yet within the year they recognized that the "articulation" arrangement with Chicago schools needed to be reexamined. Both for camaraderie and the learning experience, a dozen or more MBI students often would enroll in the same off-campus class. The togetherness didn't sit well with the resident students, who viewed the visitors like a small invasion. In addition, some students from Moody would challenge premises and conclusions of teachers, especially in the sciences. "Twenty kids would get on the [subway], go down to Harold Washington College and take over a biology class," recalls Larry Davidhizar, present dean of the undergraduate school. "They would argue with a professor. Some of those dynamics just weren't good."[11] And a significant number of students chose not to enroll at the Chicago schools at all, wearied by inconvenient travel times or the worldviews being espoused by instructors.

**MBI IMPACT** ( "They See a Need and They Want to Do Something" )

In 2009, 384 students enrolled in the department of world missions and evangelism—one of every five undergraduate students—but all 1,763 undergraduate students learned to think and pray missionally.

It has been that way since at least 1964, when all students automatically became members of the Missionary Union upon enrollment at MBI, although attendance at meetings and participation remained voluntary. Missionary Union had its beginning in 1900 as the Missionary Study and Prayer Union (chapter 2).

According to former missions department chairman Ray Tallman, student participation in missions increased dramatically after Missionary Union became the Student Missionary Fellowship (in 1981). The name change eliminated some false impressions. Some students considered Missionary Union a club one had to join first, a "holy club" for the missions elite. In contrast, "Fellowship" implies that all students can be part of the missionary vision, even those who are not missions majors or planning on a missionary career.

Through the annual SMF project, students continue to make tangible contributions to international missions. For example, in 1985 students sent hundreds of reference books to Chinese pastors in mainland China. Working with the African Inland Mission, they shipped Bibles to Zaire (now the Democratic Republic of the Congo). More recently, students contributed $11,000 in 2009 to the construction of a school building in Mong Park, Burma, for rescued child soldiers. In a project named "About-Face," SMF partnered with the missions agency Divine Inheritance for the education and holistic healing of former child soldiers.

In 2010 students contributed $17,000 to International Sanctuary, an agency that aids victims of sex trafficking. The monies went to building a center in Mumbai, India, where rescued girls between ages thirteen and eighteen would receive shelter, vocational training, counseling, and spiritual healing as they transition to a normal life.

Those two projects featured creative fund-raising efforts. When the daily chapel program moved to a Tuesday through Thursday schedule in the 2000s, student organizations no longer could present opportunities and updates during chapels. Instead they led Friday assemblies, where student attendance was optional. SMF found the lower visibility meant less funds and responded with innovative approaches. The "About-Face" campaign began with a benefit concert, and included the sale of specially designed T-shirts, as well as colorful woven bags made by the rescued child soldiers. For the iSanctuary project, the campus coffee shop, Joe's, gave SMF prime sales space. And it gave customers the option of using the free insulated sleeve around the paper coffee cup or buying a handmade Coffee Cozy, a colorful sleeve knitted by one of several women. At $3.00 each, the sleeves decorated the cup, while providing a comfortable grip and better insulation, and they brought hundred of dollars to the SMF project.

"They sold like hotcakes," recalls Joe Gonzales, associate dean of student programs. "And it's not so much the money that's generated, but the thoughtfulness. This is where this generation is at. They see a need and they want to do something about it."

All students attend the annual Student Missions Conference, a three-day gathering each October that replaces classes in order to shine the spotlight on missionary trends and opportunities. More than seventy missionaries and mission agency representatives lead seminars where students can interact with and even challenge speakers in these small encounters. In addition they attend plenary sessions to hear a missionary spokesman. Many students respond: in 1983, 52 percent of the students indicated they were seriously considering missions service or sensed God's call to serve Him in missions. More recently, students have been asked for a public response at the closing missions meeting. One in five students responded in 2009.

Instead they would take courses at home during the summer.

The undergraduate school began to offer some of the courses on campus. The first course, Introduction to Western Civilization, was taught by Professor Tom Cornman, who would soon become vice president and dean of the undergraduate school. The students loved the convenience of staying on campus; they appreciated the Christian worldview underlying the presentation, and they sometimes entered into animated discussions with Cornman. Then, "in 1991 the board of trustees voted that the undergraduate school would service all general education requirements," Davidhizar noted.

## ACHIEVING AN INTEGRATED CURRICULUM

Bringing general studies courses onto campus enabled uniform teaching from a Christian worldview and assured a natural progression of courses over four years across an integrated curriculum. Several courses were already in place, including classes in writing, literature, biblical languages, music, philosophy, anthropology, and introduction to psychology. With Western civilization under way, the next year MBI added Spanish and French. (German joined modern-language offerings in 2010.) One challenge remained: How would MBI develop science courses, since the school did not have the contemporary facilities and equipment for lab courses? In fall 1994 the undergraduate school added a non-laboratory course that focuses on issues of science, "which has a critical thinking spin on it, which includes logic," says Davidhizar. Two courses now offered are quantitative reasoning (understanding the scientific method, quantitative research techniques, and developing critical thinking) and contemporary issues in science and Christian thought (understanding current issues in the physical and life sciences from a scientific and theological perspective).

Undergraduate school leaders placed the general education courses throughout the four years instead of the typical first and second year to achieve an integrated learning structure. As Davidhizar explains, "The literature course can come in the third year. It has a theological framework around it, so it makes more sense for students to take it then than during their freshman year." Similarly, the school offers Introduction to Philosophy for second- and third-year students, and Contemporary Issues in Science and Christian Thought is a fourth-year course. "The Higher Learning Commission [of the North Central Association] noticed that we had made the course progression more vertical" and commended the approach, Davidhizar reports.

This integrated approach begins in the first year, with several prerequisite courses to ground students in Christian life and community. In addition, the courses provide students with essential Bible knowledge and spiritual guidance at an early point in their undergraduate education. Beyond such foundational courses as Spiritual Life and Community, and Studying and Teaching the Bible, most freshmen take Old Testament Survey, New Testament Survey, Introduction to Disciple-making, the Church and Its Doctrines, and Speech Communication.

## WELCOME TO MOODY BIBLE INSTITUTE–SPOKANE

The first branch campus of the undergraduate school opened in fall 2006, when the former regional classroom in Spokane, Washington, became Moody Bible Institute–Spokane. Regional classrooms, the successors to the evening school, provided a service to "rooted learners," students whose job or family commitments kept them from coming to the main campus to take courses at night. (See "A Name Change and a Whole Lot More," page 131, on how regional classrooms improved on the evening school concept.) But as a regional classroom, the Spokane campus had been unique—all its classes met during daytime hours, allowing students to earn associate or bachelor's degrees in just two or four years. The campus previously had been Spokane Bible College (founded in 1972 as Inland Empire School of the Bible), and both faculty and students had grown accustomed to and liked the day classes. SBC leaders had approached Moody in an attempt to continue its evangelical history amid financial debt and dwindling enrollment. The declining enrollments reflected its inability to achieve academic accreditation.

Once SBC resolved its debt, Moody agreed to acquire SBC as a regional classroom. Enrollment stabilized—but it took off after MBI

## MBI IMPACT

( Passion and Awareness:
A Portrait of Today's Student )

In a recent interview, Tim Arens, dean of students from 1986 to the present, described today's Moody student and found much to commend.

*Twin passions.* "Students who come to us have a passion for the Word of God. They also have a passion for ministry. That is something that I don't think has changed since I've been here. I think with this younger generation this may have increased even a bit because many of our students care a lot more about justice issues that play out today, like AIDS in Africa."

*The Internet and global awareness.* "They are more capably aware, and maybe this has to do with the fact that they're technologically connected. They are the global Christian, thinking, 'Maybe I can have some kind of an effect on sex trafficking with women' [the 2010 Student Mission Fellowship project]. I didn't think about that when I was in college. I think it's because of the Internet. They're more connected."

*Fears and hopes.* "This is the post-9/11 generation. A lot of our students were little kids when the terrorist attacks on America happened, and we're still fighting the terrorism and there's that underlying stress."

---

decided to make the Spokane site Moody's first branch campus. Moody Aviation had been in Washington since 2003, funneling freshmen into the regional classroom to complete their Bible and general requirements. As non-aviation students were completing BS degrees in biblical studies and aviation students were earning a BS degree in missionary aviation technology, the synergy soon became obvious to Chicago leaders. Meanwhile, admissions officials had watched increasing numbers of qualified students being turned away from Chicago earlier in the application year as student capacity reached its limit.

The solution was another learning venue. In fall 2006 MBI opened its first ever branch campus, Moody Bible Institute–Spokane.

... We don't know what will happen or what the Lord has in all of this. I think it's more of a well-being kind of a fear—they're pretty secure in what they think about their station with the Lord. But college campuses aren't quite the safe havens they once were. Just look at the way our campus has changed with [security that requires] IDs and fobs to enter buildings."

**Social relationships.** "They're always connected to somebody, texting or Facebooking, or they're on their cell phone. One of the things that I spend a lot of time talking about with this generation is, 'Are you okay being by yourself? Can you turn your cell phone off, can you not be on the computer, could you not be playing a video game, listening to music?' And that's hard for them. It's an opportunity to have the Lord speak into your life. They call it social networking, but do they really have solid relationships that go beyond this quick language of text-messaging and the like?

"They're more social in the sense that they're more of a group-oriented population; they want to do things in groups. Girls and guys don't necessarily divide into couples and go off in their own ways. They tend to do it in more of a group setting, which I think is more positive. Yet I don't know if that allows them to have close relationships."

---

There were obvious attractions for students—a much smaller city than Chicago (though not too small, with a population of 200,000, and 350,000 in Spokane County). With lakes and fields nearby and the slopes of the Rocky Mountains to the east, the campus community enjoyed a sense of the "wide open spaces," minus urban congestion.[12]

For some students the attraction was the novel one-plus-three program. Each year highly qualified students wound up on a waiting list at the Chicago campus once all dormitory space was filled. Now enrollment management began to offer a limited number of the students the option of immediate entrance to MBI at the Spokane campus. In 2007 fifty-six students were told if they attended MBI–Spokane their first year, they would be assured enrollment on the MBI–Chicago campus their remaining three years—if they had a successful first year (as measured by a solid grade point average). One-third accepted the offer. In 2008 and 2009, more students were offered admission through the one-plus-three, and more accepted.[13] Several have stayed in Spokane to complete their studies, citing the campus setting, relationships formed, and course offerings, according to MBI Director of Admissions Charles Dresser.

Enrollment grew rapidly in Spokane, with 178 full-time students in 2008, 253 in fall 2009, and 377 in fall 2010. The number of students admitted in the "one-plus-three" option was reduced in 2010 as enrollments climbed; and admissions officials expect to discontinue the offer in fall of 2011. The popularity of the Spokane campus is due as much to academics as location. The Washington State Higher Education Coordinating Board in 2009 granted the school authority to offer BA degrees in Bible, biblical exposition, international ministries, and youth ministry; in 2004 the board had authorized MBI–Spokane to award BS degrees in biblical studies and missionary aviation technology.

Meanwhile the resident full-time faculty expanded. In fall 2008, Communications Professor Michael Orr, having served fifteen years at Moody Bible Institute in Chicago, joined the Spokane staff to teach general studies courses. In 2010 John McMath, associate professor of Bible, was awarded the rank of full professor. The Spokane faculty added three instructors that year, including Professor David Beine and Associate Professor Floyd Schneider in the department of world missions. Joining the Bible faculty that year was Jonathan Armstrong, who had completed graduate studies at Trinity Evangelical Divinity School and had taught at Oxford University.

When Armstrong visited the campus to decide whether it was time to leave Oxford to teach at Moody, he not only evaluated the academic program, facilities, and location but also the spiritual life of the students. "One of the things that is both his passion and attractive to him is the spiritual life," says Jack Lewis, director of Moody Bible Institute–Spokane. One evening Armstrong met with students for a potluck at someone's home. Sixty-five students showed up "to greet him and talk about spiritual things." In turn Armstrong asked them about their prayer lives and what drove them. Later he told Lewis, "I want to be part of this."[14] In fall 2010 he began teaching courses in Bible and New Testament Greek.

## RECORD ENROLLMENTS AND RENEWED DEMAND

In fall 2001, enrollment at the Chicago campus reached a record 1,407 full-time students. Through 2005, the numbers in the undergraduate school continued to move upward each year but one.[15] When the branch campus opened in Spokane in 2006, the total number of students at the two campuses jumped to 1,565. Record enrollments have continued through the first decade of the twenty-first century: 1,604, 1,582 (a dip during the nation's recession), and 1,762 full-time students in 2007, 2008, and 2009, respectively. Total full-time enrollment for both campuses reached 1,927 students in 2010.

Yet despite the presence of a second campus, the MBI undergraduate school continues to turn away large numbers of applicants, up to three of every five applicants a year, according to the admissions department. The key reasons for this demand by applicants include fewer schools that offer undergraduate Bible training, as some of the early Bible colleges have merged, changed, or closed due to factors ranging from finances to a broadened mission. President Paul Nyquist notes that the reputation of Moody Bible Institute as a pioneer and quality Bible institute has kept demand strong.

## A NAME CHANGE AND A WHOLE LOT MORE

The evening school of Moody Bible Institute, begun in 1903, paralleled the day school course offerings only once, from 1918 to 1924. As the undergraduate program expanded, it became unrealistic to offer those courses in the evening school; the approach changed to help train the laity to better serve their church (see chapter 2). But its growth in the 1970s and 1980s brought courses taught by Moody day faculty into Chicago and its suburbs and adjunct faculty into Wisconsin, Ohio, and Florida. All were under the direction of the department of external studies.

But the term *evening school* became inaccurate when the extension campuses included Washington. The Spokane campus offered courses only during day hours, though its courses included typical evening school fare, which could lead to a certificate. Eventually bachelor of science degrees were offered at Spokane and most evening school extensions, as some of the undergraduate school courses were available.

So those directing external studies decided to rename these sixteen campuses "extension sites" and later, "regional classrooms." Today, whether students enroll in Boynton Beach at night or in Spokane in the day, they can take classes for enrichment, certificate, or undergraduate degree.

These regional classrooms also provide course credit to undergraduates, and become another "delivery system" for the undergraduate and graduate schools. That's why, in 2002, external studies disappeared and became the Moody Distance Learning Center (MDLC). The four modes of course delivery, or "venues," are online, modular (for graduate-level courses), regional classrooms, and print. The print mode is for independent studies and is the successor to the correspondence courses that had their origin in 1901.

## THE SCHOOL THAT NEVER CLOSES

Always innovative, the undergraduate school discovered in 2000 one more way for more students to attend classes—via the computer. Of the four delivery systems, only one made it possible for MBI to offer a system that would offer college credits around the clock: the online classroom. The Moody Distance Learning Center developed online undergraduate courses primarily for the so-called "rooted learner" who could not come to Chicago because of family or job commitments.

Rooted learners can earn an associate of biblical studies degree or a bachelor of science through either online courses alone or in conjunction with courses in regional classrooms (the successor to Moody's famed evening school). In addition, undergraduate students can take a limited number of college credit courses to fulfill requirements for MBI or another school.

Both the rooted learner and the college student can "attend" class any hour during either a sixteen- or eight-week schedule, joining the Internet classroom in the morning or late at night.

A MDLC survey in 2006 revealed most students wanted courses in a more concentrated format, primarily to complete their degree work sooner; and proponents of online education "are moving away from standard semester formats into five, six, eight, or ten week formats for online courses," says Kevin Mahaffy, director of MDL operations. As a result, all courses are expected to be offered under the eight-week schedule by spring 2012.

In 2009 MDLC was renamed Moody Distance Learning since MDL describes the delivery system (and there is no "center" location for the four venues). An increasing number of college-level courses in the actual undergraduate school curriculum are available online, including Old Testament and New Testament survey courses, the church and its doctrines, and speech communication. MBI faculty often facilitate the courses; sometimes skilled adjunct faculty interact with students.

That faculty expertise is just one of the reasons online courses are popular at Moody. Students can securely submit assignments for quick grading (no lag time while going through the mail), monitor their progress through the "grade center" that shows their overall points and grade to date, and enter into electronic discussions with classmates. The weekly discussion board questions "are designed to engage students in critical thinking skills and reflection upon a topic dealt with during the weekly reading or topic." Often it is superior to any discussion in an actual classroom, Mahaffy believes. "It's a great way for students to feel free to participate electronically whereas they may not have that freedom in the classroom due to more outspoken students usurping the conversation." Although the instructor monitors the discussion board, he or she will "pop in" to offer input or redirection only occasionally. "In this way the instructor does not hinder students from freely expressing themselves and interacting with fellow students," says Mahaffy.[16]

## NOTES

1. 2008–2010 Undergraduate Catalog, Moody Bible Institute, 19.

2. Men's Department of the Bible Institute for Home and Foreign Missions of the Chicago Evangelization Society, 2; cited in Gene A. Getz and James Vincent, *MBI: The Story of Moody Bible Institute* (Chicago: Moody, 1986), 66.

3. Charles Dyer, personal interview, May 6, 2010.

4. Two additional courses that began in the 1920s, the Pastors Course and Jewish Missions Course, are described in chapter 2.

5. Growth and location of Chicago Swedish population is from Anita Olson Gustafson, "Swedes," *Encyclopedia of Chicago*; at www. Encyclopedia.chicagohistory.org /pages/1222.html.

6. Raymond Tallman, personal interview, August 28, 1985, as quoted in Getz and Vincent, *MBI*, 109.

7. Getz and Vincent, *MBI*, 96.

8. Dennis Fledderjohann, e-mail interview, May 28, 2010.

9. Ken Bosma, "1984 Alumni Survey," 46, 48.

10. As cited by Fledderjohann, e-mail interview, May 25, 2010.

11. All statements by Larry Davidhizar are from a personal interview, May 7, 2010.

12. Jack Lewis, associate dean of the undergraduate school and director of Moody Bible Institute–Spokane, points out the lakes within a one hour's drive that offer fishing, boating, and waterskiing. And the five ski resorts within ninety minutes include the world-class Schweitzer Basin in Sandpoint, Idaho, "with tons and tons of ski runs," says Lewis. The campus is only twenty miles from the Idaho border.

13. Under the one-plus-three program, seventeen, fifty-four, and seventy-four additional students enrolled in Spokane in 2007, 2008, and 2009, respectively.

14. Jonathan Armstrong, as cited by Jack Lewis, May 25, 2010, personal interview.

15. In 2002, 1,414 full-time students attended MBI. After a drop to 1,364 students in 2003, enrollments jumped to 1,423 and 1,449 in 2004 and 2005. All figures are from the office of the registrar.

16. Kevin Mahaffy, e-mail interview, May 18, 2010.

# 7

# Filling the Gaps:
# Pastors and Worship Leaders
# for a New Century

D. L. Moody's call for "gap men" fueled the vision for Moody
Bible Institute in the late nineteenth century. Now, in the early twenty-
first century, MBI's pastoral studies department strives to fill a gap that
seminaries may miss. Through its department of pastoral studies, MBI
continues to fill the pulpits of evangelical American churches as it has for
more than eighty-five years.[1]

"We are trying to fill in the gaps that a seminary doesn't," says department chairman John Koessler. In seminary, most of the training focuses
not on pastoral ministry but on theological training and language study.
In contrast, the MBI program includes a theological base and biblical
languages, but the focus is pastoral skills. "We want our students to be
practitioners when they come out and to have a skill set that would
enable them to move right into ministry."[2]

Today's graduate with a BA in pastoral studies can carry that
strength directly into the pulpit—and many do. The majority of churches
are congregations of two hundred or less, Koessler reports, yet the

largest concentration of worshipers tends to be in large churches—which are fewer in number. "So what you have is the number of small churches increasing and the number of large churches shrinking, but the large churches remaining are getting larger. So you have this large number of small churches that are having trouble finding pastors. There's a real opportunity there for a young person with a bachelor's degree." Many qualified Moody graduates with a BA in pastoral studies find their credentials welcomed.

"It's probably going to be in a small church, and because they're young and don't have extensive experience, it could be in a struggling church. Or it could be in church planting. There are opportunities for our grads."

A much earlier study by the Accrediting Association of Bible Colleges supports Koessler's conclusion that the Bible institute–college movement has had a significant role in training evangelical pastors for ministry immediately after graduation, especially among small churches. In addition, the AABC study found, several denominations adhere to "the regular college and seminary pattern for ministerial preparation" and have organized Bible institutes "as a type of school that provides the educational services not available in conventional institutions."[3]

That does not mean that Koessler and his department colleagues do not prompt graduates to pursue at least some seminary training at a later point. The pre-seminary major in the department is directed toward students who plan to immediately pursue a seminary education. A 2003 survey by the pastoral ministries department found slightly over half the pastoral graduates enroll in seminary.

"The trend toward professionalization continues," Koessler says, "so we do encourage students to go on, at some point, for further education. At the same time, our goal has always been to give students a foundational base of knowledge and ministry skills so that they can move directly into pastoral ministry, should they have the opportunity to do so. And those who continue directly to seminary, I encourage to . . . find a ministry context and do whatever additional training within that context."

Nevertheless, a graduate with a bachelor's degree can expect to find churches that value his training and will be open to his candidacy as a pastor. A survey of pastors at the 2005 Moody Pastors' Conference found three out of four pastors believed a BA would be welcomed by churches. The 2005 survey asked pastors, "Do churches today require pastors to hold a master's degree, or is a bachelor's degree adequate?" and 77 percent answered that churches would expect the candidate to have a bachelor's degree; 21 percent thought a master's degree would be necessary.

## THROUGH THE YEARS

In addition to the pre-seminary major, pastoral students can choose to major in pastoral ministry or biblical exposition or one of those majors with an interdisciplinary approach. The bachelor's degree includes a minimum of forty hours of Bible and theology, forty hours of general studies, and four hours of field education. At 129 total semester hours, the all-at-Moody degree requires twenty-four fewer semester hours than the original BA program begun in 1966, when students completed ninety-three semester hours of professional studies at MBI and another sixty hours in the liberal arts in an approved college or university, a total of five years of course work. (Those general studies in another school could be earned either before or after coming to Moody Bible Institute.)

As previously noted, earlier pastoral students enrolled in a three-year Pastors Course that began in 1922. With the shift to the baccalaureate programs and a department structure in 1966, the Pastors Course was renamed the department of pastoral studies. The department continued to offer a diploma for those who completed only the MBI course work, and pastoral students could specialize in either Greek or Christian education.

During the first sixty years, from 1922 to 1982, MBI contributed significantly to pastoral service in evangelical Protestantism. More than 1,850 students were graduated from the Pastors Course and department of pastoral studies, an average of thirty-one each year. Those figures have held steady over the years. During the first decade of the twenty-first century, 271 students earned bachelor of arts degrees in pastoral training, an average of twenty-seven each year.

## WHY MENTORS MATTER

While Moody Bible Institute required each student to complete a one-semester internship beginning in 2004, a couple of years earlier the pastoral studies department already had mandated its students serve stints as interns as part of their learning experience. Today's pastoral students typically intern in a church setting, doing such varied tasks under a mentor as preaching, attending board meetings, visiting hospitals, leading a communion service, and organizing the youth.

"They are on the field," Koessler explains. Instead of being in the classroom hearing about what it's like to be in a hospital, "they are in the hospital, at the bedside, engaged in pastoral care."

Pastoral ministries students also do fieldwork every semester through their practical Christian ministries along with all other students (see next chapter). But the internship is both specific to the major and fine-tuned to the student. When they move into their internship, its focused experience is in the area of their discipline. Whether it's preaching a series of sermons, sitting in on board meetings, or planning an event, there is a series of tasks they are required to do.

Significantly, the department requires any church wanting a pastoral intern to be willing to commit to the intern's development, giving time to guide and develop the prospective pastor, rather than simply use a developing student's talent and training.

"We use a mentoring model," Koessler says. "It is not simply sending a student into a church or organization, giving them a series of tasks. We want a mentoring relationship with a ministry leader."

## MENTORING MEN . . . AND WOMEN

Those mentoring relationships extend beyond men mentoring men to women mentoring women, for the department of pastoral studies offers a women's ministries major to women only. The 2010 undergraduate catalog describes the major this way: "The women's ministries major is designed to equip female students to organize and lead church and parachurch programs that disciple, counsel, and teach women."

According to department chairman Koessler, the major traces back to the inception of the Institute. "If you look back at our roots, what is MBI today grew out of a ministry designed to train women. Emma Dryer's mission was to equip women to share the gospel." He notes that women typically comprise the majority of worshipers at the local church.[4] He points to ministries of Beth Moore, Anne Graham Lotz, and Nancy Leigh DeMoss and sees women having "a significant word of ministry to women. Women are studying the Word together." Graduates also will coordinate ministry to women in large churches; others will serve women through "a variety of parachurch opportunities," notes Koessler. In addition, he says, "Ministry by women and to women has always fueled international ministry."

Larry Davidhizar, dean of the undergraduate school, said the faculty voiced no opposition to letting women in the pastoral studies program once it became clear women were not being trained "to be a pastor of a church." The major began in 2003 with adjunct faculty member Pam MacRae, the former coordinator of MBI women's conferences in the conference ministries department. During her previous four years as conference coordinator, MacRae had connected with a number of key leaders in ministry for women and began to understand the desires and needs of women who came to hear solid Bible teaching.

"The major has been very successful in training women to minister specifically to women," MacRae says. She notes some male students have enrolled in one or more women's courses, "wanting to enhance their ministry effectiveness, aware that they impact many women." Graduates of the program help women deal biblically with such issues as careers, marriage, family, poverty, and abuse. And with their degrees, women graduates are better able to minister to women who increasingly are achieving higher academic training than men in the twenty-first century.[5]

Women can also enroll in the department's biblical exposition major, along with men. The major includes speaking and teaching courses. Why a biblical exposition major that includes women? "We would all agree that women could have the gifts of proclamation or evangelism or teaching," Davidhizar answers. He describes it as "more of a skill-set major. It does not imply the office of pastor. . . . It implies a gifting major."

Koessler concludes, "We want both men and women to be able to declare God's Word in a way that's sound."

## WHAT IT MEANS TO BE A PASTOR

The major charge of the pastoral studies department remains to train pastors. In 2009–2010, 135 men (about 10 percent of the Chicago student population) were enrolled in pastoral training. Beyond developing skills and knowledge and application for their future ministry, they learned about the challenges and opportunities that await in the pulpit. Koessler points to a mobile society with a consumer mentality that "shops churches" for specific programs or personalities.

"Anyone sitting in church who doesn't like what they hear or are experiencing can get in the car and drive to someplace that they do like. That market pressure creates an environment that can make a pastor especially vulnerable to compromise. He can become market driven rather than oriented toward being a shepherd or a leader. One of our main challenges is to help our students understand what it means to be a pastor, and to be sensitive to the needs of those they serve—without being driven by the needs of the market."

A second challenge is to remember their calling to be shepherd leaders. "There is a great deal of pressure for pastors to . . . aspire to direct large organizations rather than to be shepherds," Koessler says. "The biblical metaphor that shapes pastoral ministry is shepherd leader. . . . In our curriculum we ask, 'What does it mean to be a shepherd who cares for the flock and a leader who watches over the flock and a preacher who communicates God's Word to His people?'"

Other challenges pastors will face are the social breakdowns in a Western culture that often disrespects authority and looks out for itself, and the pressures that can undermine the traditional family. Yet some pressures are not entirely new, Koessler says.

"The rhetoric says this is the ungodliest age we've ever lived in, but I'm not convinced of it. You can't tell me that the Corinthian context was better than ours. I don't believe it. We have more challenges that perhaps are related to technology—Satan becomes more creative, more technologically astute with his abilities to deliver the goods—but I don't think that sexual immorality is more popular today than it was in the New Testament era.

"The challenges pastors face are perennial. . . . You can read the Scriptures and find all the problems the pastor faces today in the New Testament church. You can look at that and say, 'Well, there is nothing new under the sun.' All the personal problems, the spiritual problems, and the social problems are in there. The challenges the pastor faces—conflict, a sense of inadequacy, or ambition—have been issues . . . since the church began."

That's one reason Koessler still has his students read Puritan preacher Richard Baxter, who wrote more than three centuries ago. "He helps them understand what it means to be a true pastor."

## HOW SWEET THE SOUND

Here's a music riddle: What do Christian singers/composers Graham Kendrick, Matt Redman, and Chris Tomlin have in common with the music department at Moody Bible Institute?

The answer: All have had chorale arrangements of their worship songs written by Jack Shrader, sacred music graduate of 1964. The prolific Shrader is the bestselling composer in the Hope Publishing music catalog,[6] with twenty-four hymn credits in Hope's most recent hymnal, *Worship & Rejoice*. He has arranged 144 hymns, gospel songs, and worship songs. In addition to Kendrick's "Shine, Jesus Shine," Redman's "Blessed Be Your Name," and Tomlin's "How Great is Our God," his collections of arrangements range from such classics as "Great Is Thy Faithfulness," "When I Survey the Wondrous Cross," and "Because He Lives" to such worship songs as "Shout to the Lord" and "God of Wonders" and choruses like "Lord, I Lift Your Name on High," "Majesty," and "Great Is the Lord."

Shrader stands in a long line of Moody Bible Institute faculty or alumni who have become writers, composers, and arrangers for the Christian church. The line stretches back more than one hundred years to the early twentieth century, when Daniel Towner, the second director of the Musical Course at MBI (after H. H. Granaham), wrote "Grace Greater Than Our Sin" and "Only a Sinner."

# ( A Class, a Calling,
# and a Conversation )

S teve Klingbeil received his diploma in sacred music
(composition) in 1982 at MBI and his bachelor of science in sacred music (BSSM) in 1984. But more than twenty-five years later, when he thinks of Moody, his strongest memories are of one professor who prodded him to get serious and listen to God's call. He recalls David Smart, his wise composition teacher, and Virgil Smith's tuning class, but he remembers also the afternoon toward the end of his diploma program when Professor Gerald Edmonds invited Klingbeil to join him in the Coffee Cove, the small eatery on campus (in Crowell Hall basement) that preceded today's Commons.

Edmonds treated his student to a Coke and began to praise and guide his student.

"Steve, you have a ton of potential, and it needs to be harnessed."

"That particular conversation with him," Steve recalls, "really helped me focus . . . and take a little more seriously what God might be calling me to. He was saying good-bye and recognizing my potential and challenging me to ramp it up a notch. That was the impetus for me to take myself, and my calling, and my giftedness a little more seriously, and to use it as God would have me use it.

"He saw potential in me personally. At that point I hadn't necessarily figured out what to do with that potential. I was still undisciplined."

Klingbeil had finished high school early and entered MBI at sixteen. He soon knew he was to "pursue worship ministry as a worship pastor. By the time I finished I think that was the path I was being called to. . . . I knew I was gifted musically."

Edmonds had instructed Klingbeil in four classes, had directed him in oratorio chorus, and watched Klingbeil conduct the senior ensemble and perform as the featured brass soloist of the Moody Concert Band under Henry Hecht.

He heeded the professor's advice. He moved to Southern California for a multiyear internship—without course credit but offering invaluable experience at a Baptist church with 1,200 worshipers. "This let me find out what it means to be in ministry, the relational side of things, the administrative side of things. When you get to a church, the musical skills are assumed, but it's the other things—the relational skills, the administrative skills, the leadership skills—that really matter." He started a handbell choir and directed the youth choir and led them on tour.

Then he took his BSSM to Southern Baptist Theological Seminary, earning a master of church music (trombone) and then his doctor of musical arts, studying under Donald Hustad, the former MBI music chairman. Hustad had actually directed Klingbeil's mother twenty years earlier as conductor of the Moody Chorale.

Since then Klingbeil has served for almost twenty years at churches in Iowa, Arizona, North Carolina, and Indiana. In each church he has led worship while conducting the church orchestra.

He still remembers his senior recital at Moody, but not very well. As a composition major, he wrote every musical piece but largely conducted, letting others perform. He rehearsed and conducted a vocal ensemble with a pianist, "and I may have written a brass piece and then recruited a brass ensemble and then played as a part of that." Steve uses "may" because during graduate music studies at Southern, "I did scads of recitals. Moody was just the first of many, and they all just run together in my mind."

For his graduate studies, he returned to the trombone, the instrument he loved in high school. Today, at Liberty Bible Church in Chesterton, Indiana, he occasionally leads as many as eight trombonists, including the church's senior pastor, Bob Nienhuis.

One event still fresh in his mind, though, is his philosophy of music class with Professor Edmonds. "He opened up different ways of viewing worship . . . and that has been a lifelong process."

## A MUSIC TOUR WITH TOWNER

The Musical Course that began just three years after the school's founding—yes, it turned 122 years young in 2011—starts its tour with Towner. The composer of more than two thousand songs, he picked up Granaham's mantle in 1893. He developed the Musical Course while serving as a faculty instructor. He directed the program for twenty-five years, hiring teachers who were specialists in their fields. Towner's graduates became prominent song leaders and writers, including J. B. Trowbridge, I. E. Reynolds, and George S. Schuler.

Moody historian Gene Getz sees three reasons for Towner's great influence in training evangelical music leaders. First, a need existed, for no school was attempting a program in sacred music. The revivalistic movement was at its peak at this time, resulting in a demand for song leaders. Second, Towner was at Moody Bible Institute, a school that in all facets of its program was rapidly expanding and reaching out to the evangelical world. The evangelists and pastors alone who were being trained at the Institute helped create numerous job opportunities for music leaders.

Third, D. L. Moody and his song leader, Ira Sankey, were names known throughout the world for their evangelistic activities, and that probably attracted many young people to the school Moody founded.[7]

The Musical Course and later the department of sacred music have encouraged gospel songs, worship songs, and traditional hymn writing. Modern gospel songs also have been penned by MBI musicians John Peterson, Dan Wyrtzen, and Larry Mayfield. Their gospel songs and choruses became church favorites, including Peterson's "Heaven Came Down and Glory Filled My Soul" and "Surely Goodness and Mercy," and Wyrtzen's "Love Was When" and "Yesterday, Today, Tomorrow." Today Ed Childs (hymns, choral anthems, organ) and Beth Naegele (handbells) are among several MBI professors who are active music composers.

This great heritage resulted from the disciplined yet practical training offered in the Musical Course.

## THREE MUSICAL MOVEMENTS IN
## THE MID-TWENTIETH CENTURY

When MBI adopted the semester academic calendar in 1951, the course had become the sacred music course and included four programs of study: piano, organ, voice, and composition. In 1966, the school organized a separate department of sacred music, which replaced the Sacred Music Course when the baccalaureate program began.

The second musical movement came as the department began to offer its graduates an option to earn either a bachelor of arts or a bachelor of music in sacred music. For the BA degree, the student had to complete sixty semester hours of general education in an approved college or university, either before or after completing the regular program at Moody Bible Institute. A student could earn the bachelor of music degree by completing the MBI program and then studying two years (minimum forty-two semester hours) in a conservatory or other collegiate-level school of music.

The Christian education-music major appeared under the new program and allowed the student to earn a BA degree either before or after coming to the Institute.

Students could earn a BA in C.E.-music by taking additional college course work before or after studying at MBI. In both the church music and C.E.-music majors, diplomas were awarded to all students completing the MBI curriculum. Course offerings have changed through the years to allow students more flexibility, but the historical curriculum has been largely maintained. Beginning in August 1986, students could complete work for the BA in church music in four years through the new baccalaureate program.

The third significant movement in sacred music at MBI occurred in 1984, when the department of sacred music received accreditation by the National Association of Schools of Music. NASM is the professional accrediting agency for schools of music issuing collegiate and postgraduate degrees. The diploma program was accredited as meeting the standards of NASM, making MBI course credit transferable and assuring wide recognition of the MBI diploma in sacred music. Three years later, the undergraduate school would earn major regional accreditation for all their academic departments, when the Higher Education Commission of North Central Association would award the school its first accreditation status, recognizing the sustained quality of all course work and academic programs.

## WORSHIP MUSIC IN EVERY LANGUAGE

Today the bachelor of music degree still requires five years, but all courses can be taken on campus. Both the BMus and the four-year BA degree programs continue to receive NASM accreditation and to offer emphases in composition, instrument, organ, piano, and voice. But the bachelor of arts has added a sixth emphasis that has piqued the interest of some students: ethnomusicology.

Beth Naegele, professor of music and organ for more than thirty years, recommended the department offer ethnomusicology in the mid-1990s. About that time, some mission boards were starting to realize the worldwide need for musicians who could understand the musical language of a given nation to assist nationals in developing their own distinct musical expressions to worship God. Ethnomusicologists study the music of local (typically non-Western) cultures; Christian ethnomusicologists help local musicians develop "worship music in culturally meaningful styles for indigenous churches."[8]

Today ethnomusicologists work with a number of mission boards. They lead workshops for local musicians in other countries. "On occasions the ethnomusicologists themselves might write music," says Cynthia Uitermarkt, music department chairperson, "but the goal is to actually have the indigenous people write the music."[9]

If the indigenous people group is young in the faith, Uitermarkt notes, "they may say, 'My musical style can't be used by God.' But the ethnomusicologist might say, 'But this is what has meaning in your culture. Let's redeem it and use it to worship the Lord.'"

Uitermarkt points to "the rich environment of mission study at Moody and the nature of Chicago as a cultural crossroads" as parts of a vital infrastructure for the ethnomusicology emphasis at MBI.

## WORSHIP MUSIC IN BANGLADESH

At this writing, Tim and Jenny (not their real names) have devoted seven years to help Christians in Bangladesh develop their own unique forms of worship music. They teach songwriting workshops to help Bangladeshi Christians who are musicians develop the tools for writing songs for their churches.

Significantly, Tim was a composition major and Jenny a piano major at MBI, but as unmarried students they caught the ethnomusicologist's passion after taking a couple of ethnomusicology courses. In those classes they studied the building blocks of musical style. After graduation they married, took additional course work, and then headed to the Indian subcontinent.

When Tim and Jenny arrived in Bangladesh, they immersed themselves in the music to become aware of the stylistic traits of the Bangladeshi culture. They became familiar enough to play the native instruments and interact with the native musicians. "But the goal is to have [the Bangladeshi Christians] write the music," Uitermarkt emphasizes, "so that it is really theirs."

## MUSIC ACROSS THE GLOBE

For more than ninety years, MBI music students have performed for the general public. What began as in-house recitals and choral concerts has spread across America and onto several continents. Today the well-known choral and instrumental groups perform nationally throughout the school year during their winter and spring academic breaks, and internationally during alternating summer tours.

Beginning in the 1950s, public performances became a curricular requirement for all students majoring in music. Junior and senior recitals in voice, composition, piano, and other instruments are held each semester; some students will have two recitals during their years at Moody. In addition, faculty members appear in professional recitals before students and the public.

Besides individual performances, all students are given opportunity to participate in ensemble performances. Choral groups have been a part of the school's musical life almost from its beginning. In 1895, separate men's and women's choruses practiced regularly to help all students develop their voices. However, these choruses did not perform regularly.

The first public performing ensemble appeared in 1921. The Auditorium Choir sang at church services held in the MBI auditorium. Dr. James Gray presided at the four o'clock weekly meetings, designed as model services for students in the Pastors Course.[10] In fall 1946 the Auditorium Choir became the Moody Chorale, destined to become one of the most well-known collegiate choral groups in the religious world. As the first director, James Davies led the Chorale on its first extended concert tour the next year. Donald Hustad succeeded Davies as Chorale director in 1947, and during his fourteen years of conducting, the group developed an international reputation.

Most recently, Gerald Edmonds directed the Moody Chorale for thirty-two years before retiring in 2010. In 1970 Edmonds organized the Moody Concert Band (now the Moody Symphonic Band) and directed the band for nine years before picking up the baton to lead the men's and women's voices of the Chorale.

## FOUR FOR THE ROAD

Four Institute ensembles tour each year: the Moody Chorale, the Women's Concert Choir and Bell Ensemble, the Men's Collegiate Choir, and the Symphonic Band. The oldest of the four, the Chorale, traces back to 1921 and counts among its highlights performing as the featured choir at a 1953 Easter sunrise service in Los Angeles. That morning they replaced the glitter of the Hollywood Bowl with the glory of the resurrection. The Chorale has toured Europe several times, singing in packed auditoriums and churches. During their 1958 summer tour, for instance, they sang before audiences totaling 65,000. One highlight of their ministry abroad was their 1973 tour of Great Britain. They accompanied President George Sweeting on an evangelistic tour that commemorated D. L. Moody's British crusades one hundred years earlier. In England,

Scotland, and Ireland they sang before filled churches, school assemblies, and civic auditoriums.[11]

Two other choral groups joined the Moody Chorale on the U.S. tours in the 1950s. In 1955 the Moody Women's Glee Club began; one year later the Moody Men's Glee Club formed. In 1958 the Women's Glee Club became the Women's Glee Club and Handbell Choir (the forerunner of the Women's Concert Choir and Bell Ensemble) after founding director Robert Carbaugh helped to purchase a set of English handbells. (Carbaugh served as director twenty-seven years.) In the early 1990s both groups shed the term "Glee," part of the terminology of mid-twentieth-century single-gender choirs, to assume their current names.

A fourth touring group, the Moody Symphonic Band, first appeared in 1970 as the Moody Concert Band, featuring woodwinds, brass, and percussion. Forty years later, their repertoire still includes hymns, gospel songs, and other music, now supplemented with stringed instruments.

## GOING BEYOND PERFORMANCE

Like the other two choral groups, the Moody Chorale regards its concerts as ministry, not mere performances. Evangelism and encouragement are among their key goals. According to the Moody Chorale constitution, members sing in order "to bring those [listening] into a relationship with the Lord Jesus Christ by salvation and to bring Christians into a deeper relationship by consecration; and also to aid in the deepening of the spiritual lives of members themselves."

All four groups have such opportunities, and they see results. During one spring tour, the Chorale was returning from a sightseeing side trip to the Grand Canyon and began informal singing as the bus wound its way from the famous site. The bus driver interrupted the singing by taking the microphone and announcing his life was not right with God. "He asked the group to pray with him. Two weeks later the Chorale flew him to Chicago for their annual home concert. The concert crowd was moved by the genuine quality of the bus driver's testimony."[12]

H. E. Singley, director of tours for the music department as well as Men's Collegiate Choir conductor, outlines three goals for every public concert by every ensemble: (1) present the gospel, (2) represent Moody Bible Institute, and (3) expand the horizons of the students. "The tours are not sanctified entertainment," Singley explains. "In our view the music we sing ought to have the Christian message included. Obviously we amplify that with things that we say, and by having students in homes overnight, interacting with people."[13]

To represent MBI, students look for opportunities to talk about MBI during the concert and "to invite students to come to Moody," says Singley. To expand students' horizons, the summer international tours give music students "a global view of what God is doing," Singley says. He reports, "We have students serving Christ all around the world as a direct result of their visiting a specific country while touring in an ensemble."

A highlight for each musical group is an international tour to churches, arenas, and outdoor venues. Most groups go overseas every other summer, where they minister in song and word to the spiritually seeking as well as to Christians who may be in the minority. In some places they find thriving, enthusiastic churches. Students raise their own funds for these ministries across cultures.

## CHINA OR BUST

The itinerary in the twenty years ending in 2010 has been truly global. Besides the People's Republic of China, the Symphonic Band has visited Israel and Eastern Europe. Destinations for the Women's Concert Choir and Bell Ensemble have included Korea, Japan, and Singapore. In late May through early June of 1991, the Moody Chorale made a historic tour of the Soviet Union; two months later the USSR and Soviet Communism fell. Among its international stops, the Men's Concert Choir (MCC) has visited Australia and New Zealand (1999), Ireland and Scotland (2001), and the People's Republic of China (2009).

The MCC three-week tour of China included a time in Hong Kong, just under a week in Fujian province, more than a week in Shanxi province, and a long weekend in Beijing. They sang in two large Fujian coastal cities, Putian (a population of almost three million) and Fuzhou (population five million). In Putian they sang in an old theater likely built during the era of communist leader Mao Zedong. "We were singing and presenting the gospel in a place where people once could only see propaganda films."

In Fuzhou people were leaning in through the windows to hear the MCC. At the end of the concert, held at a government-registered Three Self Church, the pastor rose and presented the gospel. "About a dozen hands went up to receive Christ," Singley estimates.

The men's choir sang at more than a half dozen Three Self churches during their tour. Although the government monitors activities of the churches, Singley concludes, "There are many Three Self churches that are just as gospel preaching as any church in the United States."

The highlight for MCC Director Singley occurred in Beijing during the final Sunday in China. The men sang to four thousand Chinese in each of three services. Rather than a concert performance, they brought the special music during different points of the worship service, with the Mandarin translation projected on the wall. They also had Communion there. "I had to pinch myself as we took Communion with Chinese believers in Beijing."

## CHRISTMAS TRADITIONS:
## CANDLELIGHT CAROLS AND *MESSIAH*

Residents of the Chicago area are most familiar with the MBI choral groups through two special Christmas programs, Candlelight Carols and a performance of Handel's *Messiah*. Candlelight Carols, originally called Christmas Vespers, began in 1953 with the singing of Christmas carols and a dramatic biblical pageant that retold the Christmas story. The concert grew through the 1970s to include antiphonal singing, special visual effects, and even congregational singing. Every seat in Torrey-Gray Auditorium was filled for each of the three performances, and one MBI representative confessed, "We could fill Torrey-Gray Auditorium three more times, if the choirs could perform [the whole week]."

Instead, in 1987, the sacred music department chose to move the annual concert to Moody Memorial Church. The historic church, with its bigger spaces, stained glass windows running along each side, and classic archways, "infused Candlelight Carols with a more dramatic setting,"

Uitermarkt notes. There were logistics to consider—equipment, setup, and student practices now required a one-mile trek north to the church—but the larger capacity easily made up for the inconveniences. Almost four thousand concertgoers could fill Moody Church, double the capacity of the campus auditorium.

That ended the capacity problem that left some unable to attend Candlelight Carols, and student singers and musicians now performed at just two concerts. But the crowds kept building, and the sacred music department eventually added a third performance. Sometimes the three concert times still sell out, representing close to 12,000 spectators.

Candlelight Carols combines traditional carols, classic Christmas songs, drama, and special visual effects to tell the story of Jesus' coming to earth. Some audience members have come year after year, making the event part of their Christmas tradition. At key moments the audience joins the combined three musical choirs and the Symphonic Band in a huge carol sing.

The drama usually focuses on the Bethlehem story. In the mid-1990s the scripted drama often began in a contemporary setting, or with a historical character who explains how he or she interacted with the story of Jesus' birth. Yet Candlelight Carols "always ends with the birth, death, and resurrection of Christ. It always comes full circle to tell the complete story of redemption," Uitermarkt says.

"The goal is to tell the Christmas story in a way that draws people in who might not know the gospel, but are willing to hear it in the context of a holiday setting," Uitermarkt continues. "We know many unbelievers come. We know there are extended family groups who come. It is part of the holiday tradition for them, and they hear the gospel. And that might not be the reason every attender comes but it is what happens when they're there. So it's sharing the gospel in a comfortable setting that's appropriate to the season but doesn't shortchange the truth of the gospel."

## ANOTHER SELLOUT

*Messiah*, George Handel's famed oratorio, features the MBI Oratorio Chorus—one hundred fifty student voices from all music emphases, plus members of the three choral groups; advanced voice students are featured soloists. The oratorio is presented less than three weeks before Candlelight Carols, so the same students are involved in two big productions between mid-November and early December.

*Messiah* differs from Candlelight Carols in two significant ways: It is held in the more intimate setting of Torrey-Gray Auditorium, and there is no dramatic staging with lights or intricate script. Instead, students in formal attire perform the well-loved choruses and arias. *Messiah* also features a small orchestra, primarily of students but also including some members from the community who play additional instruments.

Yet in one way *Messiah* is just like Candlelight Carols. Year after year it sells out quickly. "The fact is more than 250 years later people of all ages are still coming to hear this work," says Uitermarkt. "The text is only Scripture and it still has such appeal."

## FINDING BALANCE IN WORSHIP

Over the years MBI music leaders have addressed the place of lyrics and content in compositions to assure Bible doctrine is neither overlooked nor incorrect. The disagreements in the early twentieth century over the value of gospel songs sound similar to those in the 1990s and early 2000s over worship choruses. Getz described the concerns to the gospel songs this way:

> Leaders believed that the content and music of certain gospel songs have a definite place in the music program of the church. However, MBI leaders also have felt that some gospel songs have been written that are not very worthy. They have recognized a degeneration in the type of content and musical expression, as well as in the way these songs have been used by various religious leaders.[14]

MBI developed the new music course in 1929 to help counteract concern over superficial or inaccurate lyrics, and, in Dr. Gray's words, "do much to restore the lost balance in gospel music." Thirty years later, music course chairman Donald Hustad wrote in the campus *Moody Memo,*

We believe the gospel hymn is a vital subjective expression of our "know-so, say-so" faith. It is our personal testimony in song, and it is effective partly because it is couched in simple words and music.

However, we are thankful that our churches are also regaining some of their lost heritage of historic hymns of worship and doctrine. I'm thankful for the example set by our church leaders here at MBI; it is not hymns or gospel songs, but both. This means spiritual, as well as musical, balance.[15]

In a scholarly journal, Hustad explained the goal of MBI musicians should be a balance between an emphasis on "personal experience and emotion" and the "inclusion of theological and Scriptural truth." He added, "We need songs of testimony, of simple faith, and of invitation; but we also need hymns of worship, of doctrine, and of admonition."[16]

His call for balance is being echoed today by the calls issued by advocates of "blended" music church services who face criticism from those who want either all-hymn (so-called traditional) or all-chorus/song (so-called contemporary) music.

Whatever the outcome, many would agree with the conclusion of Hustad and the position of the music department of Moody Bible Institute: In all our singing and playing to the glory of God, there should be "spiritual, as well as musical, balance."

## NOTES

1. Among MBI alumni in full-time Christian service who responded to a 1962 survey, 23.5 percent indicated they were serving as pastors. A 1974 survey indicated 22 percent of all graduates who were in full-time religious vocations were pastors. Glenn F. Arnold, "A Comparative Study of Present Doctrinal Positions and Christian Conduct Codes of Selected MBI Alumni," unpublished doctoral dissertation, New York University, 1977, 86.

2. All quotations from John Koessler are from a personal interview on May 12, 2010.

3. S. A. Witmer, *Report: Preparing Bible College Students for Ministries in Christian Education*, Report of the Accrediting Association of Bible Colleges, (1963), 95–116.

4. The typical congregation is 61 percent female, according to an April 2001 study of more than two thousand congregations. The survey, conducted by the religious research group U.S. Congregations, received responses from about 300,000 worshipers; "U.S. Congregational Life Survey—Key Findings: Who Worships in the U.S.?" www.uscongregations.org/key.htm.

5. In 2006 women earned 57.5 percent of all bachelor's degrees, and 60.0 percent of all master's degrees granted in the United States, according to the National Center for Educational Statistics; "Digest of Education Statistics," http://nces.ed.gov/programs/digest/d07/tables/dt07_178.asp. The NCES projects that by 2017, women will account for 59.9 percent of all bachelor's degrees and 62.9 percent of all master's degrees. See "Digest of Education Statistics," http://nces.ed.gov/programs/digest/d07/tables/dt07_258.asp.

6. http://www.hopepublishing.com/html/main.isx?sub=27&search=86.

7. Gene Getz and James Vincent, *MBI: The Story of Moody Bible Institute* (Chicago: Moody, 1986), 126–27.

8. Cynthia Uitermarkt, e-mail correspondence, May 11, 2010.

9. This and all subsequent quotations from Cynthia Uitermarkt are from a personal interview on May 13, 2010.

10. Mary Jean McKinley, "History of Chorale Goes Back to '21," *Moody Student*, April 21, 1949, 3; as cited in Getz and Vincent, *MBI*, 129.

11. Robert G. Flood and Jerry B. Jenkins, *Teaching the Word, Reaching the World* (Chicago: Moody, 1985), 92.

12. Ibid., 245.

13. All quotations from H. E. Singley are from a personal interview on May 19, 2010.

14. Getz and Vincent, *MBI*, 131.

15. Donald Hustad, "Gospel Songs Fading?" *Moody Memo*, May 1961; as cited in Getz and Vincent, *MBI*, 131.

16. Donald Hustad, "Problems in Psychology and Aesthetics in Music," *Bibliotheca Sacra* 117 (July 1960): 214.

# 8

# "Oh, You're from Moody"

For many years the clothing gave them away. The MBI dress code helped merchants and employers recognize Moody students walking the streets of Chicago's Near North Side. The men wore slacks or casual pants, but never jeans. The women wore dresses or skirts and blouses, never pants or halter tops. Then there were the smiles and friendliness of most of those students. "Oh, you must be from Moody," the clerks would say.

Over the years, the dress code moderated slightly, allowing clothing exceptions, but only for certain occasions, such as practical Christian ministries assignments and severe winter conditions. Then, in 2002, the dress code altered to permit men to wear jeans, hoodies, and sweatshirts to classes; women could add sweatshirts, dress slacks, khakis, and jeans to their daytime wardrobe. But their friendly smiles still give them away. "Hey, are you from Moody?" the server asks.

There's something about students from Moody Bible Institute that sets them apart. It's not their age, since one of every three undergraduates (35 percent) do not enroll directly from high school. And it's no longer their clothing. It's the smiles, the courtesies, and their general reputation for friendliness. The merchants love the attitude, and local employers love the reputation for reliability.

## IN DEMAND: MOODY STUDENTS

Dean of Students Tim Arens points to many affluent Chicagoans living near Lake Michigan who specifically ask for Moody students. "The Gold Coasters call for our students. That's because they trust them and know they work hard. The area businesses still look highly on Moody students. It's because the students are honest and they work. Through the years students have paved a good road. Current students continue to pave that road."[1]

Employers keep asking for Moody students because they are reliable, teachable, and have integrity, adds Pat Friedline, associate dean of career development. "They know they can trust our students." Perhaps the biggest indicator of that has been the calls over the years for students along Jewelers Row on Chicago's Wabash Avenue. Shop owners have requested Moody students to act as couriers. "They pick up diamonds and make a delivery to a client," Friedline says.

Some employers want only Moody students, and they ask for them again and again. Many female students have acted as babysitters or nannies, a job on the Near North Side of Chicago that pays well as double-income parents return home late in the evening.

"Moody women have babysat or been nannies [for children] from baby years through the teens," Friedline says. "Parents may have had four Moody girls, but they have had a Moody influence in that house for ten or twelve years. They're interacting with the kids, becoming involved in the family life."[2] Many student workers cook dinner for the entire family, with children eating in the evening and parents eating after they get home. They may take the children to afternoon activities, such as dance and gymnastics classes, driving the family's car.

Catering companies have used MBI students to serve guests at soirees or banquets at the Field Museum, the Art Institute, or a downtown corporate gathering. Some students who remained with one caterer "have worked their way up from being a server to being a captain, to being hired full time." Some may want to go to seminary but have to increase their savings, says Friedline, so after graduation they accept an offer to work full time in the main office of the catering company. Such offers come "because of the reputation of our students."

Most working students average fifteen hours per week. Friedline assists many students during their senior year as they prepare for ministry vocation and seek his help for résumé preparation, interview skills, and career advice.

## A DIFFERENT KIND OF WORKER

Some employers, though, are wary of these friendly Christians. "When people talk to our students, some might call them a little weird, because of what they believe," Arens explains. "That's what you would expect and actually hope for, because we *are* different. That's very good; our students still have a strong evangelical component.

"Some think, *Those are those Bible thumpers. They're straitlaced.* But that goes with the territory." Some student workers are rebuffed when they casually share their belief in God and His Son Jesus. Yet other employers "do ask because they notice the quality of the work. 'Oh, why don't you do that?' or 'Why do you do this? . . . Oh you go to that Bible school. What is that all about?'"

## MINISTRY THAT MATTERS

The reputation of Moody students among employers and merchants is matched by their reliability and training in their PCM assignments. Leaders in churches, kids clubs, shelters, and other ministry agencies value MBI students for their training in Bible and practical theology. Every fall, ministry coordinators welcome student assistance in Chicago and surrounding suburbs. They value equally the students' creativity, skills, and passion.

Just three weeks after PCM assignments began in fall semester 2006, one woman wrote the Moody PCM department after two students caught her attention:

I am a senior and I live at West Maple just down the street from your school. Keith Chase with LaSalle Senior Center requested some volunteer help for seniors, and he sent two lovely young ladies to help me, Jen and Eileen. These young ladies are exceptional; they are kind and gentle human beings, compassionate, patient and very hard workers. I had lived here for five years and had never unpacked a whole living room full of boxes. Jen and Eileen helped me go through 40 boxes of books and give Keith 36 of them for some library.

It was a lot of heavy work and they were really very capable. I was a manager most of my life and I appreciate good workers more than most people. . . .

Jen and Eileen prayed with me too, which was very nice. Thanks again for your kindness.[3]

Students on MBI's Spokane campus receive applause as well. One spring day in 2010, Professor Michael Orr read a letter from a small-church pastor, thanking Moody–Spokane for two woman students and requesting more help. When Orr later called the church, the pastor said, "Thank you, thank you, thank you. The two girls who did their PCMs at our church built a youth group that we've never had. They were wonderful. . . . This has served our church in ways you'll never know." In his commendatory letter, the Lutheran pastor wrote, "We consider ourselves blessed that these young ladies developed a youth program at Gloria Dei. . . . We would like to have one or two students again, gifted in the areas of Christian education and music, with good relational skills."[4]

## FROM THE BEGINNING

Students have served their community from the first year of the Institute. "Study and work go hand in hand," announced the first brochure published by the Chicago Bible institute, printed in 1889 shortly after its opening. During the early years, students had practical Christian work assigned five days a week. A few rode to their assignments by horse-drawn streetcar bus (later electrified cable cars), or elevated trains (popularly called the "el"), but most took one of the three horse-drawn Institute gospel wagons, which later would be gospel cars.

Dwight L. Moody (shown at age 47) loved his wife, Emma (top right), greatly. He also admired the sacrifice and purpose of Emma Dryer (middle), who would start the May Institute, the forerunner of the Chicago Bible institute. After the evangelist sent a letter announcing his intention to resign from the Chicago Evangelization Society to Mrs. Nettie McCormick (bottom), a CES manager and a major supporter, the two Emmas mobilized to convince Moody to withdraw his letter.

Top: D. L. Moody (rear center) and James Farwell (in top hat) catch the vision to begin the Sands Mission School to reach the neighborhood's poor children. Boys with such names as Madden the Butcher, Rag-Breeches, Jackey Candles, Smikes, and Greenhorn soon believe, bring their friends, and the school grows. Years later students at Moody's Bible institute use gospel wagons (shown in front of the 152 Building) to take the good news of Christ into Chicago's streets.

Practical Christian ministry traces back to MBI's founding. A 1926 open-air meeting draws a crowd to hear music, testimony, and preaching. Today open-air meetings are held near Water Tower Place (bottom left) and Chicago's Millennium Park, with its famous Cloud Gate sculpture.

The Board of Trustees Executive Committee—Henry P. Crowell, James Gray, and Herbert S. Ullman—meet in D. L. Moody's office (November 1930). Students in the Pastors Course gather in front of the 153 Building (July 1936).

Most of the 1934 entering class pose at Moody Church. Of the 345 entering students, 304 fill the platform and choir loft.

Board of Trustees Chairman Henry P. Crowell places mortar onto the cornerstone of the new Administration Building as President Will Houghton and architect F. J. Thielbar watch. In 1945, daughter Mary Crowell unveiled the renamed Crowell Hall. The first graduates to march through the Arch were the class of 1938 (shown below).

ALT. WOMEN'S BLDG.

**THE MOODY BIBLE INSTITUTE**
of Chicago

THIELBAR & FUGARD
ARCHITECHTS

PAT WARREN CONSTR. CO.

PHOTO No. 4  J U N E 3, 3 9

Just north of the Administration Building, the Women's Building loses fourteen feet from its front after LaSalle Street is widened. Notice the "new" 1939 car speed by at bottom left. The Women's Building, built in 1912, remains today as Smith Hall, thoroughly modernized.

Top: Looking east from Wells Street, a 1940s postcard highlights the new Administration Building, flanked by the first campus structure, the 153 Building (right), and the 152 Building and the Sweet Shop.

During the 1940s students mingle in the Women's Building reception room with Dean and Professor William Culbertson, soon to become MBI president. Leaning in above Culbertson is a young George Sweeting (class of 1945).

Bottom: Students roast hot dogs during a Lincoln Park picnic in 1925.

Today's students relax in a Houghton dorm room and study at the Alumni Student Center. Jonathan Hayashi and Anna Windle of International Student Fellowship greet new students during the fall move-in day.

Western Culture

Irwin Moon [top left] electrifies the audience as one million volts race through his body during a climactic Sermons from Science demonstration.

*City of the Bees*, one of many award-winning films from Moody Institute of Science, captures bees' behavior inside the hive and out among the flowers. Sermons from Science demonstrations drew large crowds at three Olympic games and five world's fairs, including the 1962 Seattle World's Fair.

Early Moody Radio featured popular local programs like the KYB Club (Know Your Bible) for children hosted by "Aunt Theresa" Worman (airing 1933–71). The original radio studio broadcast from the 152 Building. Today listeners can hear any owned-and-operated station on an electronic mobile device using an "app."

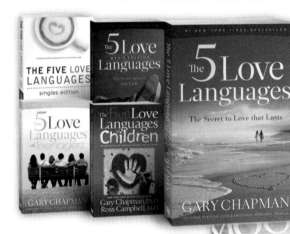

Print media began in 1894 with Bible Institute Colportage Association. BICA has become Moody Publishers and left the typewriters (1934 photo) for computers. Its bestselling *Five Love Languages* series has sold more than eight million copies. Begining in 1900, *Moody* magazine also transmitted the good news by print for 103 years.

Paul Robinson (top), founder of Moody Aviation, reviews cross-country training route with Paul Wertheimer, manager of Wood Dale Airport. In 1967 Moody Aviation relocated to Elizabethton, Tennessee (middle), where it remained until 2003. It now trains pilots at MBI–Spokane. Missionary pilot and Moody graduate Larry Montgomery lands a seaplane to serve villagers in Peru.

 Campus expansion in the late 1960s brought a new men's dormitory, Culbertson Hall (with Houghton Hall and the John Hancock Building in the background). The 153 Building was leveled to make way for a beautiful campus plaza, but its famous stained-glass window, "The Sower," now greets guests at the Crowell Hall information desk. The Sweeting Center for World Evangelization, opened in 1991, welcomes students in Chicago.

Top: The Solheim Center

Bottom left: Many community camps occur throughout the
year. Horace Grant, a member of the Chicago Bulls (1987–94),
guards his pig-tailed opponent during a summer Solheim camp.

Bottom right: Karsten Solheim and President Joseph Stowell watch the
inaugural basketball game at the Solheim Center.

Four presidents, spanning fifty years of service, gather for "Celebrating the Legacy of Moody Bible Institute" on October 15, 2010: Joseph Stowell (top, from left), Paul Nyquist, George Sweeting, and Michael Easley.

Current President Paul Nyquist chats with students outside the Alumni Student Center and poses on the campus plaza.

Some, of course, could walk to their assignments. Students sang, taught, preached, and visited hospitals, jails, and shut-ins, among other practical Christian work (PCW) assignments.

Today some students still travel to their assignments by "el" train, but bus, Institute van, or private car are also common. Open-air evangelism remains popular, and the setting can be near Water Tower Place, just eight blocks away, or Millennium Park near Lake Michigan.

But PCW is no more. In 1982 the PCW department became the practical Christian ministries department (PCM). Most Bible institutes and colleges had begun designating required service as "Christian service," and that spurred the name change. There also was concern that the term "work" was misleading.

"'Ministry' better reflects what we are all about," then-PCM Director Leonard Rascher explained in 1985. "The experience is not just part of student training but actual ministry. Students don't have to wait until they have a diploma to start ministering. And the ministry *is* practical."

## FOUR AREAS OF IMPACT

Through its PCM program, the school has contributed directly to evangelical education in the Chicago area. The impact of students on the spiritual needs of Chicago cannot be directly known, but statistics kept by the practical Christian work department suggest a positive effect on evangelical training in Chicago. Consider these four areas:

1. *Bible classes.* These classes have included Sunday school classes (the most popular type), mission classes, weekday church school classes, child evangelism classes, and released-time classes in public school. In addition to these classes in which the Bible has been taught directly, there also have been personal evangelism and teacher training classes, which have been designed to teach others how to carry out certain types of Christian work.

Statistics on the number of classes taught are available for only forty-three of the first ninety-five years (through 1984). Conservative projections reveal that Moody students have taught, since 1889, approximately 17 million individual class sessions. This equals the efforts of one thousand Sunday school teachers presenting classes every Sunday morning for thirty-three years.

2. *Visitation and personal counsel.* Through the years teams of students have regularly visited hospitals to talk with patients and offer spiritual and emotional comfort and help. During much of the twentieth century, teams of students also visited homes to converse with people regarding spiritual concerns. Statistics are available for forty different years. Projecting from these figures, students at the Institute made an estimated 2.2 million calls and visits in homes and hospitals during the first seventy years of the twentieth century.

While teaching, attending various meetings, and doing visitation, students have also counseled with individuals personally regarding spiritual matters. Statistics are available for forty-nine years of such activity since 1900. Conservative estimates indicate that over 4.7 million people have been counseled since the opening of the formal school through 1985, or about 1.3 times the number of people currently living in Chicago.

3. *Literature distributed.* Distribution of literature—including Bibles, New Testaments, Bible portions, and gospel leaflets—is usually handled person-to-person and often requires conversation. Bibles and portions of the Scriptures are usually given out to people who indicate a strong interest in learning about Christianity. More than 32 million pieces of literature were distributed from 1900–1984.

4. *Personal responses.* As noted earlier, the spiritual impact of the PCM outreach cannot be fully measured. However, objective data supplied by students is revealing. During twenty years, 1965–84, students reported that 62,000 people whom they had counseled professed belief in Jesus Christ as personal Savior, and almost 10,000 determined to live a more dedicated Christian life. Since the turn of the century, more than half a million people have made one of these two responses. Since much of the work has been carried on in rescue missions on skid row, in prisons, in mission Sunday schools, and in public shelters, many of the individuals responding did so as a result of an initial contact with students from Moody Bible Institute.[5]

More recently, students during the school year 2008–09 reported that they were aware of 704 individuals who accepted Christ through their ministry. For fourteen weeks, 1,533 students in Chicago served an average of 2.5 hours at 284 ministry sites, working with 289,600 people.

## PCMS IN CHICAGO

New ministries have arisen in the past thirty years to meet the needs of the city. In Operation Good Samaritan during the 1980s, students visited city facilities for the elderly. Here students washed windows, scrubbed floors, even took individuals shopping. Typically students work as teams, one student performing a task while the other provides companionship. Often there is a chance to present the gospel as friendships develop.

Today at Pui Tak Center in Chinatown, some students tutor students, and others help immigrants learn English, a very practical ministry for TESOL students. The Pui Tak outreach is one of many PCM assignments that assist Chinese, Hispanic, Japanese, Korean, Somali, and Vietnamese residents of Chicago, a world-class metropolis. Freshman Saul Rapalo found himself waiting at the center one afternoon for a student to tutor. "I don't have a regular student from week to week," Rapalo explained in his PCM report. As he waited, an adult approached and asked, "Are you waiting for someone specific or can you tutor me?"

"I told him it would be great to tutor him and we began our introduction of ourselves.

"Before I knew it, the Bible was brought up. To make a long story short, our entire session was spent on a quick run-through of the New Testament, and he eagerly continued to present question after question about God's plan of redemption . . . and simple questions about the Bible in general. It was the perfect ending to this semester's PCM."[6]

One of the larger PCMs is Breakthrough Urban Ministries. Its founder, Arloa Sutter, caught a vision for the poor while directing a food pantry and warming shelter at her church in the Andersonville neighborhood.[7] Today her center of operation is East Garfield Park, where she and her staff feed and shelter homeless men and women, and tutor middle- and high-school-age children while offering Bible studies and other "spiritual development activities and athletic programs to engage youth physically." It also assists women trying to escape prostitution with food, shelter, health care, spiritual counsel, employment training, and housing placement.

Twenty-eight MBI students assisted Breakthrough in 2009–10, some as after-school tutors and others in the Friday night street outreach to women in prostitution. The Friday outreach usually has two female students who meet with prostitutes, and two male students who monitor the action to ensure the women's safety. An RV serves as their base of operations and a service center. Nathan Strand, PCM operations manager, reported on an earlier visit he made with several students:

> A male student and I followed a half block behind our female counterparts. It was our task to engage in conversation any men who might try to interfere with the ladies' interaction with the prostitutes. We watched and prayed (and distracted quite a few men, most of whom were inebriated) as the two hugged, cried, and prayed for the different individuals we encountered. . . .
>
> Occasionally a prostitute will become tired of the street and come to the RV for some hot chocolate, cookies, and a ride to Breakthrough's women's emergency shelter at the Joshua Center. There is always great rejoicing when this happens.[8]

## PCM MINISTRIES IN SPOKANE

Students at Moody Bible Institute–Spokane have also had an impact on their community through its practical Christian ministries. Spokane County, with 350,000 residents, has its own urban and rural needs. Immigrants from Burma, Russia, and Vietnam have settled in the area. "There's a reason for that. Washington State has the highest minimum wage in the country," explains Dean Jack Lewis. "Spokane is the major city in the eastern side of the state, which has a lower cost of living. This makes it an ideal place to [relocate] refugees."[9]

A local World Relief chapter helps establish many refugees, and other ministries follow up with ongoing services and visits. Through their PCMs, Moody students have helped World Relief and these agencies. "That population presents a huge opportunity for our students to get involved in cross-cultural ministry, to give real service to disadvantaged people," Lewis says.

As freshmen, Spokane students first learn about and assist local churches. They receive a PCM passport, which requires students to explore churches. They visit six different churches. At each church the students will interview a staff or ministry person, and learn about opportunities to serve, the ministry's requirements, and its needs. They can also explore community service opportunities, such as a Big Brother or Big Sister program or an outreach to one of the large immigrant communities.

Sometimes after visiting three churches, a student sees an opportunity and asks if he or she can begin a ministry at the third church. Typically, if the student wants to "plug into a ministry right away, we'll waive the other three [churches]," says Lewis. "That happens from time to time."

Students in Spokane know that churches wrestle with the secular mind-set, with fewer than 6 percent of adults in Washington State attending church on any given Sunday, according to Lewis. "Spokane is much higher than that, probably about 18 percent [go to church], but that's still a lot less than many parts of the country." One of the reasons may be the great outdoors. Sixty lakes await boaters and water-skiers within a one-hour drive. In the winter five ski resorts within ninety minutes of Spokane beckon snow skiers.

## MILLENNIUM MINISTRY

Underclassmen in Chicago have assignments in at least two of four areas: service, encouragement, evangelism, and discipleship, known as SEED ministries. Entering students enroll in an introduction to ministry class their first semester to learn about the purpose and focus of practical Christian ministry assignments. As a class in an academic department (field education and practical Christian ministry), introduction to ministry "says, 'This is not off to the side. This is not student development or optional Christian service,'" explains Operations Manager Strand.[10]

PCM assignments have varied from the predictable to the innovative through the years. Juniors and seniors have proposed and won approval for PCMs that use their talents to present the gospel message through song, drama, pantomime, and magic.

Open-air evangelism, a bold and effective PCM that goes all the way back to horse-pulled gospel wagons, has left the hand organ, trombone, and choir behind to embrace paper easels with colored markers, as well as drama skits. But testimonies and gospel presentations remain part of open air. In 2009, thirty students were out in various open-air ministries on Wednesday and Friday nights.

In spring 2010, students who had made productive contacts with tourists in Chicago's Millennium Park proposed a new PCM. This latest open-air evangelism now began in fall 2010 on Saturday afternoons. As Strand explains, "Students [find the] tourists more conversational than those waiting for a train or [walking by]." The park's relaxed setting as an outdoor tourist attraction—the famed "Cloud Gate," or "Bean," sculpture, Pritzker Pavilion, and Crown Fountain are nearby—establishes a friendly feeling for casual conversations that can go deeper into spiritual conversations.

In a society that values community service and calls for volunteers, practical Christian ministries on the two campuses of Moody Bible Institute contribute much to their surrounding communities. The 1,750 undergraduate students on the Chicago and Spokane campuses put in two hours a week for fourteen weeks each semester for two semesters. That means MBI students donate 98,000 hours each academic year to serve churches, hospitals, shelters, jails, community and senior centers, and local agencies.

## WHERE "POVERTY IS A WAY OF LIFE"

Students in the Moody Theological Seminary and Graduate School complete a community internship as a requirement for graduation. Since 2002 they have ministered to the city through the annual Service in the City (SITC) day. MTS students organize SITC and recruit undergraduates and faculty to join them as they partner with the Chicago Mayor's

Office of Community and Faith-Based Initiatives. All SITC participants help residents in impoverished neighborhoods of Chicago.

The program has grown, and in 2010 more than two hundred undergraduate and seminary students linked with Campus Crusade students from Chicago-based colleges and universities to serve a special meal to senior citizens, pantry families, and the homeless; host a carnival for at-risk youths; aid seniors with difficult home chores; and complete maintenance work at a local church. World Vision and the Chicago Food Depository donated food, hygienic items, and household cleaning supplies that students distributed.

John Fuder, professor of urban studies at MTS, helped originate the program. He says the one-day SITC outreach offers students great opportunities to "apply what they are learning in the classroom to real-life ministries in neighborhoods where violence is prevalent, poverty is a way of life, and the Word of God needs to be proclaimed."[11]

## ALUMNI AROUND THE WORLD

Students automatically become members of the Alumni Association after earning fifteen hours of academic credit. Many stay four years and receive a Moody degree; some transfer; others continue with their undergraduate or graduate education elsewhere. No matter the length of their Moody education, their studies and PCMs that began in Chicago or Spokane have prepared them for a lifetime of service for Christ.

Most alumni will enter full-time vocational ministry. A 2002 survey of alumni of the undergraduate school found that 73.4 percent of graduates and/or their spouse were or had been in full-time vocational ministry. Another 4.2 percent were preparing for ministry.[12]

Many not in vocational ministry still have an impact in the church and the workplace. The same 2002 study found that among those not in full-time ministry or preparing for it, another 18.7 percent of the respondents have served in a lay ministry capacity in their church.[13] Many more, from teachers to accountants, have a vibrant witness in their communities or workplace.

**MBI IMPACT**

# ( Among Chicago's Finest )

One wintry February morning, Chicago Police Sergeant Alan Haymaker sped to a burglary in progress on the city's Northwest Side. There was light traffic on snow-covered Lake Shore Drive, but on one slick spot his squad car spun out of control. Haymaker was wearing his seat belt, as he always did, but it did not matter. The car went onto a grassy berm, struck a light pole and then a tree, trapping him inside. He was pronounced dead at a local hospital two hours later.

The MBI graduate (1980) and former assistant pastor at Jefferson Park Evangelical Free Church made a major career change when he joined the police force in 1988, following in the steps of his father and grandfather. For Haymaker, the police force presented a key opportunity for ministry, first as an officer and then a sergeant at the Austin District and later the Town Hall District.

As an officer he sometimes would drive up in his squad car and hand out almonds to the children. Several times he would buy food for people he came across. He even counseled prostitutes at times. He referred those who were interested to rescue shelters. Some made professions of faith in Christ.

"He loved people," his brother-in-law, Ron Vogelpohl, told reporters after Alan's death. "It didn't matter to him who you were. He cared about prostitutes and treated them like human beings."

After he became sergeant, he led fellow officers, even as he continued to monitor the streets. Officer Calvin Jones described Haymaker as "humble, easy to talk to. You could approach him with any situation and he would sit you down and try to make things better."

Tom Leland, who learned under Haymaker at Austin and later became a fellow sergeant and close friend at the Town Hall District, heard from district residents how Al helped during his off time, doing everything from "teaching one of the kids how to play guitar to helping people with problems they had with landlords. He went above and beyond in caring for his community. . . . As an officer and a sergeant I care about my officers and the community I serve and protect. The department would be thrilled with you just caring for those officers, for your community. Al did more than just care about them. He loved them."

At the funeral service at Bethel Community Church, Mayor Richard Daley called Haymaker "a role model for us all, not only within his family but within his profession. He believed this was a calling to serve and protect the people." Daley closed by saying, "I'm sure Alan Haymaker didn't think of himself as a hero, but he was. The way that he went about his work and his life should serve as an inspiration to all of us."

Perhaps the best tribute came from Albany Park District Commander Mike Meaher, president of the Chicago Chapter of Fellowship of Christian Peace Officers. "Al never hid his faith from anyone. He tried to make sure he was the best Christian witness he could be with the job he had."

His death continues to have an impact on the Austin and Town Hall Districts where he served. One of Al's favorite books was *Heaven*, by Randy Alcorn. His widow, Elaine Fisher Haymaker (1980), and her three daughters have talked with his coworkers and distributed booklets containing excerpts from *Heaven* at the two police districts. In August 2010 the Chicago Police Department retired Alan Haymaker's star badge. That day Elaine and her daughters placed free copies of the *Heaven* booklet on the display table for Sergeant Haymaker, reminding fellow officers of Alan's one sure hope.*

* Carlos Sadovi, Annie Sweeney, and Duaa Eldeib, "Squad Car Crash Kills Police Sgt. Alan Haymaker," *Chicago Tribune*, February 22, 2010; Antonio Olivo, "A Tearful Final Salute to a Beloved Sergeant," *Chicago Tribune*, February 26, 2010; Mal Martinez and Susan Carlson, "Funeral Services Held for Veteran Police Sergeant," CBS online, February 26, 2010; telephone interview with Tom Leland, August 31, 2010; and personal e-mail from Elaine Haymaker, August 14, 2010.

Here are several alumni, some well known, some not, who have had an impact through the years:

- Martin R. DeHaan II (class of 1968), Bible expositor on the *Radio Bible Class* and writer of many booklets for the discovery series.
- Bill Dillon (1968), founder of Inner City Impact, a ministry to the youth of Chicago's West Side. His grandfather Michael Dillon (1906) served as superintendent of Chicago's Sunshine Mission.
- Larry Feldman (1974), messianic rabbi at Shuvah Yisrael in Irvine, California, one of the largest messianic congregations in the United States.
- John Innes (1961), pianist and later organist with the Billy Graham crusade team.
- Andrea Jensen (2005), academic coordinator, K–5, at Breakthrough Urban Ministries.
- Hugo Perez (1992), manager or vice president of corporate communications at various companies, including pharmaceutical and science companies; earlier directed corporate affairs at the American Heart Association. In the 1990s he was a field producer with NBC News.
- Jonathan Smith (1979), teacher of MKs at Puebla Christian School, Puebla, Mexico, and missionary to Mexica and Mixteca tribes. Later served as camp director of *Oasis de Agua Viva* (Oasis of Living Water), begun in 1970 by his father, Samuel Smith (1959).
- Wess Stafford (1970), president and CEO of Compassion International.
- Arloa Sutter (class of 1975), executive director, Breakthrough Urban Ministries. She received the Alumni Association's Distinguished Service Award in 2007.
- George Verwer (1960), founder of Operation Mobilization, an international evangelism ministry that promotes literature distribution and relief and development programs in 110 countries.

- Gordon Whitelock and Alice Brubaker Whitelock (1937), founders of Camp Peniel north of Houston, Texas (now in Marble Falls near Austin). Founded in 1946, the camp continues to present the gospel and help "kids connect to their creator God."

## LIVING—AND DYING—FOR JESUS

Some graduates have made the ultimate sacrifice in their service for Christ's kingdom. Twenty-one alumni have died as martyrs on four different continents. The executive cabinet of Moody Bible Institute has defined *martyrs* as "those who were killed because they refused to renounce their faith or because of active opposition to their witness for Christ."[14] Three martyrs illustrate their unwavering commitment to their faith.

Ancel Edwin Allen graduated from Moody Aviation in 1956 and within three months was flying above villages for Air Mail from God. His mission was to buzz local villages to get their attention and then circle back, dropping copies of the gospel of John. Each book included an application for a correspondence course. Christian workers later would return to the village to meet with those who expressed interest in the course and the gospel message of John.

Sometimes his wife, Naomi, would sit on the rear seat, shoving out the books as Ancel flew across the village. Some of the leaders of one village resented the tactics and that someone would try to turn their people from their long-held beliefs. Just one month after he began his literature drops, he returned to the village of San Bartono. As he flew over the village, gunmen waited below. Once in range, the plane met a hail of bullets. "A couple of bullets from a high-powered rifle ripped through the plane and pierced his body."[15]

The next day Mexican believers helped Naomi bury Ancel. In her grief, Naomi felt consolation in those whose lives had been transformed by the gospel. "She was not bitter but simply wrote that the people who shot Ancel down did so because they had yet to understand the Word that he was trying to give them."[16]

John Stam first felt a burden for China and its people when walking through New York's Chinatown on his way to and from work. Betty

Alden spoke Chinese as a young child as her father served as a Bible teacher; but she did not commit to missionary service until a summer at America's Keswick, which she ended with a vow on a pledge card: "Work out thy will in my life at any cost, now and forever. To me to live is Christ."

John and Betty met at Moody during Betty's final year while attending Monday evening prayer meetings held at the home of representatives of the China Inland Mission. Their affection deepened through that year, yet Betty (class of 1931) was a year older and ready to join CIM at school's end. They sought counsel and agreed the timing was not appropriate. One year later John graduated, attended CIM candidate school, was accepted as a missionary, and later sailed for Shanghai with plans to enter China. Upon arriving in China, John was stunned. Betty was in Shanghai because severe tonsillitis had kept her there for a few weeks to recover—long enough to see John arrive. John soon asked her to marry him. She accepted.[17]

They finished language study (mainly for John) and visited several mission stations. Now married almost fourteen months and enjoying their three-month-old daughter, Helen, they moved to the city of Tsingteh and a new ministry. Just a couple of weeks after setting up house, on December 6, 1933, the Stams answered the furious knocking on their door. Several militant communists wanted entry; once inside, they demanded that a $20,000 ransom be paid.

In a faith-filled letter to CIM, John wrote, "All our possessions and stores are in their hands, but we praise God for peace in our hearts and a meal tonight. God grant you wisdom in what you do, and us fortitude, grace, and peace of heart. He is able—and a wonderful friend in such a time."[18]

The following morning the Stams and other captives were force-marched twelve miles over the mountains. That night in the town of Miaosheo, John was tied to a bed frame, Betty left untied to care for their infant daughter. The next day guards entered their room, forced the Stams to strip to their undergarments, and bound their hands. Within minutes they were marched barefoot through the town, past the townspeople summoned to watch their execution. In a grove of pine trees atop a hill, their captors taunted them. Then, at their command, John knelt. A flashing sword came down upon his neck. Betty trembled slightly and also knelt. Within a moment she was with her husband in eternity. Christians found their daughter, Helen, the next day and transported the baby in a rice basket over the mountains; eventually she made it to her grandparents' home.

Their lives and deaths had a profound impact. In a chapel service at MBI, seven hundred students rose to their feet to recommit their lives to God. At Wheaton College in suburban Chicago, two hundred students offered themselves to Christian service. "And in China, countless Chinese Christians moved by the Stams' death, put away bickering and strife, rededicating themselves to the Lord."[19]

## GIVING BACK TO MBI:
## THE ALUMNI ASSOCIATION

The Moody Alumni Association traces its roots back to 1916, when business manager A. F. Gaylord, H. W. Pope, and faculty member P. B. Fitzwater wrote separate letters to the Institute's executive committee recommending such an association be formed. By the end of 1926, 2,443 students from 40 states and 27 countries were members. Today there are 39,000 members from 50 states and 102 countries.[20]

The original purpose, according to the constitution, was "the promotion of fraternal fellowship among former students, the advancement of the interests of the Institute and cooperation." Those goals remain largely unchanged. The greatest occasion for fellowship occurs each February when alumni stream back to campus for Founder's Week. Tuesday is Alumni Day and features conference speakers who are Moody faculty and graduates. An alumni luncheon follows the morning session. After lunch there are class reunions and special gatherings for classes celebrating their tenth, twenty-fifth, or fiftieth reunions.

Each year at Founder's Week Alumni Day, the Alumni Association executive director presents an oversized check to the MBI president, representing alumni donations to all Moody ministries during the past year. It topped $2.8 million in 2007.

Since 2000 alumni have been saying thank you to their professors in a special way. Their association created the faculty endowment fund to encourage instructors in the undergraduate school (both Chicago and Spokane) and Moody Theological Seminary and Graduate School to participate in cross-cultural overseas ministry. Their goal has been to build a self-sustaining endowment of $500,000. During the first ten years, the endowment has sent faculty to Africa, Asia, Europe, and Australia. In 2010 it sent faculty to Pakistan and Afghanistan for ministry. The association looks for faculty who are either taking students with them or will be meeting with and helping MBI alumni; even better are faculty trips that will both guide students and encourage alumni. Faculty who have taught at least three years are eligible for these educational and ministry trips.

The fund balance was $130,000 in 2010. "We'd love to be able to send out twenty-five faculty in a summer," says Walter White, Alumni Association executive director. "Right now there are two going per year. When the endowment is fully funded, those faculty could take students on cross-cultural experiences and/or minister to missionary alumni."[21]

Meanwhile, White seeks to connect now with current students and recent graduates who can feel removed from the school after graduation. "In the first five or ten years alumni are getting involved in their ministry or continuing education. Many say, 'Well, I don't have anything to give,' and students even more so. Some get married and begin to have children and expenses and obligations. If we don't engage them . . . they typically don't get involved."

The association is using social networking to reach out to current graduates and students. They have a Facebook page with 1,100 fans and hope to grow it as well as a Twitter presence. "Cultivating relationships for me is at the heart of the alumni ministry," says White. "We want to cultivate relationship with students so that we are not an afterthought with students but an ongoing participant." The association plans to do so "by creating a healthy and enriched student life experience for them while they are here. My passion is to see the Alumni Association as a resource throughout their lives."

# NOTES

1. All statements by Tim Arens from personal interview, June 30, 2010.

2. All statements by Pat Friedline from personal interview, August 12, 2010.

3. Personal letter from M. Taylor to Nathan Strand, September 20, 2006.

4. Letter addressed to Professor Michael Orr, April 28, 2010.

5. Gene A. Getz, *MBI: The Story of Moody Bible Institute* (Chicago: Moody, 1969), 115–16.

6. PCM Report, May 7, 2009, to department of field education/practical Christian ministries.

7. Keri Wyatt Kent, "Arloa Sutter's Aha!" *Today's Christian Woman*, January/February 2007, 60.

8. Nathan Strand, "Site Visit Report to Director of Field Education/PCM," October 22, 2002.

9. All statements by Jack Lewis are from a telephone interview, May 25, 2010.

10. Nathan Strand, personal interview, June 3, 2010.

11. "Service in the City 2010," February 26, 2010; http://www.moodyministries.net /crp_NewsDetail.aspx?id=48915.

12. "The Critical Question: Percentage of Graduates in Full-Time Vocational Ministry," Report of the Office of Institutional Research, Moody Bible Institute, no date.

13. Ibid. Thus 96.3 percent of students responding to the 2002 survey of graduates were in full-time ministry or preparing for it or had been active in serving their local church.

14. Definition adopted by the executive cabinet of Moody Bible Institute (unpublished document, March 2001); quoted in Marvin J. Newell, *A Martyr's Grace* (Chicago: Moody, 2006), 12.

15. Ibid., 188–89.

16. Ibid., 189.

17. Ibid., 67–68, 80–81.

18. Ibid., 69–70.

19. Ibid., 70–73.

20. Getz, *MBI*, 333; Office of the Moody Alumni Association, September 7, 2010.

21. All statements by Walter White are from a personal interview, July 8, 2010.

( 9 )

# On the Air

In the year 2011, the woman with a smartphone in her purse or a netbook on her desk finds her "radio" extremely portable, as she does audio streaming of her favorite stations. Even when traveling out of state, her phone app can let her locate her favorite home station and others two thousand miles away with three or four taps on the phone.

But finding a program wasn't that easy in 1926, during radio's early days—when AM stations ruled and FM broadcasting was ten years away. Instead, competing radio stations with varying signal strength and subject to atmospheric interference at sunset jostled one another to be heard. In the midst of all the static, WMBI Chicago, the first radio station of Moody Bible Institute, struggled to survive.

It is a tale worthy of a radio soap opera, a plot filled with twists and turns and strained relationships.[1] During its first decade on the air, WMBI:

1. had to share its broadcast hours with WKBA after learning both stations had been granted a license on the same wavelength;
2. had to appear before the Federal Radio Commission to lobby to keep the station as several hundred new license applications

competed with 733 existing stations for space on eighty-nine wave channels;

3. was denied an increase in signal power and instead was warned by the FRC a "cut in power may be necessary";

4. found its station assigned to a radio zone under the 1928 Davis Amendment to the Radio Act, competing in the immediate Chicago area with twenty-one other stations for limited space in their zone; and later that year

5. learned it might be considered a "propaganda" station, after WCBD in Zion, Illinois, was so classified for its heavy religious content and fund solicitation.

## PROPAGANDA . . . OR IN THE PUBLIC INTEREST?

In the last challenge, the Zion station no longer could share time with two other stations. This final development would bring Institute leaders to Washington, D.C., to testify for the third time in a year. H. C. Crowell, reinforced by 50,000 postcards sent by MBI and WMBI supporters at President Gray's request, had successfully defended the station from challenge 2; and both H. P. Crowell and H. C. Crowell joined the Institute attorney before the FRC to win challenge 3. For this challenge, witnesses spoke on behalf of the station, as did the Institute attorney and President Gray. The attorney argued that WMBI was not a "propaganda" station, but rather an interdenominational, educational station, appealing to all segments of the religious and nonreligious community.

Although the FRC did not rule WMBI as a propaganda outlet, on April 14, 1930, it denied the request for more broadcasting hours. After the hearing, though, certain FRB members told H. C. Crowell that WMBI's case was the most organized and best presented they had witnessed.

Following the Washington hearing, the road became relatively smooth by comparison. Both in 1930 and 1931, Crowell decided to visit Washington to maintain firsthand contact with the commission and to keep the members informed as to the status of WMBI. FRB members in 1931 unanimously expressed their belief that WMBI was operating in the public interest. They assured Crowell that the station was secure as long as it was not directly attacked by another station in an under-quota state.

These were reassuring words during a time when several religious stations were being forced off the air because they were "not serving the general public." Still, more and more stations were coming into existence, power was being increased, and the overcrowding of stations on the air persisted. This continued to cause concern despite the commission's positive comments.

## COMMENDATION FROM THE FCC

On June 19, 1934, Congress authorized the Federal Communications Commission (FCC) to oversee all areas of telecommunication in the United States: telephone, telegraph, and broadcasting. This administrative change had no serious effect on WMBI. When a representative from the FCC stopped at the Institute to make a routine check early the next year, he told MBI officials that their station was in very good standing with the new commission members and that they had appreciated the care that had been exercised from the beginning in making financial appeals. He also reported that very few letters of protest had been received by the commission concerning the Moody programs. The wild soap opera seemed to be over.

Since its beginning, WMBI had taken great precautions to avoid offending listeners through strong propaganda, financial appeals, or slanderous remarks against other religious viewpoints. Outside speakers were chosen carefully and forewarned against careless speech. The station was not above criticism, to be sure, but the commission records, as reported, revealed an unusual silence, and later research among listeners also revealed a general hesitancy to criticize the station's programs.

In 1939, the Institute filed an application for full limited-time operation in Chicago, and subsequently received approval. After the signing of the Havana Treaty, an international agreement among Canada, Cuba, the Dominican Republic, Haiti, Mexico, and the United States, WMBI began expanded broadcasting on July 6, 1941. Assigned to its new operation frequency of 1110 kilocycles, the station now offered up to fourteen and one-half hours of daily programming during the long daylight hours of

June and July. Immediate steps were taken to secure an adequate program and to increase technical staff.

## FM FOR MOODY

FM radio broadcasting for educational use became available in 1936,
and Moody officials were interested. Unlike the limited hours of AM
broadcast, the FM signal would permit nighttime programs. However,
the processing of the application for a license took years, and by the time
it was approved, World War II was under way. The government sus-
pended all station construction during the war's early years, then
relented. The FM station began operation on October 1, 1943, sharing
programming with WMBI from approximately 10 a.m. until sunset.
After WMBI signed off, the Institute continued its programs until 9 p.m.
over their FM station, WDLM—the last three letters standing for Dwight
Lyman Moody's initials.

WDLM-FM was the first FM noncommercial religious station in the
country. For nearly ten years the Institute continued to broadcast on
both WMBI and WDLM. However, the FM station seemingly was reaching a relatively small audience. Though serving a very useful purpose,
FM had not caught on as was hoped, and consequently the Institute officials decided to cease broadcasting on WDLM.

The termination of FM broadcasting from the Chicago studios in
December 1952 turned out to be only temporary. FM broadcasting,
though lagging in the early fifties, soon developed into the fastest growing entertainment medium in the country. By 1960 the trend was moving
in only one direction—upward. FM frequencies were becoming scarce in
top markets, and in some localities none was available.[2]

Fortunately, the board of trustees recognized this new trend early.
On October 15, 1958, they asked permission to erect a noncommercial,
educational FM station on 90.1 megacycles. By July 1960, the station
began broadcasting once more, this time as WMBI-FM with a power of
47,000 watts, the fourth strongest FM station in Chicago. On July 28,
1965, the FM power was increased to 100,000 watts, enabling the signal
to reach as far as the signal of WMBI-AM.

## MOODY RADIO IN OHIO

FM radio, with a broadcast signal able to overcome atmospheric interference, continued to grow in popularity. A group of Christian businessmen in Cleveland, led by Harry McKee and Robert Berry, wanted to start a religious radio station that would extend through northeast Ohio. It would not be the first Christian station, but the business plan stood out: The station would not sell commercial time and would be a nonprofit enterprise. The plan echoed the ministry approach of WMBI, and the businessmen decided to ask the Institute whether it would be interested in operating the station.

As early as 1954, Robert Parsons, then director of the MBI radio department, had urged the administration to buy or construct a station in another area. At that time it did not seem feasible. The Cleveland offer in 1957 was unexpected, and there was hesitation, followed by much deliberation and prayer. After careful thought, Institute officials agreed it was time to act. They accepted the Cleveland proposition, provided that the station would be supported locally. The FCC readily approved the application, and the following year Moody was given the station license and began broadcasting November 23, 1958, on 103.3 megacycles at 21,500 watts.

By 1964 the total hours each day increased to sixteen, from 7 a.m. to 11 p.m. The name WCRF stands for Christian Radio Fellowship, and later the station expanded its programming to twenty-four hours a day. Today its signal extends beyond northeast Ohio via repeater stations to northwest Pennsylvania and southern Ontario, Canada. Listeners and management celebrated the station's fiftieth anniversary in 2008 with a series of events, culminating in a gathering at Parkside Church in Chagrin Falls and a re-creation of the first script used for the Moody radio drama "Ranger Bill." It featured worship led by songwriters and singers Keith and Kristyn Getty and a message by Pastor Alistair Begg.[3]

## THE MOODY RADIO NETWORK

One year after the Cleveland group had contacted the school asking for assistance, MBI officials themselves decided to expand within Illinois.

The WMBI-AM signal had reached west of Chicago, boosting its audience, but it had gradually decreased due to interference from other stations operating on or near 1110 kilocycles. So MBI petitioned the FCC in 1958 for a permit to build an AM station to operate in East Moline, Illinois. Leaders chose the call letters WDLM, the same call letters used from 1943–53 by the original Chicago FM station. The FCC approved the Moline application, and on April 3, 1960, the third Moody station went on the air, operating at one thousand watts from sunup to sundown. It also celebrated its fiftieth anniversary in 2010.

The addition of WDLM created what became the Moody Radio Network. (The Chicago FM station resumed broadcasting in July 1960 as WMBI-FM, the fourth station of the network.) In subsequent years, other individuals and Christian broadcasting groups have asked the Institute to start new stations or assume management of existing ones. Today thirty-five stations across the U.S. are owned and operated by MBI. They include WDLM-FM, Moline's sister Moody station, started in 1980. Together the two stations, WDLM-AM and FM, are known as Moody Radio Quad Cities, covering the four principal cities of Moline and Rock Island (Illinois) and Davenport and Bettendorf (Iowa). Their signals cover much of western Illinois and extend past the Mississippi River into southeast Iowa.

The owned-and-operated stations stretch from Spokane in the Pacific Northwest (KMBI and KMBI-FM, acquired in 1974) to south Florida (WRMB-FM, Boynton Beach, acquired in 1979). The FM signal radiates in all directions for wider coverage and nighttime reception.

## THE LOCAL TOUCH

The heart of Moody's owned-and-operated stations is its local programming. Many stations have morning drive shows, such as *New Day Florida* (in Sarasota, Lakeland, and Naples), *Fresh Start* (Boynton Beach), *John and June in the Mornings* (Tuscaloosa and Selma, Alabama), and *The Morning Ride* (Chicago). In its 1994 "Best of" contest, the *Chattanooga Times* named Bernie Miller, morning drive host on WMBW, "Best Morning DJ." Two years later the National Association of Broadcasters awarded WMBI-FM the Marconi Award as the top religious/gospel station. In 2000 WMBI won the Marconi for broadcasting excellence once more, and in 2009 the National Religious Broadcasters (NRB) awarded WMBI the Media Award as station of the year (large market). More recently NRB named WMBW the 2010 station of the year (medium/small market) for its community service, promotions and marketing, and outreach.

Through the years, most owned-and-operated stations actively assist their communities and even reach overseas. Here's a snapshot from summer 2008. In June WDLM-AM and FM collected more than one hundred gift cards to home improvement stores, restaurants, grocery stores, and gas stations. Local churches distributed the cards to victims of the spring flooding of the Mississippi River. WCRF held its fifth annual Shoes for Orphan Souls drive. They collected more than 12,000 pairs sent to orphans and needy children in Latvia, as well as for children in Cleveland's inner city. Not to be outdone, listeners to four stations in Tennessee contributed more than 20,000 pairs of new shoes and 38,000 pairs of new socks in the Shoes for Orphan Souls drive, sent to children in other countries. In September, WKES (Tampa and Orlando) organized Moody Radio and World Hope Missions Ministry. Doctors, dentists, and pharmacists, all WKES listeners, traveled to Brazil's Amazon River basin to give free medical and dental services to residents, while children's workers led kids' clubs for 183 children. Meanwhile WMBI, the flagship station, collected 5,800 backpacks filled with school supplies for children in Chicago's public schools.[4]

Two of the most creative outreaches through the years have involved Operation Teddy Bear and "One Night on the Street." In December 1991 WMBI teamed with Josh McDowell Ministry to send thousands of teddy bears donated by listeners to children in Moscow hospitals. In November 2007, WCRF hosted the "One Night," actually on two nights, with several live remotes from a downtown Cleveland church and Building Hope in the City, an urban ministry and mission in Northeast Ohio. The station interviewed ministry leaders and hosted an urban pastors' forum to highlight opportunities for listeners to serve in the city, including in children's ministry, teaching English as a second language, and working with the homeless. After the event, the station reported, "Individuals, small groups, and entire churches are all making commitments to serve Christ in urban Cleveland—all thanks to one night in the city."[5]

One of the most innovative gifts to their communities has been one week of ongoing Christmas music. Started in 1993 at WMBI, WRMB, and all owned-and-operated stations, today all thirty-five O-and-O stations suspend regular programming several days before Christmas to air the special music. In addition to playing traditional carols, Christmas songs, instrumentals, and even excerpts from Handel's *Messiah*, the stations include short stories and vignettes containing the gospel and explaining the meaning of Christmas. During their first year airing the special musical programming in southern Florida, station WRMB learned several local businesses piped the programming over their stores' intercoms for their shoppers.[6]

## WHEN MRN BECAME MBN

Owned-and-operated stations could boost their signals with translator towers that would extend each station's programs into remote areas. But after more communication satellites were launched in the late 1970s, Moody radio saw a new role for FM translators: to beam radio signals via satellite to translators across North America (including Alaska, Hawaii, and the Caribbean). This would bring Christian radio to smaller communities. In the early 1980s Robert Neff, vice president of broadcasting, and Jim Goodrich, assistant to the VP, began to investigate. Goodrich first thought of satellites' potential while a station manager in Missoula, Montana, receiving translator-fed broadcasts from KMBI in Spokane.

Neff and Goodrich presented the case to MBI administration, and in 1981 the MBI board of trustees approved satellite broadcasting. One year later MRN was renamed the Moody Broadcasting Network, and MBN became the first distributor of religious programming via satellite.[7]

But FCC rules limited translator use to rebroadcasting "over the air" radio station signals. By 1984, MBN satellite broadcasting remained limited to the owned-and-operated stations and sixty-three existing outlets that chose to broadcast some of the MBN programs.[8] That year the

FCC delayed final approval for low-cost, unmanned satellators and called for a three-year moratorium.[9]

Once more Moody broadcasting sought to influence a federal agency to benefit the radio community. Vice President Robert Neff, a graduate of MBI (1962), met with FCC commissioners four times on satellite-fed translators and other matters. Broadcasting also received counsel from two Washington, D.C., law firms to develop their case, including communications attorney Richard Wiley (a former FCC chairman and later an attorney for the National Religious Broadcasters). Of the Moody strategy, Neff said, "We go in trying to present the best case for our interests, while recognizing the concerns the FCC might have."[10]

Final FCC approval in 1988 brought the dawn of satellator stations. Moody had pioneered the concept of satellite-fed translators, or "satellators," and invested many thousands of dollars and a number of years to convince the FCC to change the rules. MBN quickly saw fruit for its labors (as future Christian radio networks would later). Satellite broadcasting revolutionized Moody radio, extending live programming beyond owned-and-operated stations to new stations that could bring Christian radio to their communities. Once satellator broadcasting won approval for regular use, many small towns and cities began to purchase the equipment. By 1990, 274 satellite affiliates received satellite feeds; in 2010, 581 received all MBN programs.

Similarly MBN outlets, which broadcast one or more of the network programs, grew steadily in the past twenty years: 383 stations in 1991, 696 in 2000, and 1,206 in 2010. The original RCA Satcom IIIR satellite, moving in a geostationary orbit 22,300 miles above the earth, received the network signal relayed from the WMBI studios atop Crowell Hall via a dedicated phone line to the satellite uplink at Monee, Illinois; Satcom then bounced the transmission back to earth to satellite receiver dishes, providing the signal to each station. The entire 45,000 mile round-trip took less than a half second! Thirty years later Moody Radio relays its broadcast signal to the SES World Skies AMC-3 satellite and back to downlinks across America in less than one second.

( "There Are People
Listening on the Other
Side of the World" )

Stations within the Moody Broadcasting Network through the years have received moving letters from listeners that show the impact of radio on individual lives. Here are two relayed to the board of trustees in reports in 1993 and 1995.

"Jail saved my life! With the nightmare of alcohol and drugs, I wanted to end it with suicide. With WMBW, Jesus has stepped in and now has 100 percent control of my life. I have freedom from sin and can put the past behind. Thank you for being there 24 hours a day."

"I have been listening to WCRF since 1977 when I escaped from an abusive marriage. This station has been a source of emotional healing and spiritual growth. I've received much spiritual guidance and confirmation from your programs."

In 1998 WMBI learned of its impact overseas, thanks to the global reach of its Internet audio stream:

> I found your station (WMBI) via Internet . . . that is awesome to listen to. . . . I am in Tallinn, Estonia, that is in North Europe. We also have Christian radio here but it is not on Internet yet. So this is just to say thanks and to let you know there are people listening also on the other side of the world.

---

New network programming developed for satellite broadcasting featuring live interviews and call-ins to hosts of such programs as *Prime Time America* (during afternoon drive time) and *Open Line* (at night). Today Christian listeners to stations stretching from Santa Cruz, California, to North Pole, Alaska, and Hilo, Hawaii, tune in to *Midday Connection*, one of five weekday programs. The most popular program in terms of stations is *Music through the Night*, an overnight program that airs on approximately three hundred stations throughout North America and the Caribbean. Its host, Mike Kellogg, has blended humor, stories of believers, and personal biblical insights with inspiring music for almost thirty years.

*Moody Presents,* the longest-running network program, was launched in 1973 on flagship station WMBI, under the leadership of President George Sweeting. The program's purpose has always been to present the gospel clearly and also "to inform listeners about the world-wide ministries of Moody Bible Institute." The format continues to include a study of the Scriptures, interviews with students and MBI leaders, and songs from the Institute's music groups. Today President Paul Nyquist is the main speaker as the program continues into its fourth decade.

MBN also has broadcast live events of interest to the American Christian community. Over the years special events have included Founder's Week Bible conferences; Moody Pastors' Conferences; Amsterdam 1983, 1986, and 2000 evangelism conferences (organized by the Billy Graham Evangelistic Association); Promise Keepers men's conferences; the triennial Urbana missions conference; and the National Day of Prayer activities held each year in the nation's capital.

## WHEN IS RADIO NOT RADIO?

Leaders at MBN watched a sea of change in radio broadcasting during the first decade of the twenty-first century. Earlier we noted how the woman with the smartphone in her purse or a netbook on her desk finds her "radio" extremely portable today. Her access to any station across America—and even stations in Europe, Australia, or New Zealand—can be credited to a marvelous tool called the Internet. The World Wide Web, the most popular portal to civilian Internet usage, is truly worldwide. Listeners can locate radio stations by typing in web addresses and within seconds hear live audio streaming across the website. Once confined to desktop or laptop computers, Internet sites are now available on more compact netbooks that specialize in web access, small computer tablets (like iPad), and so-called smartphones.

In their centennial history of MBI, *Teaching the Word, Reaching the*

*World*, Flood and Jenkins forecast missionaries overseas one day would be able to listen live to Moody's annual Founder's Week conference.[11] Their prediction anticipated satellite delivery of Moody programming in foreign countries. But with Internet, radio audio feeds of Founder's Week have already gone global.

Beyond live audio streaming via the Internet, listeners also can access previously broadcast programs at their convenience by downloading an audio file to their computer or mobile device, such as an MP3 player. Such on-demand "broadcasts" are known informally as podcasts, named after the iPod MP3 player developed by Apple Inc.

Another, newer application of Internet broadcasting is audio channels. Begun in 2007 with *The Conference Center*, MBN developed three unique audio channels that play Christian music and messages around the clock. *Praise & Worship* offers the best of praise and worship music. *Majesty Radio* showcases classic hymns and sacred music in orchestral and chorale settings. *Proclaim!* (previously *The Conference Center*) features inspiring messages from well-known preachers and teachers who have spoken at MBI conferences through the years, including Paul Little, J. I. Packer, Billy Graham, Charles Swindoll, and Joni Eareckson Tada.

## WHEN MBN BECAME MOODY RADIO

In 2008 the Moody Broadcasting Network took on a new identity—Moody Radio. The name change surprised some listeners, and "some spirited discussion" developed among network executives before they approved the change, admits Doug Hastings, manager of administration. "Some said, 'We're not just radio.' But the definition of radio is widening. It's not just an AM station or an FM station. You have satellite radio; well, what's the big difference between satellite radio and Internet radio?"[12]

Hastings expects new cars soon will offer "Internet radio right next to your satellite radio, right next to your FM radio. . . . Whether the delivery system is a transmitter, a satellite beam to a car, over the Internet, or over a WiFi network, it's all audio coming to them, and it's all migrating to be referred to as radio."

Although Moody Radio can broadcast beyond home and car radio to air programs via on-demand receivers—laptop and iPad computers, smartphones, and MP3 players—the name *Moody Radio* sticks because it derives from radio-formatted programming. "That's pretty much industry accepted," Hastings says. He points to AOL Radio. "It doesn't own radio stations. But you can go to their AOL website, and that is where all their audio channels are."

*Moody Radio* works on two other levels, according to Hastings. First, it "brands" the product. Network officials concluded it was much easier to reinforce a brand—Moody Radio—that was nationwide. "When someone turns on and hears one of our radio stations, they're going to hear the words 'Moody Radio.' They may hear a qualifier after that— Moody Radio South, Moody Radio Chicago, Moody Radio Indiana— but it's always going to be 'Moody Radio.' This reinforces the brand."

That branding means reliability for the audience. "The listener says, 'Okay, I know what I got. It's going to sound like this. . . . I am going to get this kind of content. I am going to get this kind of theology.'" It's that reliability that creates both trust and positive expectations from listeners, who come back again and again.

The name "Moody Radio" also gives a simple, clearer identity than Moody Broadcasting Network. It is an identity many longtime listeners had been using for years, Hastings says. "We realized that our constituency and our listeners were defaulting to call us that name. At an event or at church they'd say, 'Well, I heard on Moody Radio . . .' They rarely used the call letters [of stations]." Nor are call letters being emphasized in measuring radio ratings, as Arbitron has moved from the handwritten diaries in many media markets to the people meter, an electronic device that people wear. The people meter automatically records what they are listening to. They don't have to know the call letters.

He notes that many people listening to Christian radio increasingly know the network but not the station. He cites K-LOVE, another network of Christian radio stations broadcasting nationally. K-LOVE is the umbrella name for all the stations in the network. Local stations mention their own call letters infrequently, while the network announcer repeats the name K-LOVE throughout the syndicated programs. "Most people

**MBI IMPACT** ⟨ Listening on the Way to Work ⟩

The engineering executive was en route to his office in downtown Chicago close to Lake Michigan one cold December morning in the late 1970s. Turning his radio dial, he listened, trying to locate Christmas music to remind him of the season. Finally, pay dirt—an FM station playing all Christmas music, including his favorite carols and contemporary sounds that kept Christ in Christmas.

He pushed a preselect button so it would be easy to find the next time he wanted to hear holiday melodies. Weeks later, during a morning commute to the Amoco Oil building in Chicago, he was hitting his preselects and heard Bob Murfin, host of *The Morning Show* on WMBI.

"I had never heard of Christian radio before. I didn't even know it existed. I started listening and I started getting into the pastors, Don Cole [WMBI's radio pastor for thirty-eight years], Dr. Sweeting, and some of the radio guys."

He listened at times with his wife in the car, and she started listening when driving alone. "She liked Murfin's humor; she liked the biblical teaching. She became more interested.

"One day she called me at work. 'Look, I was listening to the radio station after I dropped you off. I heard this message and I slammed on the brakes and pulled over on the side of the highway. I understand now what you're talking about. I've had this experience where I'm born again.'"

That's why the executive says, "So Moody radio is a huge piece of my life. My personal biblical growth, my wife's transformation came by what [we] heard on the radio."

They became donors to WMBI in 1979, and twenty years later, this business executive listened as President Joseph Stowell asked him to leave a huge salary and a settled job and come work at Moody. Ed Cannon said yes, and today he helps President Nyquist chart the future as the chief operating officer at Moody Bible Institute.

don't know what the call letters are of the K-LOVE station. Ask them, 'Who do you listen to?' and they say, 'Well, I listen to K-LOVE.' Ask them, "What are the call letters of your station?' and they'll say, 'I don't know.'"

## LISTENING WHENEVER YOU WANT

Moody Radio is positioned well for the latest in broadcast and Internet radio developments. In late 2009 Moody released its first smartphone application, or app, to help listeners with handheld devices quickly access Moody Radio's three audio channels and local radio station streams on its owned-and-operated stations. "People are listening less to terrestrial radio and more to Internet radio, and more Internet listening is being done on mobile devices such as iPhones," explained National Program Director Denny Nugent while announcing the new app. "We are committed to using these new technological opportunities to reach . . . current and prospective listeners wherever they are."[13]

"The technology in radio is changing so rapidly that some of the things we were working on last year are not the cutting edge anymore," Chief Operating Officer Ed Cannon told a group during Founder's Week 2010. "Today you can listen to any one of the radio stations or any of the Moody-produced radio programs at any time you want—and you can store them and play them for other people."

Cannon emphasized that Moody Radio's primary focus "is proclaiming the gospel of Jesus Christ based on the truth of the Bible. We are in the business of trying to present compelling Christian material on the radio that brings a wide variety of people to a place closer to Christ than they were before they listened to the radio."[14]

Bruce Everhart, manager of Moody Radio marketing and development, predicts the role of podcasts on radio broadcasting from 2011–15 will be "immense." He cited data that in mid-2010 more than four in ten Americans owned a portable MP3 player. And according to Edison Research, in May 2010 alone, an estimated 32 million Americans listened to a podcast.[15]

Moody Radio—a pioneer in broadcasting with the first FM non-commercial religious station in the country and the first distribution of satellite religious programming—once more is ready for the challenge.

## NOTES

1. The various developments from 1926 to 1936 are detailed fully in Gene A. Getz and James Vincent, *MBI: The Story of Moody Bible Institute* (Chicago: Moody, 1986), 163–70.

2. Gene A. Getz, *MBI: The Story of Moody Bible Institute* (Chicago: Moody, 1969), 296.

3. "WCRF Celebrates 50 Years," October 30, 2008; http://www.moodyministries.net/crp_NewsDetail.aspx?id=28278.

4. "Radio Stations Reach Out," October 1, 2008; http://www.moodyministries.net/crp_NewsDetail.aspx?id=26932.

5. "One Night on the Street," November 26, 2007; http://www.moodyministries.net/crp_NewsDetail.aspx?id=10244.

6. Robert Neff, "Media Group Report to the Trustees, 1993–1994," 9; as cited in Kornel Gerstner, "The Pioneering Journey of Christian Radio Through Satellite Distribution: A Historical Overview of the Moody Broadcasting Network 1982–2002," master of arts thesis, Liberty University, May 2007, 86.

7. Gerstner, "The Pioneering Journey of Christian Radio," 72.

8. Robert G. Flood and Jerry B. Jenkins, *Teaching the Word, Reaching the World* (Chicago: Moody, 1985), 182.

9. Gerstner, "The Pioneering Journey of Christian Radio," 46–49.

10. James Vincent, "Lessons in Lobbying from Radio's Early Days," *Religious Broadcasting*, February 1987, 88. In 2001 the Alumni Association recognized Neff as the alumnus of the year. He led Moody Rado for thirty-one years.

11. Flood and Jenkins, *Teaching the Word*, 183.

12. All statements by Doug Hastings are from a personal interview on July 1, 2010.

13. "Moody Radio iPhone App," December 14, 2009; www.moodyradio.org/brd_news summary.aspx?id=6454.

14. Question and answers with Ed Cannon, Charles Dyer, Jerry Jenkins, and Paul Nyquist, Founder's Week 2:30 session, Torrey-Gray Auditorium, February 4, 2010.

15. Bruce Everhart, e-mail interview, June 30, 2010. Edison Research is a research group known for its studies and polling in elections, radio, and music.

# The Name You Can Trust

D. L. Moody scanned the shelves of the local bookstore, and his frustration mounted. He had just finished an evangelistic series in Madison, Wisconsin; now he wanted to give the new converts reading materials that would help them mature in their Christian lives. Though the shelves bulged with fiction of all kinds, he could not find a single religious book on Christian growth. Unable to find practical, inexpensive books, he decided to do something about it.[1]

## "THEIR PRICE MUST COME DOWN!"

The key word in Moody's thinking was *inexpensive*. Few people bought evangelical books once they saw the cover price.

"Their price must come down" was Moody's immediate reaction. He talked with various publishers but found little interest in preparing books that could compete with the inexpensive literature on the secular market. Finally, with the counsel and help of Fleming H. Revell, his brother-in-law who was himself a book publisher, Moody began the Bible Institute Colportage Association (BICA) in 1894. He lowered high book prices through uniform size and binding, inexpensive paper, and large press runs—the final element a risk without any obvious demand by consumers. But soon enough there was demand for economical, quality Christian books.

Incorporated into the Bible institute in 1899, BICA began to publish and disseminate inexpensive evangelical books and booklets, Scripture portions, and gospel leaflets. Two of the best-known names of the day wrote the first two books in the line. Book number one was by the famed English preacher Charles H. Spurgeon, *All of Grace*. Moody wrote the second book, *The Way to God and How to Find It*, a collection of sermons by Moody, Spurgeon, F. B. Meyer, Andrew Murray, and others. German, Swedish, Spanish, and Bohemian editions of *The Way to God* soon followed.

The first edition of *The Way to God* sold more than 100,000 copies. By the early 1980s it had sold 750,000 copies. It reappeared in a special 1996 edition and has lifetime sales of 788,000 copies.

The Colportage Library established new requirements for evangelical literature. Books had to be written in a popular, readable style by well-known authors; they would also have to be strictly evangelical and undenominational, well printed but inexpensive. The books had a uniform size and binding.

The entrepreneurial Moody brought his creative energies to BICA just as he had to his Chicago Bible institute. The paperback line kept prices down, and readers also liked the uniform pocket book size, an innovation in religious publishing. People often purchased a set instead of one book. In addition, Moody promoted the books at every opportunity. At his evangelistic meetings he encouraged people to sign up to receive books automatically as they came off the press each month. Thus he created a sort of book-of-the-month club. The first year, books were issued two per month, and the following year, one each month. Moody was far ahead of his time, since the first secular book-of-the-month club was not founded until April 1926, in New York City by Harry Scherman.[2]

Shortly after the turn of the century, more than four million colportage books had been published, including 104 different titles.[3] The major means of distribution was through "colporteurs," about one hundred men who lived in different parts of the country and sold Christian books. BICA would ship materials to twenty-four different supply depots, where the colporteurs would restock their inventory. Other sellers were "book missionaries," going door-to-door to present the gospel as well as offer books. Their literature included hundreds of gospel tracts.

BICA distributed books many ways. The gospel wagons used for practical Christian work at the Institute were imitated by some colporteurs who hitched wagons to their horses to hit the dirt roads. In 1931 a New York businessman donated a gospel car to BICA to be used in distributing literature. It really was a "house on wheels" the donor and his wife had used for several summers. By 1939 colportage workers had driven the gospel car 45,000 miles in the central states, made 20,500 calls in homes, and distributed 67,400 gospel tracts. As a result of the gospel car, 917 accepted Jesus Christ as Lord and Savior.[4]

In 1941, forty years and 17 million New Testaments and Scripture portions after BICA began, the Colportage Association became Moody Press and continued the printing and sale of books that would encourage Christians and evangelize the lost. As BICA had, Moody Press continued to return profits to MBI to help defray tuition costs for students, effectively keeping the Press a nonprofit publisher.

## MOODY PUBLISHERS:
## NEW WAYS TO DELIVER THE MESSAGE

Seventy years have passed since then. Moody Press became Moody Publishers in 2002 to reflect the publisher's entry into audio and video products (and licensing of electronic editions of the materials). Ten years earlier the first imprint had been added. Northfield Publishing began in 1992 to address non-Christians exploring the Christian faith and to present biblical principles for living to a general audience. The first Northfield books were *Family Budget Workbook*, by Christian financial expert Larry Burkett, and *The Stress Factor*, by counselors Paul Minirth and Frank Meier. Since then it has had a series of bestselling books, including all five titles in the Five Love Languages series.

In 1999 Lift Every Voice Books (LEVB) was established as the second imprint. Originally copublished with the Institute for Black Family

Development (in 2008 Moody became the sole publisher), LEVB explores issues facing the African-American community through non-fiction and fiction books written by and for African-Americans.

Though the publishing house changed its name after sixty-one years, as Moody Publishers its mission statement makes clear that transforming lives through the good news of the gospel, as well as equipping and encouraging followers of Christ, are at the center of the mission: "To evangelize, educate, and equip individuals by ethically publishing conservative, evangelical Christian literature and other media for all ages around the world; and to help provide resources for the Moody Bible Institute to train future Christian leaders."

More recently, the updated (2010) vision statement declares that Moody Publishers is committed to helping readers "know, love, and serve Jesus Christ."

## SHAPING AN INDUSTRY

As one of the oldest Christian book publishers, Moody Press in 1950 led efforts to launch the Christian Booksellers Association. For many years prospective store owners had contacted Moody Press almost daily for advice and information on how to open and operate Christian bookstores. William F. Moore, a Moody Press employee, and Kenneth N. Taylor, then director of Moody Press, discussed the need. Eventually they arranged several meetings with their Chicago-area dealers to determine the level of interest in a Christian booksellers' trade association.

As a result of these first meetings, the first organizational convention was held at the LaSalle Hotel in Chicago in September 1950. Two months later, on November 17, the Christian Booksellers Association (CBA) was incorporated as a nonprofit corporation in the state of Illinois. From its inception in 1950, CBA used the facilities of Moody Press in order to operate its office, paying its own salaries, postage, and other expenses. In February 1959, the association moved to its own office in suburban Chicago, where it remained until 1970, when it relocated to Colorado Springs. The former Christian Booksellers Association, whose members sell much more than printed books, is now simply CBA. It attracts thousands to its annual International Christian Retail Show for training and meetings with fellow retailers and industry suppliers, including Christian publishers.

According to Moore, the growth in "the entire Christian bookselling and publishing industry . . . [was] a direct result of the Christian Booksellers Association," as well as an indirect contribution of Moody Bible Institute. The association not only came into being as a result of the vision of Institute leaders, but its growth and progress had been directly related to the interest shown by Moody Press.

## CELEBRATING A CENTENNIAL

As Moody Press, the publishing house turned one hundred in 1994. It celebrated its centennial by recalling its "cheap beginnings," when it sold books for ten to fifteen cents, by offering the D. L. Moody classic *The Overcoming Life* at its original price of twenty-five cents. That year the Evangelical Christian Publishing Association presented Moody Press with the ECPA President's Award for "the standard they have set for excellence, integrity, and accomplishment."

In a special newspaper distributed at the CBA convention, former Moody Press directors Ken Taylor (1948–61) and Jerry Jenkins (1981–87) reflected on their tenures with and the impact of the publishing house. Taylor, who had left Moody Press to start Tyndale House Publishers, pointed out that booksellers in the 1990s were better trained and located, having moved their stores from the "backstreets or upstairs in an old building" of the 1950s. He appreciated the managerial control granted him by President William Culbertson and Robert Constable, his immediate boss. Constable "trusted me with the decisions."

He was grateful that "Moody Press did pull its weight and was profitable, so there wasn't a drag on the Institute. At the same time, Moody Press was performing a wonderful service to the Christian public. It grew and formed a solid base for its later rapid expansion."[5]

Jenkins, who eventually served as vice president of publishing at MBI, later was named MBI's writer-in-residence before entering a full-time writing career that would feature bestselling biographies and novels, including the blockbuster Left Behind series. He recalled signing Larry Burkett to a three-book contract. "Among the three titles was *Your Finances in Changing Times*, which has sold more than one million copies. I had no idea how big his books would become," Jenkins said. "I thought he would like us because of our policies—that MBI refuses to incur debt and is ministry oriented. He was not the type who would demand a six-figure advance." Five years later Moody Press published Burkett's *The Coming Economic Earthquake*, about the national debt and its threat to the country's well-being. The book shook up the industry and the reading public and won the first Book of the Year award handed out by the CBA (awarded in 1993).

Jenkins described the bookselling industry in his 1994 interview as "learning to choose better authors; they have A-list authors; that's how dealers live and die. The big authors are still publishing a lot of titles. But I think the selection is deeper rather than wide at this point."[6]

## "BEDROCK TRUST"

Moody Publishers continues to enjoy a high standing among Christian retailers. Its slogan, "The Name You Can Trust," is now trademarked and began not with a marketer's idea but the comments of customers. Erwin Hiltscher, a retired regional sales manager, remembered hearing comments shortly after joining sales in 1966, just a couple of years before the slogan appeared.

"On almost every call I made, the dealer said, 'I'm so thankful we don't have to read your books cover to cover. We can trust what's inside.' That was a common phrase that just recurred. There's a publisher you can trust. They publish things that are in the mainstream."[7]

Whether theology, Christian living, fiction, church life, reference, social issues, or spiritual growth, many regard Moody Publishers as an evangelical publisher that is rooted in solidly biblical principles. As Jenkins said during the 1994 centennial, "There is the bedrock trust . . . in the industry, and we certainly appreciate that."[8]

## THE PRICE YOU CAN AFFORD

Through the years, Moody Publishers has sought to keep books inexpensive. That would seem to be a challenge for any publisher as inflation persisted over the years, yet MP has found ways to keep costs down, while still making a profit. During the early 1980s when America was suffering through an extended recession, Moody Press released what they called "The Affordables." These were valuable titles in their reference line with simplified covers and type layout to cut costs. As paperback versions of bestselling classics the *Unger's Dictionary* and *Unger's Handbook* as well as the *Wycliffe Bible Commentary*, they cost half the amount of the original hardback books, making these reference tools available to everyone.

More recently, this keep-it-affordable attitude has affected pricing of Moody Bibles, which have had nominal price increases over the years. In 2008, all existing *Ryrie Study Bibles* got the valued-added treatment when free DVD software was included with every Bible. The DVD included the *New Unger's Dictionary* and *Handbook*, as well as bestsellers such as Charles Ryrie's *Basic Theology, Strong's Concordance, Nave's Topical Index*, the *Matthew Henry Commentaries*, and other study aids valued at more than $400. Today the reference works are still provided through free digital downloads.

## BIBLES BY MOODY

MP is not often thought of as a Bible publisher. Zondervan has published the *New International Version*, Thomas Nelson the *New King James Version*, Tyndale the *New Living Translation*, B&H the *Holman Christian Standard Bible*, NavPress *The Message*, and Crossway the *English Standard Version*. All are original translations or paraphrases. Yet Moody Publishers has been printing Bibles since the 1940s.

Moody Press entered Bible publishing with the Charles B. Williams translation of the New Testament, titled *The New Testament in the Language of the People*. The Williams translation became an immediate success. In one sense, this was a pioneering venture, since conservative people had been well known for their veneration of the King James

Version and their reluctance to read other translations.

When the Lockman Foundation produced its *New American Standard Bible* in the 1960s, Moody Press became one of five major publishers to print the Bible. One Moody Press version of this Bible, called the Thinline edition, featured thin yet durable paper that made the NASB lightweight and compact.

In 1978 Moody Press introduced its major contribution to Bible publishing, the *Ryrie Study Bible*, with theological, historical, and cultural notes by Dr. Charles Ryrie, a noted theologian and former professor at Dallas Theological Seminary. With its thorough book outlines, numerous charts, colored maps, numerous footnotes, and marginal cross references, the Ryrie Bible quickly became a bestseller. Published in the King James, New American Standard, New International, and now English Standard versions, it has sold more than 2.6 million copies.

"We identify ourselves more as a niche Bible publisher," says Greg Thornton, vice president and publisher. "We don't own a translation, like Zondervan with the NIV or Tyndale with the *New Living Translation*. But when we have something unique to offer the church, we will."[9]

The Institute and Moody Publishers made a significant commitment to Bibles in 1995 with the expanded edition of the *Ryrie Study Bible*. MP added graphics to the text and detailed maps from *The Moody Atlas of Bible Lands*. (The RSB now contains sixteen full-color maps.) The topical index expanded to complement the comprehensive concordance, while new articles appeared, including "A Brief Study of Church History." The RSB now contains 10,000 explanatory notes of specific verses.

In 2011 Moody Publishers released the *Ryrie Study Bible* in its first new translation in twenty-five years (since offering the NIV in 1986): the English Standard Version of the Bible. Like its four predecessors, it included the popular SoftTouch cover of simulated leather that featured a burnished cross on the cover and 2 Timothy 3:16 (the Institute's theme verse) in the chosen translation on the back.

"It is a very portable study Bible," Thornton says of the new Ryrie in the English Standard Version. Moody Publishers is "taking one of the premier study Bibles of all time—the *Ryrie Study Bible*—married with one of the more popular new translations, the ESV."

## ACADEMIC VERSUS REFERENCE

Like all ministries at MBI, Moody Publishers has modified and updated its offerings—in this case, product lines—to make them more effective, and when they are no longer viable, to end them. That was the case in 1993 when after nearly forty years the publishing house ended its academic line. At its height, more than 150 titles appeared in the textbook list, covering Bible study, comparative religions, theology, Christian education, church music, church history, missions, archaeology, psychology, biblical languages, and homiletics.

Academic, or scholarly, books seemed a natural for a publisher affiliated with a Bible institute. But with the increasing competition in the marketplace and the required costly investment in academic works, leadership made the decision to leave the field. MP retained many of its classics, which are still available, including *Angels: Elect and Evil*, by C. Fred Dickason, former chairman of Moody's department of theology, and *Jesus Christ Our Lord*, by John Walvoord. It continues to publish its one-volume classic, the *Wycliffe Bible Commentary*, which has sold hundreds of thousands of copies.

Although MP is no longer in academic publishing, its presence in reference publishing—resources for personal Bible study—continues unabated. In addition to the *New Unger's Bible Dictionary* (1988) and *New Unger's Bible Handbook* (2005), each with lifetime sales approaching one million copies, it updated its award-winning *Moody Atlas of Bible Lands* by Trinity professor Barry Beitzel in 2009 with the *New Moody Atlas of the Bible*, featuring the latest in mapmaking techniques. It won the coveted ECPA Christian Book of the Year in the Bible study and reference category, as well as the "Best Book Atlas" category at the 37th Annual Map Design Competition sponsored by the Cartography and Geographic Information Society (CaGIS). The CaGIS award, open to all mapmakers in the United States and Canada, recognized "significant design advances in cartography."

"We have remained a strong player in reference publishing," Thornton notes. "That is in keeping with our own history and with our own opportunities to know audiences and to serve them with resources that reflect well on Moody's unique position in the body of Christ." The publisher has refreshed some of its classic products. The next step will be to expand digital offerings of the reference works. "With the iPad and its four-color screen, there is the opportunity to make the *New Moody Atlas of the Bible* and the *New Unger's Bible Handbook* and the *New Unger's Bible Dictionary* really come to life in full color, electronically, just as they do in the print editions."

Meanwhile after twenty-eight volumes published since 1983, *The MacArthur New Testament Commentary* continues as one of the most popular Bible commentaries of all time, selling more than one million volumes and an additional 112,000 complete sets. Written by John MacArthur, pastor, author, and radio host of *Grace to You*, only the gospel of Mark and a portion of the gospel of Luke remain to complete the set.

In the fall of 2011 MP plans to release the *Moody Bible Commentary*, a complete one-volume commentary aimed at the Bible study leader, the Sunday school teacher, and the serious student of God's Word. It will feature the scholarship of the MBI undergraduate and graduate school faculties.

## FRONTLIST, BACKLIST, AND BESTSELLERS

In the publishing industry, most houses want to release titles that become bestsellers. Those that do will drive sales revenue and prompt retailers to come back to reorder the title—and other titles at the same time. New releases are termed "frontlist," the new titles that appear at the front of each sales catalog and build excitement for new and existing products. After one year they are considered "backlist" products, where publishers hope they remain for many years. If they do, they become known as "evergreens," books that stay fresh and saleable because their messages remain useful or their stories remain appealing for decades after publication.

The ideal mix is 40 percent frontlist and 60 percent backlist, says John Hinkley, director of marketing. In 2010 the Moody Publishers' mix was 35 percent frontlist. A slightly higher percentage would mean current releases reflect readers' concerns, but Hinkley is fairly satisfied. Four of the top eight all-time bestsellers in the publisher's one-hundred-year-plus history have been released in the past twenty years. Gary Chapman's *The Five Love Languages*, the all-time leader with more than six million copies sold, is joined by *The Five Love Languages of Children* (number three, approaching one million copies sold), coauthored by Gary Chapman and Ross Campbell. Nancy Leigh DeMoss's *Lies Women Believe* is number five on the all-time bestseller list; and *An Anchor for the Soul*, a straightforward presentation of the gospel by pastor-speaker Ray Pritchard, is number eight. In the past five years the bestsellers have included familiar names to the book reading marketplace: Chapman, DeMoss, J. Oswald Sanders, and Erwin Lutzer.

But most gratifying to Hinkley and others in MP sales and marketing are the unexpected "big rocks," books that exceed all sales forecasts and take off. Ironically, the biggest bestseller of all, *The Five Love Languages*, began that way, with low expectations and an average marketing budget. (See the side story "Up, Up, and Away.") Hinkley remembers Burkett's *The Coming Economic Earthquake* doing that. "It was a smashing success both because of the messenger, Larry Burkett, who had a radio program for years, and [his message about] signals pointing to a lot of economic trouble." He called *Earthquake* a book "to prepare people for something."

More recent big rocks have included *When Helping Hurts* (2009) and *Why We're Not Emergent* (2008). *Hurts* offers ways Christians and agencies can help the poor and oppressed. *Not Emergent*, featuring a young senior pastor whose church is across the street from Michigan State University and a member of his congregation (Kevin DeYoung and Ted Kluck), combined humor, insight, and theology to point out flaws in the emergent church movement and remind Christians of the true gospel. Its quality matched its popularity, as it received a *Christianity Today* Book of the Year award in 2009.

## "BOOKS CHANGE LIVES"

As pleasing as strong sales are, Vice President Thornton finds the greatest satisfaction in changed lives. "It's hearing from readers the impact of a book in their lives. To change their thinking, to help them

**MBI IMPACT**

# ( Up, Up, and Away )

No one saw it coming. Gary Chapman, an alumnus of Moody Bible institute (1958) and a family counselor for more than twenty years, had written one book for Moody Press, *Hope for the Separated*, that had average sales, and he recently had submitted (in 1992) a manuscript entitled *The Five Love Languages*. Marketing decided to designate an average amount for promotion, and the sales staff was hoping for 10,000 in sales. It sold 17,700 the first twelve months. Impressive. The second year, when a book's sales typically taper off, the sales increased 22 percent.

That caught the eye. Marketing decided to back the book more aggressively. It was apparent Gary Chapman's seminar, then called "Toward a Growing Marriage," was selling copies of the book. But word of mouth was at play as well. People loved the book and were recommending it to friends at work and church. The next fiscal year, ending June 1995, sales increased 147 percent to 56,000 books.

"Most of it the first two years was word of mouth. People read it and started talking about it. The concept itself is simple to grasp, it makes a lot of sense, and when you apply it, it works," says John Hinkley, MP marketing director. "All that really generates word-of-mouth buzz." And like most marketers, Hinkley feels that is the most effective promotion.

During 1995 a new, attractive cover was added, Gary continued his radio interviews and conferences, and more readers recommended the book. The next year sales more than doubled again. The following year the book sold almost 169,000 copies. For the next eleven years, from 1992–2008, the book continued to increase its sales each year—adding up to an unheard-of sixteen years' growth.

Marketing did its part, with hefty budgets devoted to the flagship title that became a profitable franchise, with three new covers during its first eighteen years. In 2004 Chapman's popular online love languages assessment tool was included in the book itself. The next year annual sales surpassed 500,000 for the first time. Meanwhile Dr. Chapman wrote *Love Languages* books for children (with Ross Campbell), teens, and singles, as well as a men's edition. By year-end 2010 *The Five Love Languages* had passed six million copies sold. Along the way the other four books in the series sold an additional two million combined.

On October 2, 2009, *The Five Love Languages* became the number one bestseller on the *New York Times* paperback advice list. It had been on the top fifteen *New York Times* list for months and has remained on the list 160 weeks, most of them consecutive.*

The ranking is less important to Hinkley in terms of sales and more important in terms of the book's message. "People watch these bestseller lists and want to know more. They will do a Web search, explore Amazon.com." They will learn the book's basic message and understand the concept.

The book has allowed Chapman to explain the concept of knowing the key language that makes your spouse (or child or teen) feel loved at conferences across America and abroad. A few years ago he traveled to the United Nations in New York City, where he addressed delegates from several nations. He has spoken at U.S. military bases all over the world and twice to military officers and civilian workers at the Pentagon. Chapman enjoys speaking and counseling with soldiers, Hinkley says, because he knows war and separation often strain the husband-wife relationship.

Hinkley hopes eventually Chapman's message will reach more readers who are just getting married. "There are over two million weddings a year in the United States. We are good at reaching and communicating to people thirty-five to fifty-five years old. But we need to speak to a younger age frame with this message." In 2010 Chapman released his latest book with Moody Publishers, *Things I Wish I'd Known Before We Got Married*. It's targeted for single and engaged couples. "This book may become one of those open doors to this group," Hinkley says. Chapman, the open, compassionate, and personal marriage counselor, is ready to spill the beans—with his wife's permission—and invite a new generation to learn how to communicate and experience deep love in their marriages.

---

* The 160 weeks on the bestseller list is as of September 2010. It returned to the number one position on the *Times* advice list on August 29, 2010. All statements by John Hinkley are from a personal interview, August 31, 2010.

adjust their behavior. But ultimately [it's] to see God use these messages
. . . to transform lives by the power of the Spirit of God. That's why I
remain in publishing. I love doing publishing in the context of MBI."

Thornton says, "Everything that is said about literature and learning
is true and more. 'Books change lives.' 'Great leaders are great readers.'
Because we are a publishing house that is mission driven and committed to Christ, we are seeking to publish messages that help people learn
and grow. But we ultimately are concerned about individual readers
growing in their love and understanding of God, and their love and service to fellow men. The e-mails and letters that come are certainly the
wind in our sails at Moody Publishers."

Thornton reads letters to staffers several times each year during
monthly "highlights" meetings. Some are addressed to the publisher;
many to the author. One reader of *Lies Women Believe* wrote Nancy
DeMoss:

> Through MUCH prayer and seeking, the Lord has put your book
> *Lies Women Believe* in my life. There are no words to let you know
> the depth He has reached in my life as a result of your book. Only He
> knows. I question why I haven't realized these Truths before. His
> timing is perfect. Thank you so much for walking with Him and
> being so used by Him.

The letter was signed, "Changed a little more, ____."

## "THE CONTENT GOD IS TRUSTING TO US IN THE FORMATS READERS ARE LOOKING FOR"

Like their counterparts at Moody Radio (chapter 9), Thornton and
his management team are in a changing media landscape, and he is
unsure of the impact that electronic publishing will have on printed
books. He believes the two can coexist, but he watches as new advances
to electronic reading devices spur interest in digital downloads of books.
He traces the breakthrough in e-books to Amazon's release of its first
Kindle e-reader in November 2007. E-books were around in the mid-

1990s, but the Rocket e-reader never took off. Heavy and bulky, its e-ink technology had not been perfected, and made for "muddy" reading, according to Thornton.

Kindle was a turning point because "the hardware was right." Moody was one of the first to order the Kindle. The moment he received his Kindle, Thornton remembers, "there was a sense they had done it right. It's lightweight, and the e-ink technology is not backlit, so the reader is not having glare come into their eyes as they do with a computer screen." Ordering additional books by digital download was easy as well. Kindle was, as they say, "the game changer." Now the third version of the Kindle reader is available, and its competitors such as the Sony Reader, the Barnes & Noble Nook, and others are making advances as well. Meanwhile, "There are some who say this e-ink, black-and-white, read-only device will never make it. That the whole world will be tablet. It's going to be the four-color [Apple] iPad world," Thornton says.

Although Thornton is unsure whether dedicated black-and-white— or color—e-readers or larger handheld computer tablets awash in color will eventually win out, he believes digital delivery of content is here to stay. "The delivery of content through the Internet [will allow] enhanced e-books." Authors and editors can embed audio clips, video clips, and hyperlinks to extend the reader's understanding and experience.

"Every publisher has to wrestle with this question, 'Where is digital going?'" Thornton concludes. Moody Publishers is prepared—by year-end 2010, 700 of their backlist titles had been converted to digital format, and all new titles are prepared as print and digital media. "We are trying to provide the content God is trusting to us in the format readers are looking for," Thornton says. In the meantime, Moody Publishers remains committed to acquiring, developing, and producing books that can help readers "know, love, and serve Jesus Christ."

## NOTES

1. "A Brief Story of the Bible Institute Colportage Association," pamphlet, n.d., 3; A. P. Fitt, *Preaching the Gospel in Print* pamphlet, n.d., 2. He would start the Bible Institute Colportage Association (BICA).

2. Joseph N. Kane, *Famous First Facts,* 119; as cited in Gene A. Getz and James Vincent, *MBI: The Story of Moody Bible Institute* (Chicago: Moody, 1986), 136.

3. Gene A. Getz, *MBI: The Story of the Moody Bible Institute* (Chicago: Moody, 1969), 234.

4. "These Forty Two Years," pamphlet, Moody archives, 1937.

5. "Moody Press Turns 100," promotional newspaper distributed at 1994 CBA convention, 2.

6. Ibid., 3.

7. "'Bedrock Trust' in 'The Name You Can Trust,'" in "Moody Press Turns 100," 4.

8. "Moody Press Turns 100," 3.

9. All statements by Greg Thornton are from a personal interview, August 25, 2010.

( 11 )

# Seminary in the City

Most in the audience who filled Torrey-Gray Auditorium for commencement exercises on May 27, 1988, came to watch their own son or daughter, brother or sister, or spouse graduate with a valued bachelor of arts degree from Moody Bible Institute. They were unaware they would be treated to history as well. Six students had completed course work for a master of arts in ministry (MAMin). The undergraduate students had received their diplomas. Now each graduate student was about to receive his master's hood.

The six were the first graduates of Moody Graduate School. One by one they were called to the stage, and bowed their head slightly as Dean of Education Howard Whaley placed around their shoulders a hood edged in scarlet, symbolizing theological studies. The hood's inner lining of maroon and white reflected the MBI school colors. (Today the school colors are blue and white.)

Earlier in May, Vice President and MGS Dean B. Wayne Hopkins revealed that his excitement at the first academic hooding in MBI history would be for the graduates themselves, not for the historical nature of the occasion. "Those graduates represent hundreds of other students. All those students are influencing others."[1]

The six who received the first MAMin degrees consisted of three pastors, two administrators, and one missionary. "They are symbolic of our enrollment," Dean Hopkins pointed out. He noted that among all students enrolled in 1988, 70 percent were pastors, 15 percent were administrators, teachers, and others, and 15 percent were missionaries.[2]

## GROWING AND GROWING INTO A SEMINARY

Three years earlier, in June 1985, the graduate school had begun with eighty-one students. By the time it was twenty-five years old—in the year 2010—it had achieved several notable successes. Student enrollment had grown to 622 students that fall semester, almost an eightfold increase. The six full-time faculty (1991) had grown to fifteen, of whom one-third (33 percent) were non-Caucasian (including African-American, Chinese/Dutch West Indian, and Indian professors), meeting the goal of an ethnically diverse faculty. And the Moody Graduate School had become Moody Theological Seminary and Graduate School, or MTS.

MTS came to life less than two years after the Michigan Theological Seminary (Plymouth, Michigan) approached the Moody Graduate School in summer 2008 to ask about a possible merger of the two schools. A nine-month process of due diligence found the two schools compatible in theology and educational philosophy. The MBI board of trustees approved the merger in spring 2009, and the Higher Learning Commission of NCA gave provisional approval to the merger at their October 29 meeting.

On January 1, 2010, MGS formally became Moody Theological Seminary and Graduate School. Shortly after the Higher Learning Commission of North Central Association had given approval to the merger of the two schools, Jerry Jenkins, chairman of the MBI board of trustees, described the compelling reason for the combining of the two schools: "[Michigan Theological Seminary] and Moody not only align theologically and doctrinally but this merger combines two schools with the same mission to train and equip students for ministry. As a single entity we can be more effective for the Kingdom."[3]

On January 1, 2010, with official approval from HLC, Michigan Theological Seminary became Moody Theological Seminary–Michigan. At the time, Rick Warren, the former chairman of the Michigan seminary's board of trustees, called it a time of great opportunity: "We are excited to officially merge with a school as respected as Moody, while continuing to provide a solid biblical education in the Detroit area. This merger will provide new opportunities for both schools to be more effective in preparing students for ministry and advancing the Kingdom."[4]

The merger benefited all students, according to then-Provost Charles Dyer. The Michigan campus, located in suburban Detroit, "brings a well-established counseling program and Moody brings an effective online education program; combining the two schools offers students access to courses and ways of studying they may not have had otherwise," Dyer said.[5] At the time of the merger almost two hundred Detroit students joined the four hundred Chicago students.

## DEGREES OF CHOICE

Today prospective students can choose from many graduate-level degree programs. Through MTS–Michigan, students can earn a master of arts degree in Christian Education (MACE), or counseling/psychology (MACP), a master of theological studies (MTS), or a master of divinity (MDiv). Moody Theological Seminary now is one of only four schools offering an MA in counseling/psychology, which can lead to licensed legal counselor certification to become a professional counselor.

Meanwhile, students with a baccalaureate from a general or Bible college admitted to either campus can earn a master of arts in one of four fields: biblical studies, intercultural studies, spiritual formation and discipleship, and urban studies (known as MABS, MAIS, MASF/D, and MAUS). A ninth graduate degree option appeared in the fall of 2010, a master in ministry leadership (MAML). This new degree program provides "advanced training in leadership for current and future pastors, ministry leaders in churches, managers in Christian organizations, business-as-mission entrepreneurs, missionaries, teachers, administrators and evangelists."[6]

All those master's programs require sixty credit hours, but a tenth master's-level program offers a professional degree and requires ninety-six credit hours: the master of divinity. The MDiv program began on the Chicago campus in fall 1999, the same year the MAUS began. (The MAIS and MASF/D began in fall 2000.) Today the MDiv offers four emphases: pastoral, spiritual formation/discipleship, ministry leadership, and intercultural/urban studies. The program seeks "to provide in-depth biblical and practical preparation for those desiring to minister in churches or parachurch organizations, whether in the United States or abroad."[7] Graduates of the program include pastors as well as associate pastors, Christian education directors, youth pastors, and women's ministry directors.

## CERTIFICATES OF CHOICE

The school also offers graduate certificates for completing one year of graduate-level studies. The one-year curriculum had originated in 1971 as the Advanced Studies Program, which offered special classes through the undergraduate school. ASP helped prepare college graduates without Bible training for missions and ministry as Bible teachers. In fall 1990 the ASP joined the MGS and became the first graduate certificate program.

Today the graduate certificate program is anchored by the certificate in biblical studies (the former ASP), and includes certificate programs in intercultural studies, spiritual formation and discipleship, and urban studies, as well as ministry leadership. Graduates of the program march with MA and MDiv grads on commencement day but simply receive their graduation certificate.

## WHY A SEMINARY?

Some have wondered why the Moody Graduate School became a seminary. After all, D. L. Moody began the Institute with the idea it would not compete with the seminaries of its day. Vice President and MTS Dean John Jelinek explains that the focus of the seminary aligns with the vision of MBI's founder: "We are going to continue to be MGS in the sense that we offer urban studies, intercultural studies, and ministry leadership."

**MBI IMPACT** ( The First Graduate )

Of the six students who marched to the platform in May 1988 to receive their MAMin degrees and academic hoods, Rob Jones may have been the most patient. He had earned his degree in December 1987 but waited six months to receive his diploma, choosing to march with five other classmates duirng the official ceremony held the following spring.

Jones had heard about the impending graduate school while attending the 1983 MBI Pastors' Conference as pastor of Cornerstone Bible Church in southern Ohio. Two years later he enrolled in the first classes, and he would become the first (and only) graduate of Moody Graduate School in 1987. He called the MGS program with its weeklong modular courses several times a year God's answer to "the desire of my heart—a quality education without leaving (or moving) family and ministry."

The one-week modulars, with their pre- and postcourse assignments, continue today, offering convenience for those in full-time ministry. Jones describes the postclass projects as "so practical that I never felt any class was merely theoretical. Most of the projects eventually took the form of church ministries that helped us toward our part in accomplishing the Great Commission."*

Upon graduation, Jones accepted the call to pastor Judson Baptist Church, a largely Caucasian church located in a heavily African-American neighborhood in nearby Oak Park. He came with a vision "to reach our community for Christ." When he left five years later, "the congregation was happy with its new identity and its 45 percent African-American composition," he says.

"The graduate school had prepared me for a cross-cultural ministry." Then the first MGS grad adds: "It turned out that God used even me—an Appalachian hillbilly—to build up this wonderful body of believers."

*Rob Jones, "They Said It Couldn't Be Done," *MGS Servant*, June 1995, 9.

Jelinek acknowledges that MBI was founded "to fill a gap that the seminary was not filling." The new seminary now "is more of the ideal place to fill that gap. . . . It fits hand in glove with Moody's mission if you look at what we're doing in terms of urban studies and intercultural studies, our evangelism classes. We go out and witness right outside the Jewel store. Our faculty take the student right out on the street. It's that academic, professional, relational component." [8]

Seminary training is vital in the twenty-first century, and Jelinek says students in post-baccalaureate studies appreciate Moody's heritage and reputation. "While other seminaries are in the area offering a master of divinity, there is something about the Bible gold standard in Moody that makes it more attractive, [so we] offer an MDiv."

Today each professor comes "field tested." More than academicians, their background in the field, whether as missionary, pastor, or parachurch leader, makes them practitioners who also are scholars. So, unlike the graduate school's original team-teaching model (see page 88), students find in each instructor the prof/practioner combined. Students can choose to take several courses online and many in the one-week modular format. Modular courses are essential in classes that require face-to-face interaction, Jelinek says, "where you can objectively validate character." Although students may enjoy online coursework for its scheduling convenience, there is limited interaction. He points out that a total online program could produce a graduate who is "academically qualified to answer a set of questions and [has] no people skills whatsoever. I don't want to send out a student who has completed every course online but lacks every social skill you can imagine."

## INNOVATIVE FROM THE BEGINNING

From the very beginning, the Moody Graduate School—now Moody Theological Seminary—was innovative. The modular format that offered one-week intensive courses with pre- and postcourse assignments was ideal for students already in ministry. Courses were offered once a quarter in either Chicago or Florida during the first five years, and MGS was essentially a commuter school. In 1987, nearly 90 percent of students were at least thirty years old and 75 percent had been in full-time Christian service at least ten years.[9]

The one-week modular form continues today, but for students in residence, weekly three-hour class meetings are also available. In 1990 the graduate certificate program and MABS curriculum had introduced a new paradigm in MGS education model. Students were invited to remain on campus the entire semester, taking sixteen-week courses. This attracted younger students who could devote full-time to their graduate studies. (In 2010, the percentage of students at age thirty or more was down to 65 percent, the rest being in their twenties.) They could live in campus housing or off-site. Both students in residence and who commute may take certain courses online. MAMin students created strong bonds during the one-week modules, the intensive classes preceded and followed by at-home studies. But for students in classes for more than three months, even closer friendships developed.

The graduate school began in 1985 after an exploratory committee formed in 1984 at the urging of President George Sweeting and under the leadership of Dean of Education Ken Hanna. The committee included four undergraduate school professors, educational consultants from seminaries and missions agencies, and MBI educational administrator Richard Patterson. They completed research, compiled results, and soon launched the school. Upon his retirement, Dr. Hopkins revealed that Hanna asked him three different times to become the graduate school academic dean and leave his position as a professor of Bible in the undergraduate school. Though he hesitated twice, Hopkins said, in the end "I took it, and I have loved it for the past fifteen years."[10] He retired in 2001 and was succeeded by Joseph Henriques, who served through 2007. In 2008 Dr. Jelinek became the third dean of the school.

## A DISTINCTIVE EDUCATIONAL PHILOSOPHY

Hopkins and his team developed a distinctive educational philosophy, which has been refined under Academic Deans Henriques and Jelinek. In 1990, with the inauguration of the Graduate Studies Program with its one-year certificate studies, Hopkins introduced total person training (TPT), which emphasized the triad essential to complete learning: *knowing, being,* and *doing. Knowing* required course work, *being* required the development and evaluation of character, and *doing* required practice in the field. Later the three became the *cognitive, character,* and *competence.* Today they are known as the *academic,* the *relational,* and the *professional.*

No matter the labels, the ideal of training the whole person—going beyond head knowledge to affect every element of the person's life—has appealed to both faculty and the students they prepare. Former professor Richard Calenberg once wrote, "How thrilled I was to join the faculty of a school to implement such an educational approach!" Professor John Fuder joined the faculty in 1995 and concludes the school has always sought to "prepare its graduates with a strong biblical, academic grounding. The Word of God would be front and center, but we also would be deeply after your character." And Professor Bill Thrasher, who has taught at MTS for twenty years, believes the threefold emphasis on academic, relational, and professional training has attracted many international students.[11]

Originally students met with a professor and fellow students in their emphasis during a weekly colloquium to discuss challenges. The meeting featured interaction, honest disclosure, and a time of prayer. It became a key component for faculty and students to measure character (the relational). In another weekly meeting, called a practicum (held in connection with a student's internship), faculty and students measured their capability (the professional). Later the colloquia were renamed spiritual integration labs. Today they are known as biblical spiritual formation labs, taken in conjunction with the course Biblical Spiritual Formation. The idea is that the teacher will be more than a scholar; he is a mentor and leader as well.

## CHARACTER COUNTS

Male professors lead male students in the weekly labs; female professors and wives of professors lead female students. "Picture a one-hour gathering of seven or eight students with a faculty member [or faculty wife]," says Professor Fuder, "and the primary agenda is character related:

spiritual disciplines that they would be working on, prayer focus together, and accountability." It is part of the curriculum and required. Other elements that help students develop and faculty evaluate character are chapels and private meetings with advisors.

Today students in most master's programs complete an internship. Field education remains a key way of evaluating relational (character) and professional growth. At one point students completed three internships. At this point most do one or two, depending on their master's program. MGS Dean Hopkins outlined several of the benefits of field education in an interview shortly before he retired:

> Students need to get on the field. They need to stub their toes, to fall down, and have an arm put around them, or a pat on the back. Someway, somehow, they need to do the work of the ministry.
>
> It is vital to have various environments in addition to the classroom. We use the local church, the marketplace, the group, one on one, to provide different settings. When you do this, students are more teachable.[12]

Character is displayed through outreaches and ministry. During such ministries students can be inconvenienced or face confrontational or even hostile attitudes, according to Fuder. "I watch students responding humbly, handling a little bit of ridicule. A lot of character is measured beautifully in those settings. Hands-on ministry is a way of measuring character."[13]

Similarly, mentors in a student's fieldwork are asked to evaluate a student's character. Mentors evaluate how well students performed assignments and also their character. "Part of performance is character," Fuder says. "We basically act as who we are in Christ. If a church is going to hire an associate pastor or a youth pastor, we will want to know as much about their character as about their skill set—to preach, teach, lead music."

## SERVICE IN THE CITY

Moody Theological Seminary is not the only seminary in Chicago, but with its location one mile from the center of downtown and its desire to honor the urban outreach of founder D. L. Moody, its urban focus is unmistakable. Emphases in urban studies are available in its graduate certificate program and in the master of arts. Its heart for the city is seen most dramatically in its annual Service in the City day, open to MTS students in residence on the Chicago campus. (See page 166–67 for a description of SITC in 2010).

The first SITC began when the annual winter retreat for students had to be cancelled when the facility had a conflict. With no alternate location but the date open, the MGS team planned a day of service. The school contacted several ministries where they had internships and long relationships. "Can you use some Moody students?" MGS leaders asked. "We have this opening on our calendar."

"We met on campus, prayed up, teamed up," says Professor Fuder. "We went into the communities and served as needed."

"It was a total hit," Fuder recalls. He returned to the graduate school to propose a new spring outreach. MGS embraced the idea, which became Service in the City. Today students plan SITC to help existing ministries, especially churches, that serve throughout Chicago. They ask fellow students in local churches to see if their congregations want help. The activities range from planning a youth program and doing a construction project, to helping Christian agencies to work with refugees, to helping churches in diverse religious communities to reach out to Muslim or Buddhist neighbors.

The all-day event, led by MTS faculty and student leaders, often has students eating lunch in an ethnic restaurant in the community. At day's end students return to the Alumni Student Center for a debriefing on what happened in various neighborhoods, view a PowerPoint of pictures taken that day, give testimonies, and conclude with a time of worship through music and prayer.

## A MOTTO FOR MINISTRY

In 2010 MTS moved from the third floor of Smith Hall to the first floor of Fitzwater Hall. The new location brought greater prominence to MTS, with new signage on the front of the building, declaring "Moody Theological Seminary" and easier access for students and guests. At the same time a seminary motto appeared: Transformational Scholarship for Exceptional Ministry Leadership.

"By 'transformational scholarship' we mean that we want personal study and research to impact the person's life," says David Woodall, chairman of the department of Bible and theology. "We want the biblical text to first change our lives and bring us to a position where we can then minister effectively to others. It's not scholarship for the sake of scholarship. It is the impact of that on one's life."[14]

Woodall and Eric Moore, chairman of the practical ministries department that oversees field educational programs (assisted by internship director Jayanthi Benjamin), review course syllabi, confer with professors, and bring faculty ideas and concerns to the seminary administrative team. The two chairmen and the rest of the administrative team coordinate accreditation of the school. MTS has accreditation from the Higher Learning Commission of the North Central Association and the Association for Biblical Higher Education. MTS–Chicago is also pursuing accreditation with the Association of Theological Schools.

Looking at the MTS educational model of academic, relational, and professional components, Dr. Woodall emphasizes the school's desire for balance. "We want to be balanced in every area. Solid biblical interpretation transforms the character of the student and leads to excellence in ministry practice."

Dr. Jelinek calls this educational model the Ezran Archetype. "Ezra made a purposeful resolve: he would fervently study the law of God, practice it in his daily life and then teach others what he learned (Ezra 7:10)," Jelinek explains in a letter to students in the MGS catalog. "Our programs are designed to help you not only to study the Word, but also to apply it personally and then incarnate its truth, as Ezra did."[15] To remind faculty and students of these three goals, Ezra 7:10 is written in

Hebrew on the wall adjacent to his office for all to see as they enter his door.

## A DIVERSE FACULTY

From its beginning, the MTS faculty has maintained and eventually increased its ethnic diversity. Among its first six full-time faculty, one (17 percent) was African-American. Today a full one-third of the fifteen full-time faculty are non-Caucasian. They are of African, Chinese/Dutch West Indian, and Indian backgrounds. They reflect the cultural diversity of America and indeed the global church as they prepare students to serve in the United States and around the world.

The diverse faculty also reflects the intentional approach of the three academic deans who have led the graduate school. For example, in 1999, Dean Hopkins asked recent MABS graduate Berlean Burris, an African-American, to become a faculty member and direct the MGS internship program. Mrs. Burris left her position as vice president for community affairs at National-Louis University (Chicago), and she directed the internship program and counseled students at the graduate school for six years.

Joseph Henriques, the second dean of the graduate school and himself Portuguese, maintained the focus on a diverse faculty, telling students, "MGS faculty, staff and students will reflect the ethnic diversity of both Chicago and the nation."[16] He coauthored the book *Cultural Change in Your Church: Helping Your Church Thrive in a Diverse Society*. Current vice president and dean John Jelinek is Native American and has maintained faculty diversity, with 33 percent of academics being non-Caucasian in 2010.

## A DIVERSE STUDENT BODY

Significantly, MTS students reflect a similar diversity of backgrounds. Among domestic and international students, 34 percent of all enrollees were non-Caucasian in fall 2008, according to Randall Dattoli, associate academic dean of MTS.

Dattoli believes the underlying success in attracting a diverse student body comes partly from ongoing prayer and the Moody reputation. "We believe in prayer and asking God to bring the people of His choosing." All three academic deans have focused on prayer among the faculty and staff, notes Dattoli.

The Moody reputation is about name recognition and respect, says Dattoli. He notes that many minority students have come to know and respect MBI after hearing broadcasts on Moody Radio or reading books by Moody Publishers. "And the Moody Science films cannot be ignored in terms of the Moody name in the international arena," attracting overseas students to MBI.[17]

Professor Thrasher agrees the Moody brand attracts both domestic and international non-Caucasians. But he believes the intentional recruiting of a diverse faculty set the tone from the beginning.

He traces this value to the exploratory committee. "Dr. Hopkins was the leader of the committee, but the committee was on board with [this value]. There was a great agreement in educational philosophy, trying to serve the whole body of Christ. We wanted a diversity that fit with us theologically and educationally." Each dean has been intentional in trying to include a diverse, multinational faculty, according to Thrasher.

Professor Fuder also attributes the ethnic diversity to the school's early influence in the Chicago community. "A lot of [the diversity] dates to those early connections, when students came because they sensed the graduate school was committed to the city." He says the intentionality for a global mix goes back to Dr. Hopkins. "There was a heart for the city from the beginning here." He also recalls that Dr. Henriques, the second dean of the graduate school, prayed for a student from every nation to come.

Today Moody Theological Seminary and Graduate School continues to seek students of every color, tribe, and nation who desire to know God's Word and gain knowledge (academic), develop character (relational) and apply it (professional) to a lifetime of ministry.

## NOTES

1. "First Graduates This Month," *Moody Graduate School Bulletin*, May 1988, 1.

2. Ibid.

3. "Merger Receives Approval," November 10, 2009, www.moodyministries.net/crp_NewsDetail.aspx?id=44770].

4. "Merger Becomes Official," January 4, 2010, www.moodyministries.net/crp_News-Detail.aspx?id=46524].

5. "Merger Receives Approval," November 10, 2009.

6. The MAML program has similarities to the MAMin program, and the MAMin degree no longer will be offered to incoming sudents.

7. Catalog description; online at http://www.moody.edu/edu_mainpage.aspx?id=161.

8. All statements from John Jelinek are from a personal interview on June 10, 2010.

9. "MGS: A Program for Veterans," MGS Bulletin, 1.

10. "Dr. Hopkins to Retire," MGS Servant, January–February 2000, 4.

11. Richard Calenberg, "Total Person Training," Servant, January 1995, 1; John Fuder, personal interview, November 10, 2010; Bill Thrasher, personal interview, November 12, 2010.

12. "Dr. Hopkins to Retire," MGS Servant, 5.

13. All statements by John Fuder are from a personal interview on November 10, 2010.

14. David Woodall, telephone interview, November 24, 2010.

15. Moody Graduate School Bulletin, 2010–2011, 4.

16. Joseph Henriques, Servant, "Learners Who Practice 'That the World May Know,'" Fall 2001, 3.

17. All statements by Randall Dattoli are from a personal interview on November 17, 2010.

# 12

# A Legacy of Innovation

The entrepreneurial spirit of D. L. Moody has pervaded the ministries of MBI since the beginning. Consider these "firsts": The Institute established the first program to train church musicians . . . offered the first three-year program in Jewish studies . . . printed and sold inexpensive books for the masses . . . and offered the first correspondence course on radio after launching the first noncommercial educational and religious radio station.

More recently, Moody Bible Institute:

- Became the second Bible college to achieve accreditation with the NCA Higher Learning Commission (1987).
- Opened an athletics center (1990) for students and staff that also operated as an urban outreach center. Today guests from youth organizations, ministries, and summer camps still play and learn on its three basketball courts and in its classrooms.
- Began audio streaming (2007) with Moody Radio, launching three audio worldwide channels with specialized, themed content.

- Began to offer digital versions of its titles (2007) for downloading e-books onto electronic reading devices that now range from Amazon's Kindle to Barnes & Noble's Nook to the ever-popular Apple iPhone and other smartphones, as well as computer tablets like the iPad.

Yet innovation needs to be rooted in discernment. The leadership of a long-lived and dynamic organization like MBI must continually assess the effectiveness of its various ministries. Has a program reached the end of its useful life? Are there other opportunities that would be a wiser use of limited resources? Is a particular ministry area "on mission"? What external challenges are impacting the ministry environment?

The 1990s and early 2000s witnessed some significant transitions in several innovative "legacy ministries": the extension department, Moody Institute of Science, *Moody* magazine, and Moody Aviation.

## WELCOME TO MOODY!

The oldest, the extension department, began in 1887 by offering classes to the public and soon included traveling speakers: MBI instructors and other Bible teachers and evangelists. Moody Bible conferences grew in the 1920s, but its signature event remained the annual Founder's Week Bible conference. At one point the conference spanned seven days, including a Sunday "Festival of Praise." It now meets five days (Monday through Friday) each year. The conference would outgrow Torrey-Gray Auditorium and at times draws crowds up to 4,000 at Moody Memorial Church, one mile north of campus.

In 1985, the extension department was renamed conference ministries, with an emphasis on specialty conferences, including pastors' conferences, marriage conferences, and men's and women's gatherings, both in Chicago and other locations across the US. In 2007, conference ministries became the conference team as it joined the newly formed event and guest services department, which was created in 2006. This department provides organization for internal and external events, campus lodging, supervision of main campus desks, and other guest services for a busy and multifaceted institution. The annual Founder's Week conference, of course, continues.

## A WINDOW ON CREATION

Many Christians recall the wonder of such films as *City of the Bees*, produced by the Moody Institute of Science. Its visionary founder, Irwin Moon, launched MIS in 1945 with a film production company linked to Sermons from Science. Those "sermons," featuring science demonstrations, humor, and spiritual applications, had begun in 1938 as part of the extension department. As part of MIS, the Sermons from Science platform demonstrations would attract large crowds in a variety of settings, including four world's fairs and three summer Olympics (Munich, Montreal, and Atlanta). Sermons from Science featured audience participation and science experiments both dramatic and revealing. (See the side feature, "Zapped by One Million Volts.")

Together, Sermons and the film studio used science as a window into recognizing and appreciating a powerful God behind all creation. The staff included scientists and engineers who developed MIS films that soon would eclipse the live science demonstrations in impact.

Moon and his team caught the attention of both the Christian and general public with their first film, *God of Creation*. Scenes of blossoms that matured in seconds instead of weeks and a caterpillar growing, cocooning, and emerging from its chrysalis in just over a minute formed a remarkable motion picture in 1945. One year later three film companies asked Moon to help them. Cinerama wanted Moon to produce a science film for them. MGM wanted to release his films. Walt Disney met with Moon to request MIS do some filming on the wonders of nature for Disney's films. Moon rejected all three, although later he agreed to let Disney have some of the footage for free.[1]

During the next fifty-plus years, more than two dozen science films screened across America and overseas, viewed by schoolchildren, American soldiers, and audiences in 130 countries. The goal all along was to show "convincing evidence that the God of creation was also the God of redemption."[2]

**MBI IMPACT** ⟨ Zapped by One Million Volts ⟩

For more than fifty years, one of three different men would step on an electrical transformer holding a long piece of wood. "Fire!" he yelled. As the sound of crackling electricity echoed through the auditorium, his body would tense. One million volts surged through his body, and within seconds fire spread from just above the handle and climbed the board.

"Off!" yelled the man after fifteen seconds, and after a moment of stunned silence, the audience broke into applause.

Dean Ortner, the last man to climb atop the electrical coil as part of a Sermons from Science demonstration, once told a reporter, "I hate standing on top of that coil. I never know how it is going to affect me or how bad it is going to hurt." He normally climbed the coil just once every four nights at the climax of his Sermons from Science presentation. During his early days, he mounted the coil at the 1976 Olympics in Montreal every night for three weeks.

He survived, as did his predecessors, George Speake and originator Irwin Moon, because the electrical frequency had been changed from the normal deadly sixty cycles to 65,000 cycles. Still, the audience could see each man's body tighten as the electrical current moved to its discharge point through his fingers, into the aluminum base, and into the board. Afterward, Ortner, Speake, and Moon were physically exhausted.

Ortner chose to climb the coil to prove a point of faith. "No other illustration shows so vividly that if you are out of tune with the source of power, you will not be affected. I am not killed on the coil because my

---

The growing popularity of home video in the 1980s prompted MIS to transfer most of their films to video, with the help of two gifted filmmakers, Lad Allen and Jerry Harned. Allen and Harned culled archives for classic scenes and continued to produce, direct, and film many of the video projects. Contemporary music and inspiring Christian hymns

body's cycles are out of tune with the coil's.

"If you are not related to or in tune with God, He can't affect you, and you can't tap into His source of power."

Dr. Moon was on the coil first as an extension department speaker and then continued a couple of years at Moody Institute of Science, before passing the baton in 1947 to Speake. But he came back for a special appearance in 1956 as host of the MIS film *Facts of Faith*.

At the end of that film Moon returns to the discharge coil, hands his suit coat to an assistant, climbs the coil, and raises the board above him. When he shouts, "On!" the electrical buzzing begins. His arm tightens, his body crouches, and a flame soon emerges, a black char line preceding it upward.

It remains a classic moment in a series of classic films, most marked by innovations. The most honored film, *City of the Bees* (released in 1962), records for the first time unique behaviors of the honeybee, including the "dance of the scout bees" that will direct worker bees along the right path to the nectar. Research and filming consumed ten years. But MIS had to halt filming early to develop special photographic equipment, including new camera lights. The lighting team had been frying the bees with their high-intensity lights. They solved the problem with a strobe unit synchronized to the camera shutter for short, quick bursts of light. This illuminated the scene but left the bees and waxy hive undisturbed.* (All science films are available in DVD format through Moody Publishers.)

---

* Gary L. Wall, "The Man on the Coil, *Moody Monthly*, March 1979, 111–12; Carin Morehead, "Moody Institute of Science: Historical Time Line," 6.

---

combined with classic scenes from MIS archives to create a series of award-winning videos. *This Is the Day* (1988) won best video of the year from the Christian Film and Video Association, and two of the next four releases earned various awards. *The Wonders of God's Creation*, a three-part series, won three awards, including best video of the year. The next year, 1993, *Reader's Digest* began a direct-mail campaign that would sell more than 700,000 sets of *Wonders.*

The 1996 MIS film—released directly to video—*Journey to the Edge of Creation,* would be the final filmed MIS production. In 1997 the Whittier soundstage was active during shooting of the first four videos of an original video series, *Newton's Workshop,* but later that year the California MIS office closed. MIS was renamed Moody Video. In 1998, all the MIS equipment, slides, films, and historical photographs were shipped to Chicago.

Moody Video would continue for five more years, earning awards and enjoying some success in the homeschooling market. Having served well depicting a "God of wonders," Moody Video closed in 2003. Yet the complete library of films remains available on DVD.

## LEGACY, MINISTRY, EXCELLENCE

There was a time when many Christian households knew MBI primarily through the monthly visits of *Moody* magazine, which over the decades evolved from an MBI-centric publication to an acclaimed general interest magazine. *Moody* magazine, more than one hundred years a part of Moody Bible Institute, boasted a storied history.

It is a measure of the magazine's importance to the Institute that R. A. Torrey and James Gray, the second and third presidents, served as coeditors in the very earliest days, when the periodical was known as *The Institute Tie.* Gray continued as editor after Torrey left the Institute. While editor, he piloted the magazine for twenty-eight years, as it became *The Christian Worker's Magazine* (1910) and later (1920) *Moody Bible Institute Monthly.*

When Will Houghton became president in 1934, the magazine had about 40,000 subscribers. In 1938 the magazine was renamed simply *Moody Monthly,* and Houghton began to vigorously promote the publication. Circulation climbed to almost 75,000 under his leadership. Paid circulation would exceed 100,000 by the early 1960s. Led by such publishing professionals as Wayne Christianson (1950s and 1960s) and Jerry Jenkins (1970s), *Moody Monthly* soon featured full-color covers and more appealing graphics. [3]

More practical articles appeared in each issue, though biblical and doctrinal teaching remained a staple. And the magazine soon earned top awards for design, themes, and articles. The Evangelical Press Association named *Moody Monthly* its "Periodical of the Year" in 1957, an award Moody would garner several times over the next four-plus decades.

Readership continued to increase. The most spectacular growth occurred in the early 1970s, as the magazine entered into a national direct marketing campaign. Within two years, by 1974, circulation was approaching 250,000, making it the leading general interest periodical for evangelical Christians.

A hallmark of the magazine, in keeping with an MBI emphasis on applying the "Word to the world," was solid reporting and analysis of current events and ethical issues. In May 1980, *Moody Monthly* published its most-circulated and perhaps most-talked-about issue ever, an analysis of the abortion controversy at a time when the issue was just beginning to appear on evangelical radar.[4] The magazine featured an interview with Dr. C. Everett Koop, noted pediatric surgeon and soon-to-be U.S. Surgeon General under President Ronald Reagan. Dr. Koop criticized abortionists and eloquently defended the rights of the unborn.

In 1990 *Moody Monthly* was renamed simply *Moody,* a nod to the fact a combined summer issue meant only eleven issues each year. While the editorial and visual quality of the magazine remained uniformly high under editors Andy Scheer and later Betsey Newenhuyse, cultural changes began to impact *Moody* and, indeed, all magazines. A proliferation of media choices and the growth of niche periodicals, even in Christian publishing, challenged readership and advertising. The magazine was no longer the chief source for Christian news and inspiration; readers had many alternatives. One magazine study team, analyzing the competition, concluded that *Christianity Today* focused on ministry professionals, *Discipleship Journal* on small group leaders and participants, *World* on Christians in society, and *Moody* on laypersons in the church. Each was competing for a slice of a shrinking "pie" of consumers—even without reckoning the growing impact of the Internet.[5]

Still, letters and e-mails from readers showed a strong loyalty to and engagement with the magazine. A 2002 cover package asking "Is there a right way to worship?" sparked lively debate in the magazine's pages. But the "perfect storm" combination of declining advertising revenue, a static subscriber base, a changing media environment, and the post-September 11 economic downturn was ultimately too much to overcome. In 2003 senior leadership made the difficult decision to close a 103-year chapter in the life of the Institute. The July/August 2003 issue would be the last.

## "THE FUTURE OF TRUTH"

The final issue featured a cover package on the "Future of Truth," with Christian leaders ranging from Billy Graham, Chuck Colson, Nancy Leigh DeMoss, and Bill Hybels to Matt Odmark of the contemporary Christian music group Jars of Clay answering the question, "How can we followers of Christ share/live out the gospel in our culture at a time when the gospel is being challenged as much as ever?" Longtime favorites Dr. George Sweeting, Joni Eareckson Tada, Jerry B. Jenkins, and President Stowell shared their final magazine columns.

In his "Front Lines" column, President Stowell revealed that evangelist Billy Graham had told him *Moody* "is the only magazine [I read] on a regular basis." Stowell then added: "*Moody* magazine expresses the very heart of the ministry of the Moody Bible Institute as it comes alongside dedicated followers of Jesus to enable . . . them to think biblically, live Christianly, serve faithfully, and share their faith effectively."[6]

A postscript: After it closed, the magazine, which underwent a makeover in 2002, won seven Evangelical Press Association awards, including honors for cover, art, photography, and publication redesign.

## A NEW FLIGHT PATH

We have already explored the growth of Moody Aviation in the postwar boom years. But eventually inflation affected the program, particularly at the turn of the new century. Operating costs for the missionary aviation technology department had always been high, due to expenses for fuel, flight insurance, flight training, and equipment. Those costs continued to climb. Students paid tuition, but program costs traditionally exceeded revenues, which the board of trustees found acceptable because of the program's contribution to worldwide missions. The trustees were willing to subsidize the Elizabethton, Tennessee, program for a significant amount. But in 2000, financial analysis revealed that the program was costing the Institute considerably more.

Then, when the terrorists hijacked and crashed four jetliners into the twin towers of New York's World Trade Center, the Pentagon, and a rural Pennsylvania field, the fallout affected all aviation. The Federal Aviation Authority grounded both commercial and general aviation. Suddenly Moody Aviation had its wings clipped—without student flight training, student income in Elizabethton disappeared, even as operating costs remained. Then premiums for flight insurance quickly soared. Finally, the economy faltered after the attacks, the stock market dropped, and a new mood of uncertainty gripped the country.

With the Institute facing significant financial challenges, senior leadership looked at more cost-effective plans for continuing the Moody Aviation program. The decision was made to relocate a restructured aviation program from Tennessee to Spokane, where a regional classroom existed and a strong Moody supporter had reported the presence of airframe and power plant (A&P) classes through local colleges and a major municipal airport, Felts Field.[7]

## REINVENTING MOODY AVIATION

The relocation was not a sudden decision, and neither was Moody Aviation permanently grounded. The premier program, which had trained at least 50 percent of all mission pilots, would soon soar again.

MBI educational leaders had found two colleges very interested in offering aircraft maintenance courses and a Moody adjunct faculty already in place, teaching Bible and theology courses in the regional classroom setting. But what could simulate hills and valleys of the mission field once the aviation program left Elizabethton and the Great Smoky Mountains? They learned the hilly terrain of the western slopes of the Rockies awaited less than fifty miles east of Spokane. The trustees approved the move in April 2003, and appointed an ad hoc aviation advisory committee to work with the administration in implementing the change.

A separate advisory council, comprising Mission Aviation Fellowship, JAARS, and other agency representatives, met with program manager Cecil Bedford. Together they began to craft a new, more responsive Moody Aviation for students who would begin their maintenance and flight courses in 2005. They chose Spokane Community College to teach most A&P courses. To reduce costs yet offer the perspective and passion of mission professionals, Moody Aviation added "seconds" from mission agencies as teachers. "Seconded" personnel are agency pilots on home assignment with their mission agency,[8] who serve their agency by teaching at a missionary aviation schools' maintenance or flight courses.

## MOODY AVIATION:
## THE PREMIER FLIGHT SCHOOL

With the help of the advisory committee composed of missionary agency representatives, the program has been sharpened in its first seven years in Spokane, as the committee advised on the curriculum and made recommendations. The famed Moody Aviation program continues its stellar reputation. Mission Aviation Fellowship believes so. Vice President of Human Resources Gene Jordan gave his Coca-Cola seal of approval in 2007 (see "From Cola to Coke"). And during a fall 2009 advisory committee meeting, MAF announced its approval of Moody graduates with a faculty recommendation and a consult flight (a flight with a missions aviation representative who observes the student pilot)[9] to attend the MAF technical evaluation (TE).

That's a sign of confidence in the quality of Moody training, Bedford says. "Historically the missions agencies require 400 to 500 hours [of flight time]" before they invite candidates to their TE camp. . . . Bedford calls MAF's invitation of students to the early technical evaluation "their seal of approval."

Today the aviation program is part of Moody–Spokane, a thriving satellite campus. In 2009–10, eighty-nine students attended classes, with

# ( From Cola to Coke )

When Moody Bible Institute relocated Moody Aviation from Tennessee to Washington, it came up with a new paradigm, and mission agencies took a wait-and-see attitude. But Cecil Bedford, Moody aviation director, knew the program had found success when a mission official told him the program was once more "producing Coke."

The first year in Spokane, Gene Jordan, vice president of human resources for Mission Aviation Fellowship, told Bedford during an early visit to the new program, "I don't know what your graduate is going to look like." Jordan compared his evaluation of Moody to his search for a reliable cola.

"When I was the South American regional director for Mission Aviation Fellowship and bought a Coke there, I always knew what I was buying. If I bought a cola, I had little idea what I was going to get. This speaks of the consistency that Coke maintains around the world.

"When we accepted graduates from the Elizabethton program, we got Coke. We always knew exactly what we were getting. When we got graduates from other programs, or through FBO training, we never quite knew what we were getting; we felt like we were getting cola.

"Right now, where Moody Aviation is in the move to Spokane, we're not sure we're getting Coke. When we take a graduate from the Moody Aviation–Spokane program, we want Coke."

In 2007, Gene Jordan came to watch and congratulate the first graduating class. After the commissioning service, Bedford called Jordan to the podium and gave him a can of Coca-Cola. "At graduation, Gene, I present to you a can of Coke."

Several weeks later, when Jordan spoke to the MAF board of directors, he mentioned the gift can of Coke he received. "He actually presented a Coke can to his board to say that Moody Aviation was once again producing Coke," recalled Bedford.

Gene has since framed a picture of the first Spokane aviation graduating class. It sits beside the can of Coke. "It is a representation of the relationship between MAF and Moody," Bedford says. "He was saying, 'When we get a Moody graduate, we know what we are getting.'"

ten awarded the bachelor of science in missionary aviation technology in May 2010. In the fall of 2010, a record 102 students were in training to become missionary pilots/mechanics and maintenance specialists.

The impact of Moody Aviation remains. A 2003 survey by Moody Aviation found that 68 percent of those graduating between 1995 and 2002 are serving in mission aviation. With four graduating classes, from 2007–2010 from Moody–Spokane thus far, many MA alumni are now preparing with agencies, even as they develop financial support. When a new survey is completed in a couple of years (2012), Bedford believes the percentage will be much higher than the 68 percent in the 2003 survey.

## NOTES

1. Carin Morehead, "Moody Institute of Science: Historical Time Line," report, 1994, MIS archives, 5. Moon declined Cinerama because (1) he felt an audience going for entertainment should not pay for an educational and spiritual storyline, and (2) there would be no opportunity for moviegoers to discuss what they had just seen. He rejected MGM because again he believed his films would not be effective in commercial movie theaters. Morehead reports that Moon eventually agreed to Disney's request because he concluded Disney's nature films indirectly revealed the Creator God.

2. "50th Anniversary," brochure, 1995, n.p. From 1945–85, the Moody Institute of Science released twenty-nine science films; for children MIS filmed twenty Bible stories and kid-friendly adaptations of several of its award-winning films.

3. Robert G. Flood, Jerry B. Jenkins, *Teaching the Word, Reaching the World* (Chicago: Moody, 1985). 222.

4. Ibid., 218.

5. "The Unique Mission of *Moody* Magazine," report to President Joseph Stowell, February 20, 2003, 12.

6. Joseph Stowell, "For Everything a Season," *Moody*, July/August 2003, 8.

7. Details of the transition of Moody Aviation from Tennessee to Washington are from Charles H. Dyer, "Reinventing Moody Aviation," October 10, 2003; a case study presented to the MBI board of trustees.

8. Missionary pilots may be on home assignment for a variety of reasons, according to Moody Aviation Director Cecil Bedford. Some are home for health reasons, some for education needs of children, some because of a closed mission field. "All are here by God's design . . . The tenure of our on-loan staff varies by mission and reason for assignment," Bedford says. All quotations from Cecil Bedford are from a telephone interview on May 19, 2010.

9. The faculty recommendation indicates to the agency the graduating student "is mission ready from the maturity standpoint as well as the technical standpoint of flight

maintenance, and we are willing to put a stamp on it that says, 'he's ready to go," says Bedford. The agency will do one consult when the student is preparing for his private license, and a second while training for his commercial license. The consult helps the student put a face to the prospective mission agency and helps MA staff evaluate the progress of our students and the effectiveness of the curriculum.

# 13

# Biblical Mission, Global Vision

A portrait of Henry P. Crowell hangs on a wall facing the office of Ed Cannon, chief operating officer of Moody Bible Institute. Sometimes Cannon feels someone is looking over his shoulder.

"It's like he's keeping an eye on what we're doing here. He had essentially my job when he was employed by the Institute. He was the chairman of the board but [oversaw daily operations]." Crowell also was chief executive officer of Quaker Oats, a company he cofounded.

"I have his picture out there to remind me of his ethics, his focus, his discipline, and his fortitude—forty years [as trustee board chairman]. It's a reminder to me: We've got to uphold the character and business acumen of that man. That's a high bar."[1]

Cannon, along with President Paul Nyquist and the present board of directors, maintain the standards begun by Crowell. In 1910 MBI became one of the charter clients of Ernst & Whinney, now Ernst & Young. Through their auditing process, the Institute has maintained strong accounting controls for more than one hundred years.[2] And although building requires funds, MBI will not take out bank loans. Instead, projects begin when 100 percent of the target amount has been pledged and at least 50 percent of the money is in hand.

## CASTING THE VISION

That conservative fiscal policy will continue as MBI leaders seek to fulfill the call of President Nyquist's inaugural address. On October 23, 2009, four months after becoming the ninth president, Dr. Nyquist cast a vision for Moody Bible Institute in his inaugural address, entitled "Biblical Mission, Global Vision." Nyquist pointed to four challenges Moody must address as it prepares students and assists the church of Christ in advancing Christ's kingdom. The four are globalization, urbanization, secularization, and pluralization. Excerpts from the address appear on pages 240–41.

The next year, four strategic planning initiative teams, representing the undergraduate and graduate schools, broadcasting, and publishing, met to formulate goals and programs that would fulfill that vision. After six months of evaluation, brainstorming, and analysis, the strategic planning initiative teams submitted their recommendations to an enterprise team for review. Subsequent revisions followed. Later the President's Cabinet adopted several of their program recommendations, which the board of trustees then approved. They will be announced during the 125th anniversary of the Institute, part of the quasquicentennial celebration.

Cannon embraces the global vision articulated in President Nyquist's inaugural address. He expects that vision to affect media and education equally. And technology advances already under way in broadcasting and publishing (see chapters 9 and 10) will greatly benefit both media. "The whole world is shrinking. Technology, broadening the audience, and going international really speak to a lot of the president's expectations on ethnic diversity, international global, and new technology and being nimble [in our responses]."

Cannon anticipates technology advances to include Moody Publishers extending their e-book offerings and responding to new digital platforms in coming years. In broadcasting, he expects the Internet to offer new opportunities via Web radio and Web video. "The purpose is to reach all sectors of the public with the gospel." Cannon senses the urgency: "What are we doing to reach this new generation?"

## THE PURPOSE OF
## THE MOODY BIBLE INSTITUTE

As Moody Bible Institute moves beyond the first 125 years, its leaders desire to remain true to MBI's purpose statement. It reads:

*As a higher education and media ministry, Moody exists to equip people with the truth of God's Word to be maturing followers of Christ who are making disciples around the world.*

Recently senior management elaborated on its purpose with a revealing amplification entitled "Purpose Statement—Unwrapped":

*As a higher education and media ministry,*
> These are our areas of ministry. Higher education includes undergraduate education, graduate education, and nondegree adult education. Media ministry is intentionally broad, and it currently includes publishing and radio. However, with ever-changing technology, Moody may utilize new forms of media that prove to be effective.

*Moody exists to equip*
> This is our core business. We are in the equipping business, which means both the proclamation of the Word to all and the development of ministry skills in people.

*people*
> Our ministry is to all people. Both believers and nonbelievers are influenced by the ministry of Moody.

*with the truth of God's Word*
> The Bible is the basis for everything we teach, broadcast, and publish.

*to be maturing followers of Christ*
> This is the impact of Moody's work—moving people along in their journey toward ministry in Christ.

*who are making disciples around the world.*
> Making disciples is the goal of mature believers. This, then, is the ultimate impact of Moody's work—contributing to the fulfillment of the Great Commission.

## MBI IMPACT

# ( "To Understand the Times" )

In his inauguration address, Paul Nyquist cast a vision for change captured in the motto "Biblical Mission, Global Vision." Here are excerpts from that address:

As Christian leaders, we do have a responsibility to understand the times. . . . I believe there are four forces shaping the world today. As world-shapers, they also impact where Moody needs to go. If we ignore these, we do so at our own peril.

First there is *globalization*. The world is . . . increasingly intercon-nected through a mobile, wireless web. Twenty-five percent of the world—1.6 billion people—is now online. Two-thirds of the four billion mobile phone subscriptions are in the emerging world. If only half these people get online access in the near future, another billion could easily join the web. This means we are all linked in real time, providing conduits for teaching, training . . . and evangelizing.

A second force radically shaping the world is *urbanization*. The first megacity in the world of over ten million people did not come until 1950 in New York City. Just sixty-five years later, by 2015, it is predicted there will be thirty-three megacities of over ten million people. However, what is most interesting is that of those thirty-three megacities, twenty-seven of them will be in the developing world.

A third force radically shaping the world is *secularization*. And while global communication has a secularizing effect on every part of the world, the most disturbing trends are happening right here in North America. . . . According to the 2008 American Religious Identification Survey . . . in just eighteen years between 1990 and 2008, the number of nonreligious people in this country nearly doubled from 8 percent of the population to 15 percent. And . . . 22 percent of those between eighteen and twenty-nine years of age claimed to be nonreligious.[3]

Lastly, a fourth force radically shaping the world is *pluralization*. . . .

The days of a monolithic culture are gone. Homogene-
ity has been replaced by diversity. Urban centers are
not a melting pot where cultures are blended but
increasingly a mosaic of different, distinct cultures
operating side by side.

The question is what does all this mean for Moody? Where
does Moody need to go, and what does Moody need to become in a world
like this?

In order to answer that question, for the first few months I was here,
I just listened. I asked for input from employees, alumni, financial supporters, students, and other key stakeholders. We collected mountains
of data and then analyzed it. . . .

After much prayer and rumination, this is what we decided. We captured the future direction in two short phrases: *biblical mission, global
vision.*

The first phrase, *biblical mission*, captures the one-hundred-[plus]-
year legacy of Moody Bible Institute that is rooted deeply in the Word of
God. We are a Bible college . . . and we endeavor to maintain that focus. And
that is to teach, proclaim, and equip people with the truth of God's Word.
This biblical mission does not end with our college and seminary. This also
provides the marching orders for our radio and publishing ministries. . . .

But the second phrase in our vision statement reveals how Moody
must change . . . : *global vision.*

No one can discount the impact Moody graduates have had around
this world. Ten percent of the missionaries from North America today
received their training right here. Line up any ten North American missionaries and ask them where they went to school. One out of that ten
will claim Moody. As one who has a deep passion for global evangelization,
I am thrilled with that statistic.

But as I mentioned earlier, the forces of globalization, urbanization,
secularization, and pluralization are progressively morphing this world
into something new. And so we have to train our students to minister
effectively in the world that is coming, not the world that has been.

## "EVERYTHING HAS CHANGED"

Months before the Strategic Planning Initiative was announced, President Paul Nyquist described the challenge of change for the good of an organization during a personal interview.[4] Years earlier he had addressed the same challenge as CEO of Avant Ministries with senior managers. Together they had pondered change in another one-hundred-year old organization. (Avant began in 1892.)

Asked whether changes can pose a peril to a long-established organization like Moody, Nyquist acknowledged a balance must be kept to preserve the tried and true yet add elements that utilize technologies to meet current needs.

"There's no place in the world like Moody, in terms of the impact it's had. There's no question that there is a rich reservoir of legacy that is deeply honored, cherished, respected, and I'm all for that. At the same time, obviously this is not the same world it was when D. L. Moody started this school 124 years ago—as I know the world was [not the same] ten years ago. I mean, ten years ago was before 9/11. Everything has changed and is continuing to [change] at an even faster pace. . . .

"I think you have two extremes, two errors a person can make: They can worship the past and stay there and become irrelevant. . . . The other extreme is to jettison the past, to not give it the due respect and honor and to just completely reinvent yourself and pretend that there is no correlation to that history.

"We can't go either way. That's why the biblical mission, the global mission parallel has developed with the inaugural. The biblical mission, that is our commitment to providing not only an education on the Word of God but also proclamation of the Word of God through radio and publishing. That is needed more than ever with our society becoming more post-Christian with, again, more unbelievers alive than any other time in history. We can't back off that. We have to stay as rock-solid committed to that legacy as ever before. The world needs that. We have to do that. At the same time, the place where we have to change is, maybe, *how* we're going to do it in this world, using that same biblical mission. And that's where those commitments that I mentioned to you came from."

Nyquist believes technology itself is neutral, though used incorrectly, it can lead to "some very, very expensive mistakes, and we don't have the resources to make expensive mistakes with technology." But he knows that the right technology can lead to effective adaptation to the culture and accelerate the global presentation, while maintaining the age-old message of the gospel of Jesus Christ. He looks to MBI's past and sees how developments in technology made a difference, and he wants to return to that mode.

"Moody was a pioneer in Christian radio. Moody was a pioneer of Christian science films. There are ways we really set the pace. Probably in the last twenty years you can't think of some of the ways Moody has set the pace in terms of technology. I want us to get back more to being friendly with technology, to figure out how we can use the rapidly changing role of technology to move us forward in our missions of training students and also interfacing with the global church."

## HONORING THE HERITAGE, ADDRESSING THE FUTURE

"I want us to become more nimble and agile as an organization so that we can adjust and adapt quicker. Not be like a gigantic aircraft carrier that takes miles to turn around in the middle of the ocean but more like a kayak that can turn around on a dime. I'm convinced that you can be large and also nimble. It's going to take us . . . time to figure it out but I think we have to."

As President Nyquist says, the goal is not to "worship the past and stay there and become irrelevant [nor] to totally jettison the past, to not give it the due respect and honor." Instead, Nyquist says, the goal remains to serve the church of Jesus Christ in effective ways—ways both proven and new. And in all this, Moody Bible Institute seeks to fulfill its grand, global vision: "to equip people with the truth of God's Word to be maturing followers of Christ who are making disciples around the world."

## NOTES

1. All statements by Ed Cannon are from a personal interview on June 16, 2010.
2. Since 2007, MBI has been audited by Crowe Chizek and Company, now Crowe Horwath.
3. American Religious Identification Survey, Table 2, "Change in the Religious Self-Identification of the U.S. Population 1990–2008; Table 8, "Age Composition of the Religious Traditions 2008; accessed at www.americanreligionsurvey-aris.org/reports/aris_2008_report_contents.html.
4. All quotations by Paul Nyquist are from a personal interview, June 11, 2010.

# Appendix A
# Organizational Charts

# OFFICE OF THE PRESIDENT

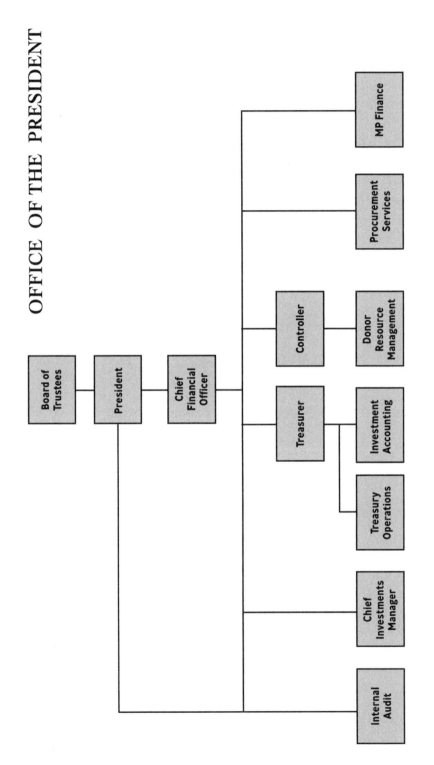

**Moody Bible Institute Organizational Chart, July 1, 2010**

# ADMINISTRATIVE CABINET

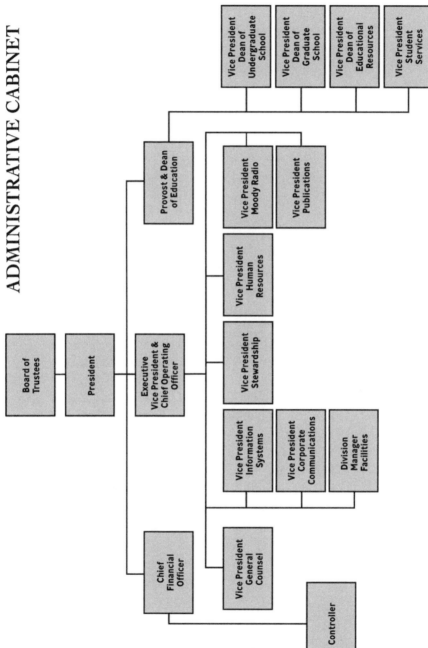

**Moody Bible Institute Organizational Chart, July 1, 2010**

# OPERATIONS

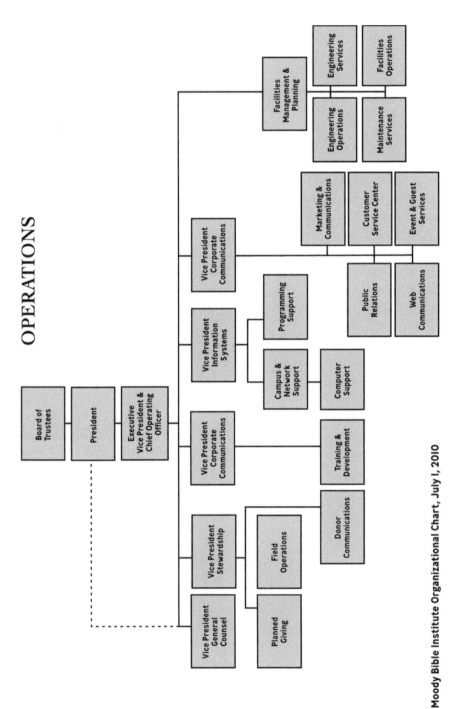

**Moody Bible Institute Organizational Chart, July 1, 2010**

# EDUCATION

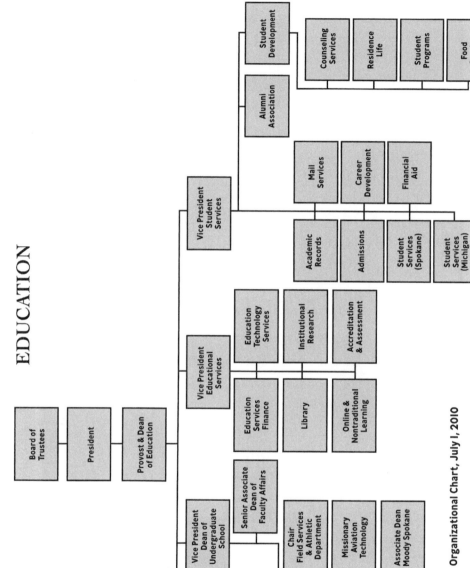

Board of Trustees

President

Provost & Dean of Education

Vice President Dean of Graduate School

Associate Dean

Vice President Dean of Undergraduate School

Senior Associate Dean of Faculty Affairs

Chair Field Services & Athletic Department

Missionary Aviation Technology

Associate Dean Moody Spokane

Vice President Educational Services

Education Technology Services

Institutional Research

Accreditation & Assessment

Education Services Finance

Library

Online & Nontraditional Learning

Vice President Student Services

Mail Services

Career Development

Financial Aid

Academic Records

Admissions

Student Services (Spokane)

Student Services (Michigan)

Alumni Association

Student Development

Counseling Services

Residence Life

Student Programs

Food Service

**Moody Bible Institute Organizational Chart, July 1, 2010**

# MEDIA

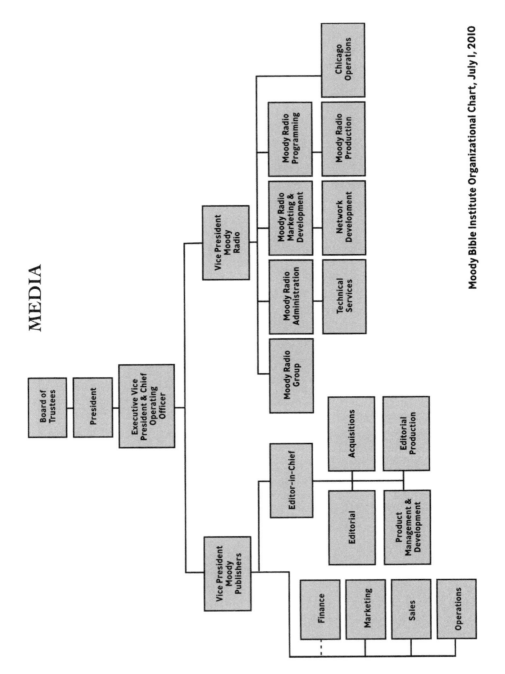

**Moody Bible Institute Organizational Chart, July 1, 2010**

# Appendix B
# Official Documents

## I. ORIGINAL CONSTITUTION OF THE
## CHICAGO EVANGELIZATION SOCIETY

(Adopted February 5, 1887)

Actuated by a desire to promote the Gospel of our Lord Jesus Christ, we hereby agree to adopt for our united government the following Constitution:

### ARTICLE I
#### NAME

This organization shall be called the "Chicago Evangelization Society."

### ARTICLE II
#### OBJECT

The object of the "Chicago Evangelization Society" shall be to educate, direct and maintain Christian workers, as Bible readers, teachers and evangelists; who shall teach the Gospel in Chicago and its suburbs, especially in neglected fields. (Acts 10:43; 2 Tim. 3:16-17; 4:1-2.)

### ARTICLE III
#### TRUSTEES AND MANAGERS

SECTION 1. The property and entire control of this Society shall be vested in a Board of Trustees who shall be Christian men, members of good standing in Evangelical churches, who willingly give prayer, time, money, effort to advance it; and only such shall be qualified for office. (Jn. 14:15-21; Mark 16:15; 2 Cor. 5:10.)

SECTION 2. The Board of Trustees shall consist of seven persons who shall be named in the Charter, self-perpetuating. They shall possess all the powers of Trustees under and by virtue of the Law of the State of Illinois concerning corporations for other than pecuniary benefit (Revised Statutes of Illinois; chapter 31, section 29-30) and shall have the management of all its concerns. They shall have power to remove their officers or members by a majority vote of the whole Board; to fill vacancies by a two-thirds vote of the whole Board; to appoint all officers; prescribe the duties of all officers not herein prescribed; construct by-laws for the government of the Work, and supervise its purposes and plans.

SECTION 3. For the purpose of more effectually advancing the "object" of this Society, the Board of Trustees shall have the power to create a Board of Managers—who shall be Christian men and women, as in Section 1, Article III—by electing nine persons, at least six of whom shall be women, who, together with the Board of Trustees, shall constitute a Board of Managers. The persons so elected to serve, shall hold their office as officers under Section 2 of this Article, until their successors are elected.

SECTION 4. To the Board of Managers shall be entrusted the operating work of this Society. They shall have power to organize Committees for the various departments of the work; to increase the members of a Committee by adding Christian men and women according to Section 1, who are not members of the Board of Managers; and such other matters as may be delegated to them by the Trustees, to whom they shall report for approval all their actions when called upon to do so, and at the regular Quarterly and Annual Meetings of the Trustees.

SECTION 5. The Trustees shall elect from their number a President, Vice President, Recording Secretary and Treasurer.

They may also appoint a General Manager, whose duties shall be to make known the Work of the organization and its object to the public; to solicit aid for general expenses and endowment funds; and to act as Corresponding Secretary for the Society.

The Board of Managers may appoint a Faculty that shall plan and supervise the daily work, direct the studies, recitations and united meetings of the workers, and their general duties in this Society and in their respective fields. This Faculty shall be appointed by ballot.

SECTION 6. All officers shall begin the duties of their offices at a time specified by the Board of Trustees.

SECTION 7. An appointee may for misconduct or neglect of duty be dismissed, and his or her position declared vacant by a majority ballot of the whole Board of Trustees at a regularly appointed meeting of the Board. Information against an accused person shall be communicated in writing and due opportunity given for defense.

## ARTICLE IV
### THE WORKERS

SECTION 1. The Workers selected for this Society shall be persons of good Christian character and ability; members of Evangelical churches, professing, in obedience to the Word of God, "to seek first the Kingdom of God and his righteousness," and "to sow the fruits of righteousness in peace," in their Christian fellowship, education and ministry. (Matt. 6:24–33; Jn. 14:15–27; Jas. 3:17–18.)

SECTION 2. These shall meet regularly, systematically to study the Holy Scriptures, the facts and truths of the Christian religion, the best ways for presenting the Gospel, and to pray for those persons in whose salvation and Christian growth they have become interested.

SECTION 3. And they shall diligently teach the Bible, declare its truths, and practice its Christian ministry in carrying out the object, principles and plans of this Society.

SECTION 4. The school for the training of Christian Workers shall be called the "Bible-Work Institute."

## ARTICLE V
### Membership

Any person in sympathy with the "object" of this Organization, who contributes annually to its support, may become a member of this Society by presenting to the Recording Secretary a written request for membership.

Notice of the Annual and Quarterly Meetings shall be sent to all such members.

## ARTICLE VI
### The Treasury

All accepted donations shall be used for the purpose for which they are given and accepted. No property shall be mortgaged. No debts shall be contracted on the credit of this Society. (Rom. 13:8; 2 Cor. 8:21.)

## ARTICLE VII
### Meeting and Quorum

SECTION 1. This Society shall hold Quarterly meetings the second Wednesday of January, April, July and October. The meeting in January shall be the annual meeting.

SECTION 2. At these meetings the Trustees shall receive reports from every department of the work, and a summary of these reports shall be kept on standing records.

SECTION 3. Special meetings may be appointed and called in the usual manner.

SECTION 4. Due notice of any meeting having been given, a majority of either Board shall constitute a Quorum.

## ARTICLE VIII
### Amendment

For the more perfect promotion of the object of this Society, this Constitution may be altered or amended by a two-thirds vote of the whole Board of Trustees.

## II. CERTIFICATE OF INCORPORATION OF THE CHICAGO EVANGELIZATION SOCIETY

### STATE OF ILLINOIS
### COOK COUNTY

### TO HENRY D. DEMENT, SECRETARY OF STATE:

We the undersigned, Dwight L. Moody, Turlington W. Harvey, Elbridge G. Keith, Cyrus H. McCormick, Nathaniel S. Bouton, Robert Scott, and John V. Farwell, Citizens of the United States, propose to form a Corporation under an act of the General Assembly of the State of Illinois, entitled, "An Act concerning Corporations," approved April 18, 1872, and all acts amendatory thereof, and that for the purposes of such organization we hereby state as follows, to-wit:

1. The name of such Corporation is the Chicago Evangelization Society.
2. The object for which it is formed is to educate, direct and maintain Christian workers as Bible readers, Teachers and Evangelists who shall teach the Gospel in Chicago and its suburbs; especially in neglected fields.
3. The management of the aforesaid Society shall be vested in a Board of Seven Trustees.
4. The following persons are hereby selected as the Trustees to control and manage said Corporation for the first year of its corporate existence, viz: Dwight L. Moody, Turlington W. Harvey, Elbridge G. Keith, Cyrus H. McCormick, Nathaniel S. Bouton, Robert Scott and J. V. Farwell.

5. The location is in the City of Chicago in the County of Cook, State of Illinois.

Signed:  D. L. Moody          John V. Farwell
         Turlington W. Harvey  Cyrus H. McCormick
         Elbridge G. Keith     Nathaniel S. Bouton
         Robert Scott

STATE OF ILLINOIS
DEPARTMENT OF STATE
HENRY D. DEMENT, SECRETARY OF STATE

To all Whom these Presents shall Come — GREETING:

WHEREAS, a CERTIFICATE, duly signed and acknowledged, having been filed in the office of the Secretary of State, on the 12th day of February A.D., 1887 for the organization of the Chicago Evangelization Society under and in accordance with the provisions of "An Act Concerning Corporations," approved April 18, 1872, and in force July 1, 1872, a copy of which certificate is hereto attached:

NOW, THEREFORE, I, HENRY D. DEMENT, Secretary of State of the State of Illinois, by virtue of the powers and duties vested in me by law, do hereby certify the said Chicago Evangelization Society is a legally organized Corporation under the laws of this State.

IN TESTIMONY WHEREOF, I hereto set my hand and cause to be affixed the great seal of State.

DONE at the City of Springfield this 12th day of February in the year of our Lord one thousand eight hundred and eighty seven, and of the Independence of the United States the One Hundred and Eleventh.

Henry D. Dement
Secretary of State

BY LAWS OF
THE MOODY BIBLE INSTITUTE OF CHICAGO
DATED THE 22nd DAY OF OCTOBER A.D. 2009

## ARTICLE I
### Name

The name of this corporation is THE MOODY BIBLE INSTITUTE
OF CHICAGO.

## ARTICLE II
### Object

The establishment of this Corporation is for the purpose of conducting
and maintaining an educational organization to include a Bible Institute
for the education and training of Christian workers, teachers, ministers,
missionaries, musicians, and the general public, so they may competently and effectively proclaim the gospel of Jesus Christ, and to promote and further the belief and acceptance of the principles of the
Christian Faith and the gospel of Jesus Christ as set forth in the Bible by
use of all available means of education and instruction, including but
not limited to:

(a) Conducting a Bible Institute for the study of the Bible and
related religious subjects.

(b) Conducting a Bible correspondence school and other educational activities for the study and training of students in the
Bible and related religious subjects.

(c) The operation, conducting, and maintaining of facilities for the
instruction and training of students in Christian missionary
aviation.

(d) The operation of one or more radio stations and related broadcasting ministries on a non-commercial educational basis to
broadcast programs of an instructional inspirational nature,

including but not limited to programs pertaining to biblical truths and subjects and promoting a belief in the Bible and acceptance of its teachings.

(e) The publication and distribution of books and literature of an educational and religious nature relating to biblical truths and subjects and promoting a belief in the Bible and acceptance of its teachings.

(f) The production and distribution of films, presentations, and programs (including radio, television, or other media) based on scientific research and knowledge, of an instructional nature and pertaining to biblical truths as they relate to man and the universe in which he lives.

(g) To have and exercise all powers necessary or convenient to effect any or all of the purposes for which this corporation is organized.

(h) To have all the general corporate powers now set forth under Chapter 805 ILCS 105/103.10 of the General Not for Profit Corporation Act of Illinois of 1986 and as hereafter may be amended, including but not limited to the power to purchase, take, receive, lease as lessee, take by gift, devise, or bequest, or otherwise acquire, and to own, hold, hold as trustee, use, and otherwise deal in and with any real or personal property, or any interest therein, situated in or out of this State.

## ARTICLE III
### DOCTRINAL STATEMENT

The following statement of faith represents the doctrinal position of The Moody Bible Institute of Chicago and shall be subscribed to annually by its Trustees, officers, faculty members, division managers, and department managers:

ARTICLE I: God is a Person who has revealed Himself as a Trinity in unity, Father, Son and Holy Spirit—three Persons and yet but one God (Deut. 6:4; Matt. 28:19; I Cor. 8:6).

ARTICLE II: The Bible, including both the Old and the New Testaments, is a divine revelation, the original autographs of which were verbally inspired by the Holy Spirit (II Tim. 3:16; II Pet. 1:21).

ARTICLE III: Jesus Christ is the image of the invisible God, which is to say, He is Himself very God; He took upon Him our nature, being conceived by the Holy Ghost and born of the Virgin Mary; He died upon the cross as a substitutionary sacrifice for the sin of the world; He arose from the dead in the body in which He was crucified; He ascended into heaven in that body glorified, where He is now, our interceding High Priest; He will come again personally and visibly to set up His kingdom and to judge the quick and the dead (Col. 1:15; Phil. 2:5-8; Matt. 1:18-25; I Pet. 2:24-25; Luke 24; Heb. 4:14-16; Acts 1:9-11; I Thess. 4:16-18; Matt. 25-31-46; Rev. 11:15-17; 20:4-6, 11-15).

ARTICLE IV: Man was created in the image of God but fell into sin, and, in that sense, is lost; this is true of all men, and except a man be born again he cannot see the kingdom of God; salvation is by grace through faith in Christ who His own self bore our sins in His own body on the tree; the retribution of the wicked and unbelieving and the reward of the righteous are everlasting, and as the reward is conscious, so is the retribution (Gen. 1:26-27; Rom 3:10, 23; John 3:3; Acts 13:38-39; 4:12; John 3:16; Matt. 25:46; II Cor. 5:1; II Thess. 1:7-10).

ARTICLE V: The Church is an elect company of believers baptized by the Holy Spirit into one body; its mission is to witness concerning its Head, Jesus Christ, preaching the gospel among all nations; it will be caught up to meet the Lord in the air ere He appears to set up His kingdom (Acts 2:41; 15:13-17; Eph. 1:3-6; I Cor. 12:12-13; Matt. 28:19-20; Acts 1:6-8; I Thess. 4:16-18).

## ARTICLE IV
### Non-Discrimination Policy

In operating and conducting the activities of The Moody Bible Institute of Chicago, it is the policy of the Institute to admit students of any race, color, national and ethnic origin to all the rights, privileges, programs and activities generally accorded and made available to students at the Institute. In so doing, the Institute does not discriminate on the basis of race, color, national and ethnic origin in the administration of its educational policies, admissions policies, scholarship and loan programs, and athletic and other school administered programs.

## ARTICLE V
### Membership

SECTION 1. Only persons who are evangelical Christians shall be eligible for membership in the Corporation.

SECTION 2. Members of this Corporation shall be:

(a) Eligible persons who have heretofore and who may hereafter be elected to the Board of Trustees of this Corporation by two-thirds vote of the Trustees present so long as a majority of the entire Board of Trustees shall concur in the vote; provided however that unless a person so elected shall within thirty (30) days after his election to the Board of Trustees accept such office, he shall cease to be a Trustee and also a member of the Corporation. If a person shall be elected to and accept the office of Trustee, he shall continue to be a member of the Corporation only so long as he continues to be a Trustee.

(b) In no event shall a member of the Corporation be a person who is not a member of the Board of Trustees of the Corporation.

As pertains to Articles V through XVI where reference is made to one person, the gender shall be understood to be inclusive.

## ARTICLE VI
### TRUSTEES

## SECTION 1. General Powers and Duties

The Board of Trustees of The Moody Bible Institute of Chicago shall control and manage the property, funds, business and affairs of the Corporation and further establish the policy and direction of the Corporation consistent with the corporate purposes as set forth in the Articles of Incorporation and applicable laws of the State of Illinois in Chapter 805 of Illinois Compiled Statutes.

## SECTION 2. Number and Qualifications

The Board of Trustees shall consist of not less than eight nor more than thirteen persons, each of whom shall be a member of the Corporation. The Trustees shall be elected from eligible persons by the Board of Trustees of the Corporation and must be men giving evidence of conversion and consecration to Jesus Christ, whose doctrinal views of Christian truth are in accord with the doctrinal statement of the Corporation as set forth in Article III hereof, and who are willing to and shall sign such doctrinal statement annually.

## SECTION 3. Trustees—Term of Office

Trustees shall be elected by two-thirds vote of the Board of Trustees for a term of three years, to be arranged so that as nearly as may be, the terms of one-third of the members of the Board shall expire each year. The election of new Trustees shall be held at the annual meeting of the Trustees, or any adjourned session thereof, or any other regular meeting of the Trustees, or any adjourned session thereof, at which time determination may also be made by two-thirds of the Board of Trustees as to the advisability of electing any Trustee or Trustees for a term of less than three years. Provision for election to a term of less than three years shall in no instance be made other than for the purpose of properly limiting the number of expiring terms to one-third in any given year during the succeeding three-year period. Board members will not stand for re-election after their 75th birthday.

SECTION 4.  Filling Vacancies

Vacancies occurring in the Board of Trustees by death, resignation, or removal of a Trustee or Trustees may be filled by election by a two-thirds vote of the remaining Trustees at any meeting of the Trustees, provided a written notice of intention to elect such Trustee or Trustees (naming him or them) shall have been delivered or mailed to each Trustee at least thirty days prior to the meeting.

SECTION 5.  Removal from Office

Any Trustee may be removed from the office of Trustee by a two-thirds vote of the other Trustees present; provided, however, that this vote shall not be binding unless a number equal to at least a majority of the entire Board of Trustees shall concur in the vote, and provided further that no Trustee shall be removed at any meeting unless a written notice of intention to consider removal of such Trustee or Trustees (naming him or them) shall be delivered or mailed to each Trustee at least thirty days prior to the meeting.


## ARTICLE VII
### OFFICERS

SECTION 1.  Officers

The officers of the Corporation shall be a Chairman and Vice Chairman of the Board of Trustees, a President, an Executive Vice President and Chief Operating Officer, a Provost and Chief Academic Officer, and one or more Vice Presidents (the number thereof to be determined by the Board of Trustees), a Chief Financial Officer, a Secretary, and such Treasurer, Assistant Treasurers, Assistant Secretaries, or other officers as may be elected by the Board of Trustees.  Officers whose authority and duties are not prescribed in these by laws shall have the authority and perform the duties as prescribed, from time to time, by the Board of Trustees. Any two or more offices may be held by the same person, except the offices of Chairman and Vice Chairman of the Board of Trustees and President and Secretary.

SECTION 2. Qualifications and Duties

The officers of the Corporation and their respective qualifications and duties are as follows:

A. CHAIRMAN OF THE BOARD OF TRUSTEES. The Chairman of the Board of Trustees shall be elected from among the Trustees and shall be the senior officer of the Corporation and shall preside at meetings of the members of the Corporation and at meetings of the Trustees, and shall do and perform such other duties as may from time to time be assigned to him by the Board of Trustees.

B. VICE CHAIRMAN OF THE BOARD OF TRUSTEES. The Vice Chairman of the Board of Trustees shall be elected from among the Trustees and shall in the absence of the Chairman of the Board of Trustees, or his inability to act, perform all duties which would be performed by the Chairman of the Board of Trustees were he present or able to act.

C. PRESIDENT. The President shall be elected by the Trustees, and shall be a Trustee and shall be the Chief Executive Officer of the Corporation. Subject to the direction and control of the Board of Trustees, he shall: be responsible for the spiritual leadership and doctrinal integrity of the Corporation; be responsible for the conduct of the business affairs of the Corporation; in consultation with the Chairman, establish and prepare the agendas and actions for Board of Trustee meetings; see that the resolutions and directives of the Board of Trustees are carried into effect except in those instances in which the responsibility is assigned to some other person by the Board of Trustees; and, in general, discharge all duties incident to the office of President and such other duties as may be prescribed by the Board of Trustees.

D. EXECUTIVE VICE PRESIDENT AND CHIEF OPERATING OFFICER. The Executive Vice President and Chief Operating Officer shall oversee the operational and administrative aspects of the Institute subject to the direction and control of the President. In the event the President cannot be timely contacted or is unable to act

due to physical or mental conditions, and if requested by the Chair
and until otherwise directed by the Board of Trustees, the Executive
Vice President and Chief Operating Officer shall perform all duties
which would be performed by the President if such person were
present and able to act.

E. PROVOST AND CHIEF ACADEMIC OFFICER. The Provost and
Chief Academic Officer shall be the chief academic officer of the
educational ministries of the Corporation, subject to the direction
and control of the President. In the event the President cannot be
timely contacted or is unable to act due to physical or mental conditions, and if requested by the Chair and until otherwise directed
by the Board of Trustees, the Provost and Chief Academic Officer
shall perform all duties which would be performed by the President
if such person were present and able to act.

F. VICE PRESIDENTS. The functions and responsibilities of the Vice
Presidents of the Corporation shall be assigned by the President, or
at his direction by the Executive Vice President and Chief Operating Officer, after consultation with such other officers to whom such
Vice-Presidents shall report. These functions and responsibilities
shall be approved by the Board of Trustees.

G. CHIEF FINANCIAL OFFICER. The Chief Financial Officer shall be
the principal financial officer of the Corporation, subject to the
direction and control of the President. Subject to such direction
and control, he shall: (a) be responsible for the maintenance of adequate books of account for the Corporation; (b) be responsible for
the oversight of custody of all funds and securities of the Corporation, and for the receipt and disbursement thereof; and (c) perform
all duties incident to the office of Chief Financial Officer.

H. TREASURER AND ASSISTANT TREASURERS. The Treasurer and
Assistant Treasurers shall perform such duties as may be assigned
by the Chief Financial Officer and such other duties as may be
assigned from time to time by the President.

I. SECRETARY. The Secretary shall be elected from among the Trustees and shall keep the minutes of meetings of the members of the Corporation and meetings of the Board of Trustees, and attend to the giving and serving of all notices of the Corporation and of the Board of Trustees. He shall have the custody of the Corporate Seal and have charge of the books, documents, and papers properly belonging to his office, all of which shall at reasonable times be open to examination by any Trustee; and shall, subject to the control of the Board of Trustees, perform such other duties as commonly appertain to the office of Secretary.

J. FIRST ASSISTANT SECRETARY. The First Assistant Secretary shall be elected from among the Trustees, and shall, in the absence of the Secretary or his inability to act, perform all duties which would be performed by the Secretary were he present and able to act.

K. OTHER ASSISTANT SECRETARIES. The duties with respect to the other Assistant Secretaries shall be specifically authorized and assigned from time to time by the Board of Trustees.

L. PRO TEM OFFICERS. In the event of the absence, inability or refusal to act of any of the officers of the Corporation, the Board of Trustees may appoint someone of their number to perform his or their respective duties.

SECTION 3. When Elected, Term, Vacancies

Officers shall be elected by the Trustees at the annual meeting, or any regular meeting of the Board, or at any adjourned session thereof in such year.

The Chairman of the Board of Trustees, Vice Chairman of the Board of Trustees, and Secretary of the Board of Trustees shall serve one three-year term which may be continued for one more three-year term at the approval of the Board of Trustees for a maximum of six years. Any such officer may be re-elected after having vacated the respective office for one year. The Board of Trustees by motion recorded in the minutes may suspend or waive such term maximums or re-election requirements as to individual Trustees and officers when determined to be in the best interests of the Institute.

All other officers shall hold office for one year from the time they are respectively elected and qualify, and until their respective successors are elected and accept office; provided, however, that any and all officers shall be subject to removal at any time by an affirmative vote of a majority of the Trustees. Before taking office each elected officer shall subscribe to the doctrinal statement of the Institute.

If any vacancy occurs among the officers, the same may be filled for the unexpired portion of the term by election by the Trustees at any meeting of the Trustees. No officer or officers shall be elected or removed at any meeting of the Trustees other than an annual or regular meeting of the Trustees, unless a notice of intention to elect or remove such officer or officers shall be delivered or mailed to each Trustee at least one week prior to the meeting at which the election is held or the removal made.

## ARTICLE VIII
### EXECUTION OF DOCUMENTS

The Board of Trustees shall by appropriate authorization or resolution, from time to time, direct and empower proper officers of the Corporation to sign, execute, acknowledge, and deliver, for and in the name of and on behalf of the Corporation, all such contracts, deeds, assignments, receipts, releases, and other documents, papers, or instruments as may be required or proper in the ordinary course of business of the Corporation.

## ARTICLE IX
### TRUSTEE COMMITTEES

SECTION 1. Executive Committee

There shall be an Executive Committee of the Board of Trustees consisting of not less than three nor more than seven members of the Board of Trustees, who shall at the meeting of the Trustees at which officers of the Corporation are elected for the ensuing year, be elected by the affirmative vote of a majority of the entire Board of Trustees, for the same term for which officers are elected, subject to removal at any time by the affirmative vote of two-thirds of the Trustees.

During the intervals between meetings of the Board of Trustees, the Executive Committee shall possess and may exercise all the powers of the Board of Trustees in such manner as they may deem to be in the best interests of the Corporation, in all cases in which specific directions have not been given by the Trustees.

Any action of the Executive Committee shall be subject to revision and alteration by the Board of Trustees, provided that no rights of any third parties shall be affected by any such revision or alteration.

The presence of a majority of the members of the Executive Committee shall be necessary to constitute a quorum, and no action shall be taken except upon the affirmative vote of a majority of the Committee.

If a vacancy occurs in the Executive Committee, the same may be filled for the unexpired portion of the term by election by the Board of Trustees.

## SECTION 2. Education Committee

The Board of Trustees shall at the meeting of the Trustees at which officers of the Corporation are elected for the ensuing year, elect an Education Committee, consisting of not less than three nor more than six members of the Board of Trustees for the same term for which officers are elected, subject to removal at any time by the affirmative vote of two-thirds of the Trustees.

The Education Committee shall function in educational matters and represent the Board of Trustees' interests and commitment to the educational mission and doctrinal position of the Moody Bible Institute, and through the President, will be responsible to represent and communicate Board policy to the educational ministries, and to represent educational interests to the Board of Trustees.

## SECTION 3. Investment and Finance Committee

The Board of Trustees shall at the meeting of the Trustees at which officers of the Corporation are elected for the ensuing year, elect an Investment and Finance Committee, consisting of not less than three nor more than seven members of the Board of Trustees for the same term for which officers are elected, subject to removal at any time by the affirmative vote of two-thirds of the Trustees, which Committee shall have charge of investing the funds of the Corporation which are available for investment, and from time to time changing such investments.

The Investment and Finance Committee shall make a report on all investments and budget matters at the regular annual meeting of the Board of Trustees and at such other times as the Trustees may request. The Investment and Finance Committee also shall be responsible for monitoring the administration, regulatory compliance and financial performance of the Institute's pension plan and other employee benefit plans.

## SECTION 4. Audit Committee

The Board of Trustees shall at the meeting of the Trustees at which officers are elected for the ensuing year, elect an Audit Committee, consisting of not less than three nor more than six members of the Board of Trustees for the same term for which officers are elected, subject to removal at any time by the affirmative vote of two-thirds of the Trustees. No salaried officer of the Institute shall serve as a member of the Audit Committee.

The Audit Committee shall determine on a regular basis that the Corporation's financial statements are reliable and are in accordance with generally accepted accounting principles, and shall establish and monitor adequate financial controls and procedures. The Audit Committee shall evaluate both internal and independent audits performed, and report thereon to the Board of Trustees.

## SECTION 5. Other Committees

From time to time the Board of Trustees may appoint any other committee or subcommittee of the Trustees or appoint advisory groups including persons who are not Trustees for any purpose or purposes, with powers as shall be specified in the resolution of appointment.

SECTION 6. Board and Committee Procedures

The meetings of the Board of Trustees and its committees shall be conducted consistent with Roberts Rules of Order as interpreted by the chairman of the meeting. Meetings of the Board of Trustees and its committees, excluding the Annual Meeting, may be conducted through the use of a conference telephone as provided by state law. In the event of a vacancy on a committee, the position may be filled for the unexpired portion of the term by appointment by the Executive Committee of some member of the Board of Trustees.

ARTICLE X

MEETING OF MEMBERS AND OF TRUSTEES

SECTION 1. Annual Meeting of Members of Corporation

The annual meeting of the members of the Corporation shall be that regular meeting of the Board of Trustees held during the second quarter of the calendar year at its principal office, 820 North LaSalle Boulevard, Chicago, unless by action taken at a meeting of the Board of Trustees, or by consent of a majority of its members, some other time or place shall be designated. Notice stating the time and place fixed for said meeting shall be mailed to all members not less than ten (10) nor more than forty-five (45) days prior to the date of such meeting.

SECTION 2. Adjourned Meetings

An adjourned meeting, or adjourned meetings, of the members of the Corporation may be held at such time or times, and in such place or places as may be voted at any regular meeting or adjourned meeting of the members of the Corporation.

SECTION 3. Special Meetings of Members of Corporation

Special meetings of the members of the Corporation may be held at such time or times and in such place or places in Chicago, Illinois, as may be called by the direction of the Chairman of the Board of Trustees, or of any two members of the Board of Trustees.  Notice of each special meeting, indicating briefly the object or objects thereof, shall be delivered to each member of the Corporation, or mailed to him at his last known place of residence by certified, return receipt mail at least one week prior to the meeting, but such notice may be waived by any Member.

SECTION 4. Quorum at Meetings of Members of Corporation

One-third (1/3) of the members of the Corporation but not less than five (5) members shall constitute a quorum for the transaction of business at any annual or special or adjourned meeting of the members of the Corporation.

SECTION 5.  Proxies

At any such meeting the members of the Corporation may take part and vote in person or by proxy.

SECTION 6.  Regular Meetings of the Trustees

A regular meeting of the Board of Trustees shall be held at the principal office of the Corporation, 820 North LaSalle Boulevard, Chicago, Illinois, during the first, second and fourth quarters of each calendar year unless by action taken at the previous meeting of the Board of Trustees or by consent of a majority of the Trustees some other times or places shall be designated.

SECTION 7.  Special Meetings of Trustees

Special meetings of the Board of Trustees shall be held at such time or times, and in such place or places in Chicago, Illinois, as may be called by the direction of the Chair of the Board of Trustees, or of any three Trustees.  Notice of each special meeting, indicating briefly the object or objects thereof, shall be delivered to each trustee or mailed to him, at his last known place of residence by certified return receipt mail, at least one week prior to the meeting, but such notice may be waived by any Trustee.

SECTION 8.  Quorum at Meetings of Trustees

One-third of the Board of Trustees of the Corporation but not less than five (5) Trustees shall constitute a quorum for the transaction of business at any regular or special meeting of the Board, but if at any meeting of the Board there be less than a quorum present, then those present, whether one or more, may adjourn the meeting to a stated time and place.

## ARTICLE XI
### POWER OF TRUSTEES TO BORROW MONEY
### AND PLEDGE CORPORATE PROPERTY THEREFOF

The Board of Trustees may from time to time authorize and direct designated officers of the Corporation to borrow money for and on behalf of the Corporation for its uses and purposes, in such amounts and on such terms as the Board of Trustees shall determine, and if required, pledge therefor personal or real property of the Corporation.

## ARTICLE XII
### AUDITOR

The Board of Trustees shall at its annual meeting, or may at any regular meeting, appoint a certified accountant, or firm of accountants, to audit the books of account of the Corporation, and to report concerning the same to the Board of Trustees.

## ARTICLE XIII
### CORPORATE SEAL

The Corporate Seal shall have inscribed thereon the names of the Corporation and the words, "SEAL, FOUNDED 1887, ILLINOIS," as per impression on this page.

## ARTICLE XIV
### Amendment of By Laws

These by laws, or any of them, may be modified, altered, amended, or repealed, or new by laws adopted by the Board of Trustees at any regular or special meeting of the Board, by the affirmative vote of two-thirds of the Trustees then in office; provided that notice of the Board's intention to modify, alter, amend, or repeal the by laws, or any of them, or to adopt new by laws, shall have been mailed or delivered to each of the trustees at his last known place of residence by certified, return receipt mail at least one week prior to the meeting, but such notice may be waived by any Trustee.

## ARTICLE XV
### Change or Amendment
### Of Articles of Incorporation

The Articles of Incorporation of this Corporation may be changed or amended in the following manner:

The Board of Trustees shall adopt a resolution setting forth the proposed amendment and directing that it be submitted to a vote at a meeting of members having voting rights, which may be either an annual or a special meeting. Written or printed notice setting forth the proposed amendment or a summary of the changes to be effected thereby shall be given to each member entitled to vote at such meeting within the time and in the manner provided in The Illinois Not for Profit Act (Chapter 805 ILCS Act 105 Article 10.) for the giving of notice of meetings of members. The proposed amendment shall be adopted upon receiving at least two-thirds of the votes entitled to be cast by members present or represented by proxy at such meeting.

Any number of amendments may be submitted and voted upon at any one meeting.

In the event of any change in the Articles of Incorporation of this Corporation, certificates thereof shall be filed in the office of the Secretary of State of the State of Illinois, and filed for record in the office of the Recorder of Deeds of Cook County, Illinois, as required by law.

## ARTICLE XVI
### DUTY OF LOYALTY AND AVOIDANCE OF CONFLICTS

The policy of the Board of Trustees of The Moody Bible Institute of Chicago is that all Trustees shall disclose any and all duality or conflict of interest affecting their service to the Corporation and shall avoid any action which would advance their financial or personal interests or that of a separate ministry or organization at the expense of the interests of the Corporation. Trustees shall serve as stewards of the ministries, assets and reputation of The Moody Bible Institute of Chicago and with a commitment to fulfill their responsibilities in a manner consistent with such responsibilities, biblical principles and requirements of the Illinois Not for Profit Corporation Act (Chapter 805 ILCS Act 105/108.60).

All Trustees shall be bound by a fiduciary duty of undivided loyalty to take actions and make decisions at all times in the best interests of the Corporation and not in their own interests by exercising their best skill, care, attention and judgment on behalf of the Corporation and under circumstances which do not create or imply conflicts of interests, self dealing or impropriety.

All Trustees shall annually certify in writing that they are in compliance with and committed to such principles.

# Index

# A Passion for Souls

ISBN-13: 978-0-8024-5181-1

Moody was a model of biblical passion, vision, and commitment. Examine the life of this great evangelist probing his
strengths and weaknesses, virtues and faults, triumphs and
struggles, to find a man after God's own heart.

MOODY
PUBLISHERS
www.MoodyPublishers.com

# A Generous Impulse

ISBN-13: 978-0-8024-4024-2

Sweeting is a unique part of Moody's history being the only graduate to serve both as senior pastor of Moody Church and as president and chancellor of the Moody Bible Institute. Readers will be touched and challenged by this remarkable story about a man whose life has touched thousands.

MOODY
PUBLISHERS
www.MoodyPublishers.com

# A Martyr's Grace

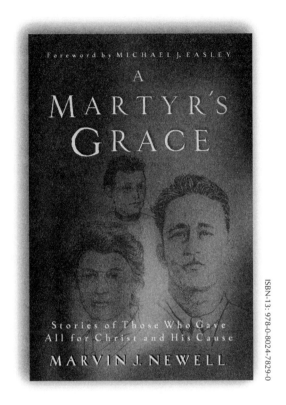

ISBN-13: 978-0-8024-7829-0

As a former director of TEAM in Indonesia, Marvin Newell knows the challenges and dangers of missionary work. Now he tells the story of messengers of Christ who didn't survive to tell their own. Newell takes a sobering look at 21 graduates of Moody Bible Institute in Chicago reminiscent of DC Talk's *Jesus Freaks* and the major motion picture *The End of the Spear.*

MOODY
PUBLISHERS
www.MoodyPublishers.com